D0180672

Endorsements

For those wandering in a sea of confusion, having themselves been involved, or having heard of strange or miraculous experiences, Julia Loren's and James Goll's book, *Shifting Shadows of Supernatural Experiences*, will come as a beacon of light, settling the heart and mind into rest from a dark and confusing world. The mysterious will never surrender to complete understanding. God's ways are higher than ours and they are often inscrutable. But Julia's and James' research, including cataloging of types and meanings as well as instructions for testing and application, can bring sensibility and balance—and the comforting message that they are not alone and not crazy after all. If they are, they're in good company! My suggestion: read and find rest; there are good and holy purposes behind what we experience that go beyond our ability to understand.

John Loren Sandford
Co-founder, Elijah House Ministries

"In today's world where anything goes, one needs to be greatly discerning so you can know the true from the imitation and the real from the fake.

This book will guide you through the maze of many types of spiritual experiences into the genuine article of the Holy Spirit where true power and lasting fruit abound. I commend this inspirational manual to you."

Elizabeth Alves
President of Increase International
Author of Mighty Prayer Warrior

"With an edge for adventure mingled with sound Biblical understandings, Shifting Shadows of Spiritual Experiences will both ground and guide you into a supernatural life with God. Your faith soars as you read the pages of this exhilarating book."

Barbara J. Yoder
Senior Pastor, Shekinah Christian Church
Ann Arbor, Michigan

God is equipping a generation to walk in His power and demonstrate His glory. All over the world the saints of God are hearing this clarion call and are hungry to understand the spirit realm so that they can more effectively expand His Kingdom here on Earth. James Goll and Julia Loren have done an amazing job in helping us understand how to walk in the celestial realm without falling prey to false spirits and New Age philosophies. This book is deep! It is not a light-hearted book with a few supernatural stories. *Shifting Shadows of Supernatural Experiences* will stir you to think, beg you reach for deeper spiritual experiences, and agitate you out of your comfort zone. If you are ready for a major shift in your spiritual walk with Jesus, this book is for you.

Kris Vallotton
Founder, Bethel School of Supernatural Ministry
Author of *The Supernatural Ways of Royalty*,
Basic Training for Prophetic Ministry, and
Developing a Supernatural Lifestyle

SHIFTING SHADOWS
OF
SUPERNATURAL EXPERIENCE

SHIFTING SHADOWS
OF
SUPERNATURAL EXPERIENCE

A Manual for Experiencing God

JAMES GOLL AND JULIA LOREN

© Copyright 2007 – James Goll and Julia Loren

All rights reserved. This book is protected by the copyright laws of the United States of America. This book may not be copied or reprinted for commercial gain or profit. The use of short quotations or occasional page copying for personal or group study is permitted and encouraged. Permission will be granted upon request. Unless otherwise identified, Scripture quotations are from the HOLY BIBLE, NEW INTERNA-TIONAL VERSION Copyright © 1973, 1978, 1984 by International Bible Society. Used by permission of Zondervan Publishing House. All rights reserved. Scripture marked (NASB) is taken from the NEW AMERICAN STANDARD BIBLE®, Copyright © 1960,1962,1963,1968,1971,1972,1973,1975,1977,1995 by The Lockman Foundation. Used by permission. Please note that Destiny Image's publishing style capitalizes certain pronouns in Scripture that refer to the Father, Son, and Holy Spirit, and may differ from some publishers' styles. Take note that the name satan and related names are not capitalized. We choose not to acknowledge him, even to the point of violating grammatical rules.

DESTINY IMAGE® PUBLISHERS, INC.
P.O. Box 310, Shippensburg, PA 17257-0310

*"Speaking to the Purposes of God for this
Generation and for the Generations to Come."*

This book and all other Destiny Image, Revival Press, Mercy Place, Fresh Bread, Destiny Image Fiction, and Treasure House books are available at Christian bookstores and distributors worldwide.

For a U.S. bookstore nearest you, call 1-800-722-6774.
For more information on foreign distributors, call 717-532-3040.
Or reach us on the Internet: www.destinyimage.com

ISBN 10: 0-7684-2497-6

ISBN 13: 978-0-7684-2497-3

For Worldwide Distribution, Printed in the U.S.A.

1 2 3 4 5 6 7 8 9 10 11 / 09 08 07

Dedication

We dedicate this book to the spiritual forerunners and pioneers (both known and unknown) who have paved the way for this next chosen generation to emerge. Indeed, their ceiling is truly becoming this next generation's floor. We thank the Lord for the sacrifice, dedication, and faith of those who have gone before us. To you we dedicate this book.

Blessings to you!

Julia Loren and Dr. James (Jim) W. Goll

Contents

Preface

Jesus promised that the wind and the rain of adversity would fall on all houses. The issue is not *whether* it will fall, but *when*! How you build your house will determine whether it stands or falls. Jesus is the One who said we must be careful how we build.

In the days when spiritual experiences are abounding and on the increase, it is imperative that we be grounded believers in the Word of God and Church history, and that we are connected to others in a practical manner in the Body of Christ. But do not fear! You can trust the third person of the Godhead! In fact, the Holy Spirit Himself will be your teacher, guide, comforter, and gift-bearer, and He will lead you to the true source of life!

As you read the pages of *Shifting Shadows of Supernatural Experiences*, Julia Loren and I want you to be both stretched and challenged, grounded and guided. Yes, for some of you, the contents of this book will be outside of your current comfort zone. For others—it will but whet your appetite and leave you hungering for even more. We have attempted to bring you truths from various schools of thought and wed them together. But ultimately our goal is to point you to Christ Jesus Himself and He, in turn, to our Father God.

It is my trust that when you combine the efforts of this award-winning journalist, Julia Loren, and my years of being in the middle of the prophetic river, you will find a biblically based treatise full of real lively experiences that will cause you to fall in love with Christ Jesus all the more. Let His light fall on your life and the only shadow seen be that of our Friend and the Lover of our soul—Jesus Christ the Lord.

Saturated with His love,

Dr. James W. Goll
Co-founder of Encounters Network
Author of *The Seer*, *Dream Language*, and *The Lost Art of Intercession*

Introduction

Like a child, we stretch out our hand and find the fingers of God gently closing around ours. In that simple touch, our hearts receive a rush of His love. He reveals Himself to us through a vision or a dream, or a quiet awakening, and the experience becomes the gift of knowing Jesus Christ, the depths of His personal love, and the realities of the spiritual kingdom that He dwells in—in Heaven and on Earth.

If you receive one touch of His exquisite Presence, you know what pure love feels like. If you inexplicably find yourself under the waterfall of His Presence, annihilated by love, you cannot help but walk away different. You become captivated by this mysterious love. Something inside of you awakens a longing to know Him more.

As with any relationship, you gradually take your eyes off of your needs and wants and begin to see what He sees and feel what He feels. The gift of knowing Him becomes, in turn, a gift you release to others—a demonstration of His Presence in our midst. You become concerned with the things that are on His heart, as He gives you little intuitions about people, as He shows you visions of what is to come—concerning yourself, others, or perhaps even the world. He invites you to share in His work through intercession—praying about the things He shows you. He calls you to be with Him. And the more you are with Him, the more you will experience the realms where He dwells. For He longs to lift you up into the heavenly places where He dwells and give you a different perspective.

You are His child. And He delights to show you the Kingdom of your inheritance. His supernatural kingdom of angels and spiritual entities, like cherubim and seraphim, are just a little slice of Heaven that He gives you a glimpse of—to show you that there is more beyond the realm of your senses, that Heaven is real, and He is Lord of all. His power transcends our understanding.

Many of the spiritual experiences we encounter in this life are given to us so that we may know Jesus Christ, the depths of His compassion and love that longs to save the lost, heal the sick—He knows how fragile we are, and treats us gently. It comes in the form of a God encounter that corrects our misguided and warped images of Jesus and unveils Him in all His glory. It heals our wounds and awakens our destinies. The God encounter releases the gift of knowing Jesus and deepens our relationship with Him.

I am convinced that all authentic spiritual experiences are given for two reasons only—to increase revelation of who Jesus Christ really is to us individually and to impart faith. The combination releases a demonstration of His Presence and power to us and through us. Those who see visions of Christ, talk with angels, become entranced by the bizarre appearance of heavenly creatures, catch glimpses of Heaven, hear music from nowhere, or find themselves transported by the Holy Spirit from place to place, discover how easy it is to become captivated by the experience rather than the Person and purpose that underlies the experience.

Examined under the light of God's love and scriptural examples, many spiritual experiences are given to impart faith and the understanding that He wants you to release a demonstration of His power. A vision or a dream, a visitation or teleportation, is just the packaging that surrounds the gifts of the Holy Spirit listed in First Corinthians 12—the word of wisdom; the word of knowledge; faith; gifts of healing; the working of miracles; prophecy; the discerning of spirits; tongues; inter-pretation of tongues. They are gifts that He wants to give you, not for yourself, but to give away to a specific person or groups of people so that they, too, may catch a glimpse of Jesus and enter into salvation. The meaning within spiritual experiences all too often fall by the wayside as people focus on the glitter of the package they come wrapped in. It takes spiritual maturity to know what to do with the things God shows to you. It also takes maturity to discern when an experience may not be from God.

In this book we are going to focus on answering the three questions commonly asked by Christians who encounter God through supernatural experiences.

1. What are the types of spiritual experiences that are common to humankind?

2. How can you tell if an experience comes from the Holy Spirit or from somewhere else? In other words, what is a figment of our imagination? What arises from our minds and psychological or emotional states? Or what, perhaps, may originate in the demonic realm?

3. What do I do with that experience?

So, come along with us on our journeys and know this: it is the Father's good pleasure to give you the Kingdom. You just may find that some of our experiences have also been your own.

CHAPTER 1

Experiencing the Kingdom of God Like a Child

BY JULIA LOREN

I'll never forget the time I met Mahesh Chavda, an internationally known healing evangelist. I was attending a conference that was being held at his home church in South Carolina as part of my research for an article I was writing about his ministry. Perched at the edge of the stage and mopping his brow after praying for dozens of people, he tilted his head and looked at me. "Come here and give me a hug," he said. I really wasn't interested in hugging a large, sweaty, silver-haired man in a conservative black preacher's suit who had a prophetic knack for knowing exactly what was going on in someone's life. It didn't even feel like a particularly "huggy" moment, so I thought it was an odd request. But I complied.

As I leaned toward him, I suddenly tumbled into "Narnia," feeling like my 3-year-old niece must feel as she innocently hugs her dad, laying her head on his shoulder, not a care in the world, absolutely secure in his presence. And all I wanted to do was lift my little hand and touch the sparkles on Mahesh's face—little flakes of gold dust that glittered on his skin in the light. I felt myself being gently pushed away and realized that I was also feeling quite "stoned," for lack of a better word. The Presence of God that was released through him impacted me greatly. I stood before Mahesh absolutely stupefied; I was in an altered state of consciousness, and I was unable to carry on a normal conversation.

Days later, I realized that that hug was one of the most profound supernatural experiences I had ever encountered. It had healed something deep in my heart that had to do with trust, innocence, and wonder. The childlike ability to embrace faith that I had lost somewhere along the road to adulthood had been restored. The hug also gave me a glimpse of Mahesh Chavda's heart. It was a glimpse that no lengthy interview could have ever imparted to me. For this man had learned to love by ministering for years to severely mentally and physically handicapped children, holding them and asking God to release His love through Mahesh's touch. And he knew that only love could make a miracle of healing happen in any of our spiritually handicapped lives. Just one brief encounter with God can change everything.

What if Jesus walked up to you and said, *"Give me a hug."* Would you? Can you even imagine it? Or have you completely lost your sense of trust, innocence, and wonder along the rocky road to rational adulthood and become spiritually handicapped in the process?

C.S. Lewis's *Chronicles of Narnia* have led more adults than children into a greater revelation of the personality and nature of God. His series helped readers go "further up and further in" to the Kingdom, experiencing realms of the spirit through the eyes of four young children who tumbled through a wardrobe in the ordinary world straight into the wondrous world of Narnia.

Through these books, the deep truths and miracles of the Kingdom were not revealed to the wise and learned, but to children. (See Matthew 11:25.) More to the point, to the child hidden within us all—beneath wrinkles and aches, financial responsibilities, and relational stressors—the child who longs for release into another Kingdom.

Even still, those of us who read Lewis ponder ways to step out of our everyday lives and into the extraordinary realm of the Kingdom of Heaven. But how do we get there? According to Matthew 18:2-4, the one who approaches Jesus like a child is the one who will enter into the deep things of God; like a child whose eyes are open to seeing the realms of Heaven, whose spirit is ready to receive the deeper truths of who Jesus is and what this life is all about, joyfully delighting in visions and increasing in faith, as he or she sees miracles working in everyday life.

> *He called a little child and had him stand among them. And he said: "I tell you the truth, unless you change and become like little children, you will never enter the kingdom of heaven. Therefore, whoever humbles himself like this child is the greatest in the kingdom of heaven"* (Matthew 18:2-4).

Children receive instruction without debating the outcomes, hold your hand when they cross the street, jump up in your lap just to cuddle, and speak so freely about what they see and hear that it bypasses the defenses of adults. They enter easily into the Kingdom of God because their young hearts are wide open to fresh experiences. Every day is full of new adventures. Every adventure creates a longing to see, hear, and touch more, and ask "Why?" a thousand times, as they try to process their awe and wonder at the mysteries of life that are unfolding in front of them.

Children not only seek to understand the natural world; they are spiritually alive, as well. One looks at the sky and wonders who made the stars. Out of the mouths of babes unexpected wisdom leaps to stop adults in their tracks with some truth they could not possibly have known. They are back-door prophets who slip in the back door, behind adults' defenses, and surprise them with prophetic and revelatory words.

Some chat with angels; they bounce on their beds while talking to Jesus; they receive just the right "word of knowledge" that unlocks the heart of an adult, opening it up to receive Christ; they venture as a group into realms of Heaven; and, having been so powerfully touched by God's Presence, their touch passes the power of God along to others. God always initiated these experiences and He always had a purpose in mind before releasing spiritual experiences to children.

As you read their stories, let their innocence tenderize your heart and awaken a longing to experience the Kingdom of God as easily as they did—by simply receiving and enjoying encounters with Jesus, angels, dreams, and visions. Let the purity of children's experiences and their experiential knowledge of the deep truths of the gospel lead you into the wonder of the Kingdom of God and the ways of God.

The Spiritual Sight of Children

Many people reflect on their childhoods and remember some sort of spiritual awakening, an encounter that set their hearts ablaze with love for God through the hug of a Sunday school teacher or a vision that they have long since dismissed as a child's imagination run wild. Then again, some children are experiencing encounters and visitations that are so real that no one can deny that the unseen hand of God is at work in their lives.

Scripture sets a precedent for children encountering God. Samuel, a young Jewish boy who was raised among the priests but did not yet know the Lord for himself, heard an audible voice calling his name in the night. (See First Samuel 3.) The voice released a message that Samuel was to give to the main priest. It also established the gift of prophecy in the young boy's life. Jesus, at some point prior to the age of 12, experienced a profound encounter that made Him realize that He needed to be about His Father's business—not as a carpenter, but as the Son of God (see Luke 2:41-50). While we don't know how Jesus received that revelation—through a dream, a vision, or perhaps an angelic messenger—we do know that something remarkable happened within Him in the years between His birth and His visit to Jerusalem at the age of 12.

Since then, many children throughout history, some from Christian backgrounds and others from agnostic families who gave them no religious training, have received visions of Jesus or have encountered God in some way and received extraordinary gifts and callings. Their experiences caused them to understand that they were born for a purpose, that God knows their names, and that He can break through painful life experiences to reveal Himself as Healer, Provider, and the greatest love one can ever know.

Joan of Arc, a young French peasant girl who lived in the 1400s, experienced her first vision at the age of 14.[1] She reported that Michael the Archangel appeared to her along with two women who were known in the Catholic faith for being saints. Their messages fueled her desire to help save the Kingdom of France during a low point in its history and released a faith that motivated the military to victory. She is largely credited with being a national hero who saved a nation by becoming a military strategist to King Charles VII. Those who rose to power through her divinely inspired intervention burned her at the stake when she was only 19 in order to solidify their position.

More recently, Akiane Kramarik, the young prodigy from Sandpoint, Idaho, received her calling as an artist of lifelike artwork when she received her first vision of Jesus at the age of four.[2] Now approaching her teenage years, she has received critical, worldwide fame for her talent. One morning, Akiane was found gazing through the window at the sky, her face glowing, her eyes sparkling. Asked what she was doing, she simply answered, "I was with God again, and He told me to pray continually. He showed me where He lived. I was climbing transparent stairs; underneath I saw gushing waterfalls, and, as I was approaching Him, His body was pure and intense light. What impressed me the most was His hands—they were gigantic! I saw no bones or veins, no skin or blood, but maps and events. Then He told me to memorize thousands upon thousands of wisdom words on a scroll that did not look like paper, but more like intense light. And in a few seconds I got somehow filled up. From now on I will get up early to paint. I hope one day I'll be able to paint what I was shown." Today she gets up at 5:00 A.M. five or six days a week to get ready to paint in the studio and write, and she works for about three hours a day.

Unknown children are also experiencing or have experienced ongoing visions of Jesus and the realms of Heaven—some during difficult times in their lives or in the lives of their families. One mother in Louisiana confided to a Christian co-worker (a friend of mine who later told me the story) that her 8-year-old son seemed to be having spiritual experiences, claiming to see angels and even Jesus. She entered his room one day and saw him bouncing on his bed and talking excitedly to some unseen guest. Laughing, he told his mother, "I'm talking to Jesus." His astonished mother then heard him say that she was going to have another child soon. A few weeks later she discovered that she was indeed pregnant. The child's foreknowledge helped the mother to cope with certain stressors in her life. Neither of the parents are Christians, however, but they are accepting their son's unusual, ongoing encounters with the realm of God and his new gift of predicting the future.

Along our information superhighways of Internet reporting, and through many charismatic conferences, people are talking about an increasing number of children's encounters with God—children who are lifted up to Heaven, romp and talk with angels, or see angels in their rooms at home. Lucas Sherraden, pastor of a church in Texas, recounts these stories about children in his church who seem to be open to seeing into the supernatural world surrounding us. The stories share a common theme of what others say children are seeing and experiencing in their communities around the world:

> At a Friday night Dwelling Place service in our church, this young child was with his mom in the preschool area and starts saying, "Mommy, let's go look at the angels!" He drags his mom into the auditorium and begins pointing, "There's one! There's one!"
>
> His mom wisely responded, "Mommy doesn't see them, but that doesn't mean they're not there. Show me all the angels." The boy began pointing out all the "blue-green angels" all over the auditorium. Then he pulled his mother by the hand and began to point them out in the parking lot, too.
>
> I have heard that blue-green, or turquoise, is the color of intercession and it just so happened that at that Dwelling Place service that evening there was a heavy anointing to intercede.
>
> Another child in our congregation came up to me the other day and told me that when I was on the platform she saw sparkles all around me. This one was eight years old and I believe God was opening her eyes to see into the supernatural dimensions.[3]

Supernatural Experiences Among Whole Groups of Children

God has visited not only individuals but whole groups of children throughout history. During these historic revivals, children have always entered into a greater sense of God's Presence, understanding His ways and His love. Sometimes, children have even led adults in revival or led the way in standing up for reform in various segments of society as a result of a God-encounter.

The British Isles

John Wesley and Jonathan Edwards, two great reformers and preachers of the 1700s, regularly wrote of remarkable things they observed in the children in their meetings: children falling into trances, having visions of Heaven and hell, and going into deep intercession for the lost with weeping and travailing. Some as young as three and four years old wept before the Lord or rejoiced before Him for literally hours and days. Both leaders observed that the children had far deeper experiences and more constant fellowship with God than most of the adults they encountered.

David Walters writes about historic revivals of the 1700s, a time when childhood ended early, as children often died in childhood or were sent out to work like adults from a very young age. He reveals the faith of the youngest of children in this quote from John Wesley's journals:

January 27, 1771

I buried the remains of Joan Turner, who spent all her last hours in rejoicing and praising God, and died full of faith and of the Holy Ghost, at three and a half years old.[4]

Children and teens alike felt the impact of Wesley's teaching:

August 6, 1759—Everton

Alice Miller, fifteen years old, had fallen into a trance. I went down immediately and found her sitting on a stool, and leaning against a wall with her eyes open and fixed upward.... Her face showed an unmistakable mixture of reverence and love, while silent tears stole down her cheeks…. I asked, "Where have you been?"

"I have been with my Savior. In heaven or on Earth, I cannot tell; but I was in glory!"

"Why then, did you cry?"

"Not for myself, but for the world; for I saw they were on the brink of hell."[5]

According to Wesley, the experiences of children encountering God during his preaching spilled over onto the adults of the regions and ignited revivals.

June 8, 1784—Stockton-on-Tees

Is this not a new thing in the Earth? God begins His work in children. Thus it has also been in Cornwall, Manchester, and Epworth. Thus the flame spreads to those of riper years; till at length they all know Him, and praise Him, from the least to the greatest.[6]

China

In the 1920s, 40 orphaned children under the care of a Christian missionary couple in China experienced a great outpouring of the Holy Spirit. H.A. Baker's *Visions Beyond the Veil*, records the story of these Chinese orphans in his mission, the Adullam Rescue Mission for boys ranging in age from 6 to 18. Some of the boys had lived the hard life of street children, doing anything they could to survive. As these children fell to the floor under the power of God, they came into an awareness of the depths of their sin and cried out to be saved. While in the Spirit, they met Jesus and felt His love overwhelming them. They saw so clearly into the realms of Heaven that it was as real to them as our reality. They saw angels and talked with them; they played in the parks of paradise; picked fruit from Heaven's trees and tried to bring it back to Earth for Mr. Baker and his wife. Much to their surprise, when they came out of their visionary experience and searched their clothes for the fruit, it wasn't there. Some things in Heaven apparently cannot materialize on Earth before their time.

The children entered unusual trance-like states. At first, they would be completely lost to their surroundings and captivated by what they were seeing in the spirit. Later, the boys could enter into visions of Heaven, as they walked and talked on Earth, describing to each other what they saw and heard. Throughout this season of visitation by the Holy Spirit, amazing revelations of the truths of Christ, His salvation, and the future on Earth and in Heaven were revealed to children who had little knowledge of the Bible.

The visions were often given to several people at the same time and nearly all of them were seen by a great number. Even some of the very young boys, six years of age, received them. The visions came while they were under the power of the Holy Spirit but it was not like a dream, it was very real. In many cases afterward the children came to ask if the Bible had anything to say about certain aspects of what they had seen in the visions.[7]

They saw visions of the Crucifixion of Christ and His resurrection, His appearances prior to the Ascension, and detailed accounts of Heaven and hell among other biblical truths. It was just as common for them to see demons and cast them out in the power of the Holy Spirit as it was for them to speak with angels. The end result was a tremendous evangelizing of the lost in their city, as the boys felt compelled by love to reach out to the others.

Why would God take children into visions of Heaven and hell? Especially hell, where they could see demons? Children in other cultures, especially orphaned street kids, are no strangers to evil. They could not only understand the visions and the concept of justice, they needed some strong visionary experiences to help them survive in the years to come and to fulfill their callings during a pivotal point in the history of Christianity in China. H.A. Baker's grandson, missionary Roland Baker, has since met some of the surviving orphans, now aged men, and believes that the outpouring of God's Presence and the revelations of Jesus prepared the boys to become the first leaders and martyrs of the underground church under the Maoist regime. They kept Christianity alive in China, despite facing intense persecution and even death.

Indonesia

Mel Tari's *Like a Mighty Wind* depicts revival that occurred in Indonesia during the 1960s with remarkable reports of children, aged 6 to 10, who would gather daily for prayer meetings, weeping at times for the whole world. They would often lay hands on people and pray for them, and they saw many healings take place. They received words of knowledge about the secrets in adults' lives. Heaven broke into their little patch of Earth and many found themselves walking and talking with angels on their way to minister in other villages.

About 2 o'clock one Saturday afternoon a team of children started to walk to a nearby village. Nearby could mean anything from 5 to 15 miles through the jungle. This was a weekly thing. And no adult ever went with them. I asked them once if they weren't afraid.

"Why should we be afraid, brother Mel?" they asked. "There is always an angel going ahead of us, and one on the right side of us, and one on the left side of us, and one in the back. We just follow them through the trails, and they keep us safe."[8]

As adults watched the outpouring of God's Spirit upon children, they were sometimes led into deeper encounters in the Kingdom of God themselves—when they dared to humble themselves like children and enter in. Other adults mocked and persecuted the children.

After one especially hard day for the children, the Lord said to them as they were praying, "I am going to give you a surprise today."

"What is that?" they asked.

"If you sing beautifully, I will play back your voices for you so you can all hear exactly how it sounded."

Now, of course, the children did not have a tape recorder.... So they began to sing. And they sang beautifully, as unto the Lord. When they were all through, the Lord said, "Now if you will be quiet, I will play back your voices for you." So they were all quiet, and suddenly music filled the air.

"Oh, there is my voice," one said. Then another exclaimed, and another, as they picked out their voices.[9]

North America

In recent years the Holy Spirit has set the hearts of children and teens aflame in small groups across the United States and Canada. Their passion, in turn, has ignited a childlike faith to move mountains and release the influence of God into their spheres of influence.

In 1988-1989, a sustained move of God came upon the sixth-grade class at Dominion Christian School in Grandview, Missouri, and spread to many of the other students. Just like the 1920s visitation upon the Chinese orphans, kids experienced angelic activity, meeting each other in the heavens, visions, out-of-body experiences, and fresh insights into the love of Jesus and His realms of Heaven.

The school happened to be affiliated with a large church called Kansas City Fellowship, a church that not only believed such things could happen but welcomed spiritual experiences. During that time, I went to Kansas City as part of the ministry team that was accompanying John Wimber, the former pastor of the Anaheim Vineyard Christian Fellowship. We held a special ministry time at the school for the children and watched as the power of God engulfed many of the children, laying them out on the floor and releasing visions of Jesus and Heaven to them.

Later in the evening, a couple of the children came to the house where I was staying, and I asked them what they had seen and felt. A 3-year-old girl said, "I saw angels like in a movie. And then I fell asleep."

"What did they look like?" I asked.

"Like this," she replied. Holding her little fingers in front of her, she wiggled them and spread her arms wide, lifting them upward as if shimmering angel wings were taking flight before me.

I knelt down to her level as I asked, "And what did you feel?"

She cocked her head as if annoyed by questions she hadn't the vocabulary to respond to, thought for a moment, and then stretched out her hand until it touched my forehead. "Like this," she said, as the most exquisitely sweet and delicately loving Presence of God flowed down through my head and body, making me feel as light as a feather that could float to the ground and not feel a thing upon impact. It was the kind of feeling I could imagine Jesus giving to young children to bring them into revelation of how loving and kind He really is to everyone. And, come to think of it, the child's touch imparted the same feeling I felt years later when I hugged Mahesh Chavda and tumbled into "Narnia," as my heart opened to experience the Kingdom of God like a child.

Children Touching Others

As children experience a touch from God, visions that heal their hearts, or encounters with angels and Heaven, they have also received an increase in childlike faith to reach out to others, expressing the love and power of Jesus Christ to heal the lost and the hurting.

Church-based youth ministers and itinerant ministers like Jennifer Toledo, of the Global Children's Movement, offer amazing testimonies about seeing the lost, abused, broken, starving children of other countries turned loose to bring about transformations within their own communities and countries. According to her Website[10]:

> Scripture teaches us that you must be born again and you must become like little children if you are to enter the kingdom. Children are humble enough to receive the kingdom and therefore are powerful enough to change their societies. Teams of our children travel and minister in other cities.... Our children are being trained how to preach, worship, intercede, minister to the sick and oppressed, and prophesy. They walk in such purity and simplicity that oftentimes what can take adults hours to do, the children can do in just a few minutes.

> Richard is a nine year old little boy from the Turkana tribe in Northern Kenya who found his way off the streets and into a missionary home. As Richard and the other children were becoming

more confident in who they were in Christ, we decided to take them out to the hospital to let them put to use what they had learned. The very first time we ever took the children to the hospital, Richard was one of 12 children that had been selected to go. As the leader of the group, I decided that I was not going to lead out in ministry—but was going to let the children hear from God and take the lead. As soon as we walked into the first ward, the children were a little overwhelmed by all that they saw. There were about 100 people crammed into a tiny room with minimal facilities. Most of the patients were seriously ill and dying. Everyone in the room turned and looked at the children as they entered the room. The kids nervously looked at me, and were unsure of what they should do. I knelt down, told them not to be afraid, and told them to ask Jesus what they should do.

After a few moments, little Richard tugged on my arm and whispered in my ear, "I think I'm suppose to sing a song." I smiled at him, and placed him up in front of the other children. He looked around the room, and everyone was silent as they stared at him. He closed his eyes, turned his heart towards Jesus, and began to sing the hymn, "I Surrender All." As he worshiped, he lifted his hands towards heaven and tears began to stream down his face. It was the purest, most beautiful worship I had ever heard. As he began to worship, the presence of God came and filled the room in the most amazing way. All over the room people began to weep under the conviction of the Holy Spirit. By the time he was done singing, the presence of God was so strong in the room that there was no other ministry that needed to be done. Every single person in the room cried out for salvation and wanted to know this Jesus that Richard was singing about. Because of his simple obedience and his pure worship, lives are being transformed. Richard has gone on to be a big part of community transformation.

Come Like a Child

Children are curious beings. If they weren't, I would worry about them, as they sit alone in a corner and fail to enter into the company of others and experience new things on a day-to-day basis. If an adult loses his or her spiritual curiosity, goes off to his or her own corner, retreats from anything new, and fails to experience the freshness of each day, I would say that he or she has leveled off spiritually and maybe has even died.

A child's heart is open to fresh revelation, new understanding, and increased experiences; he or she is open to embracing all that life has to offer on a daily basis.

When you lose that child's heart of humility and excitement and become an expert in the things of God and life, you level off in your development and stop growing. The more mature you are, the more childlike you should become in receiving the things of the Kingdom of God. When you shift from ongoing dependency on Him to an attitude that you can handle it from here, know all there is to know, and can do things for yourself now that you're "all grown up," you lose the innocence and dependency and wonder of being with Him.

Who is ready for the next revelation of God? The child. The child who stays hungry and excited to discover new things; the child who knows that all good things come from the Father.

Receiving the Kingdom of God like a child implies trust—trust that the Father won't give you a counterfeit of the Holy Spirit, a rock rather than a slice of bread, or a false vision that is designed to bring confusion, an experience that makes you feel tainted rather than being excited to be in His Presence, confident that your loving Father is indeed speaking out of the vast universe to little you. What follows are some guidelines to help you discern what's God and what's not, and what to do with what the Father shows you.

How far are you willing to let your own curiosity take you? Position yourself to receive more from God, learn more about His Kingdom Presence and power. Come like a child. And know this—it is the Father's good pleasure to give you the Kingdom. (See Luke 12:32.) Explore to your heart's content. Then give it away.

Endnotes

1. http://en.wikipedia.org/wiki/Joan_of_Arc#Childhood.

2. The young artist's life has been well documented in articles and on television.

3. Based on an interview with Lucas Sherraden, pastor of Abiding Life Christian Fellowship in Stafford, TX; Website: www.alcf.cc.

4. David Walters, *Children Aflame* (Macon, GA: Good News Fellowship Ministries, 1995), 24. Website: www.goodnews.netministries.org.

5. Walters, *Children Aflame*, 15-16.

6. Walters, *Children Aflame*, 31.

7. H.A. Baker, *Visions Beyond the Veil* (Kent, England: Sovereign World, 2000), 29.

8. Mel Tari, *Like a Mighty Wind* (Green Forest, AK: New Leaf Press, 1978), 52; Permissions: newleafpress.net.

9. Tari, Mel. *Like a Mighty Wind*, 54.

10. http://globalchildrensmovement.com/.

CHAPTER 2

Hey, Doc, Am I Nuts?

BY JULIA LOREN

In the mid-1980s, God moved into my little beach apartment, put His feet up on the coffee table, and settled in for several months as a delightfully unexpected houseguest. I felt His Presence dwelling with me, although I did not see Him. His manifest Presence released such an intimacy of encounter that I couldn't talk about it for years. It was too personal. Too precious. It started with a waterfall of God's love shattering my heart one day; this happened on a day when I least deserved to have Him draw near, a day when I couldn't care less about God. In fact, I had come to find Him rather boring! But He decided to show that He cared very much about me. So, He showed up in power, shattered me with His love, and moved in to talk with me, heal me, teach me, and release accurate revelations of others through dreams and visions.

After a while, I began thinking that this sense of God dwelling with me was not normal. People don't just walk around feeling slightly euphoric unless they are manic. Or do they? They don't hear voices and see spiritual beings unless they're schizophrenic. They just don't live with the sense that God is very present within and all around, feeling an overwhelming sense of

His love, peace, and security unless they're deluded. After all, life is difficult and worrisome. We need to stay in reality to cope with life's challenges, not run into spiritual fantasies. Despite the fact that I wasn't a professional counselor at that time, even I knew that crazy people tend to either fixate on sex or religion. Religion, specifically being with Jesus, seemed to be the primary focus of my mind.

Yet I could focus on my work as well and even earned more money in a few short months that I had in my business the previous year. I could get up from the Presence of God, step outside and hold a normal conversation with the grocery store checker. The only comments I heard from people who seemed to discern that I was not in a normal state of mind were not that bad. One told me that I seemed to glow. Another stated that I seemed so peaceful and asked what kind of guru I was following. For a while complete strangers boldly walked up to me at church and asked me if I had a prophetic word for them, despite the fact that the only time I ever spoke out loud in church was during a weekly prayer meeting. Apparently, people were taking notice of something different about me.

After a while, I began wondering how long this season was going to last and felt a little strange about the attention I was starting to attract. Was I nuts or was this God?

On the heels of my wondering whether I was crazy or not, I discovered the writings of certain Catholic mystics who talked about visitations of Jesus and visions and dreams. They saved my life, as I came to understand that others had encountered God in similar ways in the past. Also during that time, a pastor named Mike Bickle, who was from what was then called Kansas City Fellowship, brought some additional teaching and awareness to my home church (then the Anaheim Vineyard Christian Fellowship in California) about everyday people experiencing dreams, visions, and visitations of the Holy Spirit, as well as angels, and I realized that I was, indeed, normal.

Despite the fact that spiritual experiences had been common to me just after I received the Lord and the baptism of the Holy Spirit, I had always wondered if the supernatural realms of God were to be natural places for all Christians to experience. Was the supernatural Kingdom of God to be a supernatural residence for all believers? I breathed a huge sigh of relief when I understood, through the testimonies of others and scriptural precedence, that my experience had, indeed, been initiated by God, that I was not alone, and that the supernatural realm was always meant to be as natural to us as this temporary residence we call Earth, the land of reason.

As I analyzed my experiences, however, the Presence of God gradually lifted. The season drew to a close. In the meanwhile, I had been forever touched by God and awakened to the realm of spiritual experiences, as Heaven touched my little piece of Earth; and I understood that I could dwell with Him by faith in the land beyond reason.

This revelatory season created a huge crisis in my life. I couldn't help but continue to be curious about my own experiences. I also couldn't help but wonder why the power of God seemed so weak in the church. My church and my pastor, John Wimber, were noted for signs and wonders and demonstrations of the power and Presence of God. I'd seen lots of miracles and healings. I'd prayed for lots of people with amazing results. However, I had seen little lasting change in individuals who were deeply emotionally scarred and spiritually crippled. I was also perplexed by constant supernatural experiences and a variety of revelatory encounters I had received in such a condensed amount of time. So, I decided that a little graduate study was in order. Therefore, I launched into a Master's degree program in counseling psychology at a Christian university, just to settle some questions that were raging in my mind.

After thousands of dollars and several years of intense study, I came to the conclusion that, no, we are not nuts if we're experiencing God in dreams and visions and otherworldly revelatory encounters. Everyone has the same capacity to receive God's healing, miracles, and revelation. If we are in touch with God or God touches us in some supernatural way, we're normal. In fact, those who are most in touch with Jesus should be the most mentally and spiritually healthy people on the planet. But still we wonder about some...

Schizophrenics, Manics, and Mystics

In the 1990s, churches all over the world began encountering the Presence of God and experiencing a variety of manifestations, as the Presence of a big God met with their little bodies. People shook like rag dolls, fell to the ground in trances, saw visions of Christ that released great emotional and spiritual healing to them, danced, twirled, and stood on their heads. As a result, many believers took to the streets and to their communities with increased revelation and anointing to heal. After a while, life intervened and controversies abounded, dwindling the passion of many of those who had been touched by God's Presence during that time.

Was it all God? Or were the physical manifestations of the Presence of God that caused people to act out in bizarre ways merely reflections of their soul, the state of their heart and mind, or evidence of an erupting mental illness? It was, actually, all of the above—God ministering deeply to people, people's states of mind and heart manifesting in bizarre ways, as soul clashed with spirit, and, in some, mental illness coming to the forefront.

By then I was involved in a church plant in inner-city Seattle. Renewal lit a group of people on fire and I watched them burn. Two psychologist friends of mine really embraced this season. It was the first move of God they had ever experienced, and it was wonderfully liberating for them to set psychology aside and wade into the middle of God's Presence. I was fresh out of graduate school and more reserved, more inclined to watch and minister to others than to participate myself. Having experienced prior moves of God, I waited to see how this was different and only occasionally stuck a toe in the river of the Holy Spirit, which was washing through our midst. They ended up leading a group of young adults during this time.

One day, one of my colleagues came to me with the story of a young woman who was so caught up in visions of God that she spoke incessantly of Jesus to everyone she met. She spent all night in prayer, receiving visions and words of knowledge. God would tell her to go to a certain place at a certain time and witness to a specific person. As she followed the instructions literally, amazing encounters occurred. The visions proved to be accurate. The words of knowledge were stunning in their effects on the persons she gave them to. A few people met the Lord through her witnessing. It seemed total-ly God.

I listened for a while and became concerned enough to ask a few questions. How long had she gone without sleep? Was she going to dangerous places alone and just flying off by herself without telling anyone where she was going? Could she carry on a lengthy, normal conversation that involved listening to others speak without interrupting them? And finally I asked the key question. Knowing that mental illness often rears its ugly head for the first time as young adults launch out on their own and the stress of life overwhelms them, altering their brain chemistry and triggering any genetic predisposition, I asked if she had ever experienced a manic episode or if this was her first one?

As a result of that conversation, the psychologists drew her closer to the group and kept a watchful eye on her. Within a few days, the young woman was indeed hospitalized, as her manic episodes became increasingly bizarre and destructive; she spent some time recovering.

Renewal is stressful to the body and to the fragile brain chemicals that keep us ticking along normally and productively. If one is vulnerable to a mental illness through family history, stress will generally cause it to rear its ugly head. While this young woman received accurate revelations from God during that phase of her manic episode, her brain chemistry was pushed over the edge by the stress of the real Presence of God moving in her life and in her environment. The last I saw her, she had been to Bible school and looked healthier, carried on a more normal conversation, seemed very stable, and was serving God.

Despite the fact that there are mentally ill and demonized people in our society, it doesn't mean they cannot experience God in a wonderful way. In fact, they may be even more able to experience God's loving Presence and power because they often are more spiritually open.

During the renewal season of the 1990s our city held inter-church gatherings of praise, worship, and prophetic ministry. I often attended and had the privilege of ministering prophetically during many of those meetings.

When the meetings were held at St. Luke's Episcopal Church in Seattle, I usually ran into a young man who was clearly mentally ill. He had been diagnosed with schizophrenia. Rather than finding his symptoms worsening during the meetings, he discovered that the voices in his head stopped speaking when he was in church. When I talked with him outside the church building, however, his agitation returned. The voices waited for him outside the door. I don't know if he ever received total healing, despite an abundance of prayer.

Anytime a person experiences a manic episode, a schizophrenic episode, or a delusional disorder, it will eventually be discovered that it is not God increasing their capacity to receive spiritual experiences. Rather, it is their chemistry, or perhaps something demonic, pushing them over the edge. A thin membrane lies between what is a demonic affliction and what is chemical and somewhat controllable by the responses of the afflicted one. Body, soul, and spirit are difficult to separate from one another and healing just one aspect may not impact the others. One thing is clear—we are fragile beings.

Delusions and hallucinations are so vastly different from valid spiritual experiences that they can easily be discerned. Like schizophrenia and manic episodes, delusions and hallucinations tend to be prolonged, sustained episodes that last for days and even weeks. People who experience visions, dreams, and trance states that bring them into the Presence of God, and other valid spiritual experiences, tend to receive them as individual, time-limited encounters—lasting seconds, minutes, or hours, but not lasting for weeks at a time. They will also focus on worshiping and glorifying Jesus rather than themselves and grandiose delusions about how great they are and stressing the importance of the revelation they are receiving, dropping names of famous people who will validate their greatness, or react to rejection in their life by speaking "prophecies" about the judgment of God rather than focusing on the grace and mercy of God. Paranoia, grandiosity, and negativity have no place in a valid spiritual experience. Visionary states are occasional, not constant; the latter falls into the category of hallucinations.

How can you tell the difference between one who is having a valid spiritual experience and one who is mentally ill? A person who is in the middle of a valid spiritual experience will later talk about it clearly. A person experiencing a psychotic episode can barely describe what they saw or what they experienced. They will either try to withdraw or talk so bizarrely, acting so disorganized, that it becomes immediately evident that this is not God. A person who has had a valid spiritual experience can afterward function normally and can generally go about their day. They cannot help but dwell on the encounter and may even be swept up in a spiritual crisis, depending on what they saw or experienced. But they can function.

Many of us who have encountered dramatic revelations of Jesus or visions of impending disasters, have been so wiped out by the emotional aftereffects that it was hard to function for days, perhaps even a week or two, as we took time out for intercessory prayer. But that is the aftereffect, not a prolonged experience. A prolonged experience that takes control over a person's life is not usually God. Instead, it may be the first appearance of mental illness, such as schizophrenia, a manic episode, a delusional period, or hallucinations.

There are always exceptions, however. Those who give themselves entirely over to the pursuit of God, such as monks, nuns, mystics, and prophets, tend to experience more prolonged encounters with God's Presence and revelation than the ordinary housewife, student, or worker. In Ezekiel 3:15, the prophet sat in a trance for seven days. And so have others since then.

John Crowder's book, *The New Mystics*, details the lives of strange and wonderful mystics and miracle workers whose personality quirks caused them to be either shunned or revered by religious society. Among the strangest are the desert fathers, radical monks and hermits who lived in solitude, choosing intimacy and prayer over relationship with the Eastern societies they came from. Their prophetic wisdom and miracles became known throughout the Middle East, causing political and church leaders to make long treks into the deserts to seek their wisdom.

Crowder recounts the story of St. Simeon Stylites who lived atop a stone column for 36 years and ate only one meal per week. Another, Abbot Sisios, was prone to raptures and afraid that if he didn't lower his hands during prayer, that he would be carried away to Heaven, never to return. Another desert father found himself suddenly translated from one side of a river to the other. Another stretched out his fingers while talking to a fellow hermit. Immediately, his fingers glowed like flames of fire. Crowder also talks about modern-day mystics who are given to prayer and fasting and see miracles of healings and other signs and wonders accompanying their ministries.

Brain Research

Skeptics of spiritual experiences and the reality of God are always searching for some biological or rational explanation. Is there a place in our brains where we manufacture God or spiritual experiences? Not that we know of; however, brain research continues to unveil interesting facts about our brain activity. Although researchers are trying to prove that our brains manufacture God, those of us who come from a distinctly Christian worldview believe that God manufactured our brains; that the desire for God has been genetically encoded since the beginning of creation; and so has our capacity for spiritual experiences. An article in the *Washington Post* summarizes current brain research and conclusions:

> Using powerful brain imaging technology, researchers are exploring what mystics call nirvana, and what Christians describe as a state of grace. Scientists are asking whether spirituality can be explained in terms of neural networks, neurotransmitters and brain chemistry.

> What creates that transcendental feeling of being one with the universe? It could be the decreased activity in the brain's parietal lobe, which helps regulate the sense of self and physical orientation, research suggests. How does religion prompt divine feelings of love and compassion? Possibly because of changes in the frontal lobe, caused by heightened concentration during meditation. Why do many people have a profound sense that religion has changed their lives? Perhaps because spiritual practices activate the temporal lobe, which weights experiences with personal significance. "The brain is set up in such a way as to have spiritual experiences and religious experiences," said Andrew Newberg, a Philadelphia

scientist who wrote the book Why God Won't Go Away. "Unless there is a fundamental change in the brain, religion and spirituality will be here for a very long time. The brain is predisposed to having those experiences and that is why so many people believe in God."[1]

God created our brains, and He knows just where to tap when He wants to reveal something about himself and His Kingdom and connect our emotions with His. But our brains are so much more than a mass of gray matter predisposed to spiritual experiences. I believe that just as we may be genetically predisposed to some diseases—both mental and physical—we won't necessarily become afflicted with them. It takes environmental factors to bring about diseases. It also takes environmental factors to bring about positive experiences and health. Our free will also leaves us open to experience more than we ever dreamed.

All of our religious experiences cannot be explained by neuroscience or brain chemistry. Just because areas of our brains light up with activity doesn't mean that the specific experience or activity was pre-programmed into us, encoded prior to birth.

Another article reveals the current weaknesses in such research studies namely, that spiritual experiences, including the sense of deep intimacy or "union" with God, cannot be mapped to a specific location in the brain. Only the emotions connected to the experience can be remembered and reflected in brain scans. Researching healthy subjects who have not experienced temporal lobe epilepsy or brain injuries of any sort also rules out the hypothesis that those who experience mystical dreams and visions and the sense of God's Presence are merely brain damaged.

Dr. Beauregard and his doctoral student Vincent Paquette are recording electrical activity in the brains of seven Carmelite nuns through electrodes attached to their scalps. Their aim is to identify the brain processes underlying the Unio Mystica the Christian notion of mystical union with God. The nuns (the researchers hope to recruit 15 in all) will also have their brains scanned using positron emission tomography and functional magnetic-resonance imaging, the most powerful brain-imaging tools available.

Dr. Beauregard does not, in fact, believe there is a neurological "God centre." Rather, his preliminary data implicate a network of brain regions in the Unio Mystica, including those associated with emotion processing and the spatial representation of self. But that leads to another criticism, which he may find harder to rebut. This is that he is not really measuring a mystical experience at all—merely an intense emotional one.[2]

While we cannot separate body, soul, and spirit entirely, the spirit of a human doesn't seem to be located in the brain. Given the right environment and through enlarging our faith, our spirits flourish. Our brains are meant to contain the mind of Christ—all that He sees, feels, and experiences in Heaven and on Earth. But our brains are not manufacturing God.

The Creative Mind of Christ

I believe that spiritual experiences arise from the creative mind of Christ, not from our own minds. They originate in the thoughts of God toward us and about us. And His thoughts of us outnumber the sands of the sea.

Genesis chapter 1 tells us that in the beginning—out of nothing—God created the world. Earth was a chaotic mass and, as He brooded over the mass, He separated light from darkness. Separating light from darkness was the first thing He did! We, too, are a chaotic mass, and as we let Him hover over us, as we enter into His Presence, darkness separates from light.

God went on to create Earth and sky, sea and land creatures, "singing the world into existence," as C.S. Lewis writes in *The Chronicles of Narnia*. He then gives Adam, the first human, the task of naming those plants and animals that God created. He gave humankind the privilege of co-creating with Him as the world came into being. And we are still invited to use our imaginations and create meaning in what we see and the experiences He gives us.

God is very imaginative. Ever notice colorful and bizarre tropical fish with their neon dots and stripes, giant lips, or beaks that break coral? Ever notice a tiny flower near an Alpine lake? Why are they so small that you can hardly see them? Maybe the flower exists for God alone. God appreciates it.

In fact, He is quite pleased with His creation and the tiniest details still give Him pleasure.

Not only is God creative, He transcends time, space, and the material realm, according to Proverbs 30:4. Who else but God goes back and forth to Heaven? Who else holds the wind in his fists, and wraps up the oceans in his cloak? And what about Jesus? Who else but Jesus transcends the laws of physics and walks on water?

God gave us an imagination when He created us out of His imagination. We can only create out of something that exists. God, however, created form and substance out of His imagination, *ex nihilo*, out of nothing. He is not a construct of our imaginations. We are constructs of His. And He reaches out to us in ways He knows we will understand, individually and personally. Archetypal images of angels in white robes, brilliant light surrounding the throne of God, and jewels in Heaven not only seem in line with the Scriptures but are validated by others' experiences.

He comes to us through our imaginations and reveals mysteries of Heaven in packages that won't frighten us—at least at first. As our imagination and faith embrace God-encounters, the resulting revelatory experiences will increase our capacity for the bizarre reality of the universe God lives in that encompasses all of the heavens and the Earth. The reality of Heaven, in all its sensory glory and bizarre array of heavenly creatures, is so unimaginable, that if we saw it all at once, we would never recover.

And yet, God values little you and little me enough to prepare a place for us.

God is still creating. The first Earth is done. Now He is all about making a city, the New Jerusalem, which is referred to in Revelation 21, where the gates of the city are made of huge pearls. The city contains glittering gems as its walls and streets of gold. Do you ever wonder where the mines of Heaven are? Who is working those mines? What kind of an ocean produces the oysters that create these giant pearls?

I believe that modern church teaching is so focused on *doing* something that we forget what it means to meditate on Jesus—not to be like Him in the doing—but to *see* like Him in the being. Not to petition Him for something, but to see Him creating all and calling all that He created beautiful—even you. The color, smell, sound, sight of you, are all unique, down to your very fingerprints. If He created you, can He not recreate you, brush off the dust of the world, and brighten you up? He invites you to enjoy creation and He invites you to participate in creating, to enter into His thoughts, step into His mind, and see what He sees.

First Corinthians 2:16 states, *"For who has known the mind of the Lord that he may instruct him? But we have the mind of Christ."* It takes faith to tap into the mind of Christ in us. It takes submitting our minds to the mind of Christ. It takes coming into agreement with Him that we are "seated in heavenly places" and invited to experience all of His Kingdom in Heaven and on Earth.

Bill Johnson, an internationally known pastor and teacher, has this to say about how we can know the mind of Christ. It is through faith:

> Faith is born of the Spirit in the hearts of mankind. Faith is nei-
> ther intellectual nor anti-intellectual. It is superior to the intellect.
> The Bible does not say, with the mind man believes! Through
> faith, man is able to come into agreement with the mind of God....
> When we submit the mind of man to the things of God, we end up
> with faith and a renewed mind.[3]

In order to participate in His Kingdom, we need to know the creative mind of Christ. Through faith, we believe that spiritual encounters with the risen Christ and the realms of Heaven are not only possible, but many have gone before us and we can follow. The only way to know the mind of Christ is to dwell in His Presence.

His Presence—the Realm Beyond Reason

Tangible signs of God's mind breaking into ours—through dreams, visions, angelic appearances, and various signs and wonders—are wonder-ful to experience. Yet, our spiritual DNA created a longing for the greatest sign and wonder of all—the manifest Presence of Jesus Christ, overwhelm-ing us with His love, peace, and joy. It is a manifestation that comes like a smothering kiss, causing the beloved to swoon and fall or laugh and dance with joy. It is this sign and wonder that inflames passion for Christ and His Kingdom come, more than any other spiritual experience.

When the Church experiences the manifest Presence of Christ, the power is undeniable. The shifting shadows of doubt and unbelief are blown away by the kiss of God. Healing and deliverance come as natural byproducts during meetings, such as the ones described in my book, *Shifting Shadows of Supernatural Power*. The Presence releases a revelatory atmosphere of Heaven that often imparts to individuals a sense of calling and personal destiny, visions of things to come, angelic visitations and experiences of the revelatory realms of Heaven. When we welcome His Presence, we welcome His creative mind releasing spiritual experiences so that we may encounter Him and know His ways, His truths, and His life.

No one who has experienced such intimacy of encounter with the tangible, sensory awareness of the Presence of God can deny that He exists and that He is the God who is love. All other gods pale in comparison to Him. All other shadows flee. When His Presence manifests more fully, no one will be lost in darkness or stand gazing at supernatural signs. Instead, they will be on their faces in worship and burning with love, as they see the greatest sign and wonder enveloping them all—Jesus. And there, in worship, they step into His unpredictability. Or, as Bill Johnson calls it, they step into the realm beyond reason:

> In New Testament terms, being a people focused on His presence means that we are willing to live beyond reason. Not impulsively or foolishly, for these are poor imitations for real faith. The realm beyond reason is the world of obedience to God. Obedience is the expression of faith, and faith is our claim ticket to the God realm. Strangely, this focus on His presence causes us to become like wind, which is also the nature of the Holy Spirit (John 3:8). His nature is powerful and righteous, but His ways cannot be controlled. He is unpredictable.[4]

We become people who know and express the creative mind of Christ when we become willing to focus on His Presence and live there, in the land beyond reason.

What Do You Do With What God Shows You?

I am convinced that all authentic spiritual experiences are given for two reasons only—to increase revelation of who Jesus Christ really is to you personally, and to impart faith that releases a demonstration of His Presence and power through you to others. He wants to release what's on His mind and heart to you so that you can first receive it, then give it away.

During the season of visitation I experienced so many years ago, most of the revelation I received through dreams, visions, and long hours of prayer, while I was caught up in the manifest Presence of Christ in my tiny living room, were all about me. He showed me pockets of pain in my heart and talked me through the deeper issues so that I could release the past and embrace the future. He pulled up the weeds of sin and gently asked, *"You don't need this anymore, do you?"* And, as I recognized those weeds as sinful responses that had become habitual thoughts or behaviors, I was able to let them go. It was a cleansing and healing time that lasted for several months and was almost entirely focused on me, while I focused on Him through worship and dwelling in the Presence of God.

I also received many dreams and visions that pertained to others. As I prayed about what I should do with each revelation, sometimes God nudged me just to intercede. At other times, I felt prompted to call someone and tell them about the dream or vision. Once I dreamt that a friend's young daughter dashed out between parked cars in the large parking lot at church and was hit by a speeding car. Since my friend believed that God does talk to us if we're listening, I felt a freedom to call her and let her know about the dream. She became especially vigilant over her daughter that week. Sure enough, while standing in the church parking lot later that week, her young daughter spotted a playmate and let go of her mother's hand to dash away and greet her friend. The mom quickly reached out and caught the girl just as a car sped by. Another second's hesitation on the part of the mother and the child would have been hit!

Once a week, I attended a corporate intercessory prayer meeting at the church. Because I had spent so much time in prayer prior to the meetings, praying over the dreams and visions I was receiving, a special anointing entered into my prayers. They became prophetic prayers that were empowered by a "spirit of prayer."[5] And those who heard me pray aloud during the meetings talked with me later about how my prayers impacted them. The Presence of God simply overflowed from me and watered the dry hearts and downcast spirits around me, correcting some and encouraging others. During this revelatory season, the grace of the spirit of prayer that was on me became a gift to others.

Unwrap the Gifts for Others

Revelation of who He is and demonstration of His plans and purposes for the spiritual experience all too often fall by the wayside as people focus on the glitter of the package they come wrapped in. Some people have such a high need for significance and belonging that they will run around talking about the glittering image of the package they just received. It is as if the dream, vision, or spiritual encounter so excites them that they run off saying to anyone who will listen, "Look at what I have! Listen to what I just received! I may not understand it but isn't it neat!"

It is imperative that you do understand the supernatural experiences God gives to you. You must value the importance of revelation and understand what to do with that revelation. Cherish the revelation, ponder the gift wrap, and then go deeper for a look inside.

Examined under the light of God's love and scriptural examples, many revelatory experiences are given to impart faith and the understanding that He wants you to release a demonstration of His power. In other words, a vision or a dream, a visitation or teleportation, is just the packaging that surrounds the gifts of the Holy Spirit that are listed in First Corinthians 12—the word of wisdom; the word of knowledge; faith; gifts of healing; the working of miracles; prophecy; the discerning of spirits; tongues; interpretation of tongues. They are gifts that He wants to give you, first for yourself, and then to give away to a specific person or groups of people so that they, too, may catch a glimpse of Jesus and enter into salvation.

I believe it is scriptural to say that God does not give spiritual experiences; rather, He gives spiritual gifts through revelatory experiences. He reveals a word of wisdom through a dream or vision and gives you the strategy to release that word through an action or demonstration of His power that increases the territory of the Kingdom of God in another's life. That is the creative mind of Christ at work, inviting you to co-labor with Him.

So, step into the creative mind of Christ and begin exploring His revelatory world, the land beyond reason. Let the following chapters and stories about varieties of spiritual experiences encourage you to pursue an encounter with God and to understand that you are not nuts. In fact, you, too, may discover that you have become a back-door prophet in your pursuit of the intimate Presence of the King of kings and Lord of lords.

Endnotes

1. "Tracing the Synapses of Our Spirituality: Researchers Examine Relationship Between Brain and Religion," Shankar Vedantam, *Washington Post*, June 17, 2001.

2. "A Mystical Union," March 4, 2004, The Economist print edition online; http://www.economist.com/displayStory.cfm?story_ID=2478148.

3. Bill Johnson, *When Heaven Invades Earth* (Shippensburg, PA: Destiny Image Publishers, 2003), 46-47.

4. Bill Johnson, *When Heaven Invades Earth*, 82.

5. Romans 8:26.

CHAPTER 3

Most Common Experiences
and Their Purpose

BY JAMES GOLL

The uncommon is becoming more common. If that is the case, then what are some of the most common spiritual experiences in history or those that are happening today, for that matter? Well, let me open the door into that vast room one step at a time. In this chapter, we will take a quick glance at a variety of expressions of both visions and dreams in particular, and we will consider things I call spiritual perception, pictorial vision, panoramic visions, simple dreams, and experiences containing audible messages. But for the appetizer, let's focus on the purposes of these prophetic gifts. This ought to get your saliva glands flowing!

Wow! That is just the starter! Just wait till we get further into the full meal in our next chapters on things like trances and so forth. For those of you who know me, I am going to ground this material in the Word of God, occasionally bringing Church history quotations to bear, and then adding contemporary experiences. After all—remember—what God did before, He is doing again! Ready? Here we go!

Come On, Catch Me if You Can!

I once had a very intense dream that seemed to last all night long. It featured a man who was dressed in a white robe and at first appeared to be an angel, but who I later realized was the Lord. When I first saw Him, He was standing far away and looking at me. Then He turned, ran away a certain distance, and stopped, looking back at me in an enticing way, as if to say, "Come on, catch Me if you can." I ran after Him, but just before I caught up with Him, He took flight again. After putting some distance between us, He stopped again, looked at me, and motioned with His arm for me to try to catch Him. Once again, I took off after Him and, once again, He ran away just before I caught Him. This scene played out over and over again: He would run; I would run; and He would let me just about catch up to Him before running away again. The entire dream probably lasted no more than five minutes, but when I awoke, I felt as though it had gone on for hours.

The dream had no words—only a continuing cycle of run-stop-pursue. What was this revelatory experience all about? Why did the Lord keep running away, only to stop and egg me on to follow? This dream was a lesson in how the Lord wants us to be in passionate, hot pursuit of Him. He is saying to all of us, *"Come after Me; come catch Me; come be where I am."* Then, as He whets our appetite, He moves farther off so as to stir up our desire to pursue Him. He seems to be saying, *"You must understand, I have more for you—much more. I'm going on ahead of you to prepare it. Come after Me."*

For me, this particular revelatory experience had a twofold purpose: first, to create in me a greater appetite and a stronger hunger for the Lord Himself; and second, to reveal the simple truth of Matthew 5:6: *"Blessed are those who hunger and thirst for righteousness, for they shall be satisfied"* (NASB). This dream was a teaching tool to demonstrate how the Lord creates within His people a deep-seated craving and yearning for more of Him. Once aroused, that appetite is never satisfied: the more we get, the more we want. Indeed, arousing a ravenous appetite for God's Presence is the ultimate purpose of all true prophetic revelatory experiences.

Ten Purposes of Revelatory Prophetic Graces

Having said that, I want to consider ten supplemental purposes for God's revelatory graces—along with some scriptural examples—that serve the ultimate purpose of drawing us closer to Him.

1. Dreams and visions are used to reveal God's promises.

In Genesis 28.10-15, we find the account of "Jacob's ladder." Fleeing home out of fear of his brother Esau's wrath, Jacob stops at a particular location in the wilderness for the night. Using a rock for a pillow, Jacob falls asleep and dreams of a ladder that links Heaven and Earth and has God's angels ascending and descending upon its steps. Atop the ladder, Jacob saw the Lord, who gave him a wonderful promise:

> *...I am the Lord, the God of your father Abraham and the God of Isaac; the land on which you lie, I will give it to you and to your descendants. Your descendants will also be like the dust of the Earth, and you will spread out to the west and to the east and to the north and to the south; and in you and in your descendants shall all the families of the Earth be blessed. Behold, I am with you and will keep you wherever you go, and will bring you back to this land; for I will not leave you until I have done what I have promised you* (Genesis 28:13b-15 NASB).

God's promise to Jacob was a reaffirmation of the promise He gave to both Abraham and Isaac, who were Jacob's grandfather and father, respectively: Their descendants would become a great nation and would inherit and occupy the land of Canaan.

This dream had an immediate, profound impact on Jacob. Upon awakening, Jacob was filled with awe and fear, and said, *"Surely the Lord is in this place, and I did not know it...How awesome is this place! This is none other than the house of God, and this is the gate of heaven"* (Gen. 28:16-17 NASB). Taking the stone he had used for a pillow, Jacob established a memorial to his God-encounter; then he anointed it with oil and worshiped the Lord. Jacob vowed that if God would protect and provide for him, then he would serve the Lord.

Jacob's transformation was not completed overnight, but that one dream sent him well on his way to being changed from *Jacob* (whose name means "deceiver") to *Israel* (whose name means "prince of God").

2. Supernatural encounters often give direction, especially at major turning points.

Consider Joseph's dilemma in the first chapter of Matthew. Betrothed to Mary, Joseph learns that she is pregnant and, not wishing to disgrace her publicly, plans to divorce her quietly. That is, until an angel visits Joseph in a dream and gives counsel that changes both his mind and course of action: *"Joseph, son of David, do not be afraid to take Mary as your wife; for the Child who has been conceived in her is of the Holy Spirit. She will bear a Son; and you shall call His name Jesus, for He will save His people from their sins"* (Matt. 1:20b-21 NASB). Joseph's revelatory experience gave him direction to help him make the right decision.

In Acts 16:9, apostle Paul receives a vision in which a man appeals for him to come to Macedonia. This experience leads to the first evangelistic thrust into Europe. Prior to Paul's vision, he and his companions had tried to take the gospel into both Asia and Bithynia, but each time the Holy Spirit forbade them from doing so. Only Paul's Macedonian vision gave them direction to know where to go.

3. Revelatory experiences give warnings.

In Matthew 2:12, a dream warns the wise men not to report back to King Herod, so they end up returning home by a different route. In the very next verse, an angel warns Joseph to take Mary and Jesus and flee to Egypt to escape Herod's murderous rage. Sometime after Herod's death, Joseph is told in another dream that it is now safe to return home.

In Acts 22:17-21, Paul relates how—while praying in Jerusalem—he fell into a trance and a vision of the Lord warned him to flee because the Jews would not accept Paul's testimony about Him. In God's plan for His people, there is a time to stand and a time to flee. In this instance, the time was for

Paul to flee. As Paul indicates in verse 21, this warning from the Lord first propelled him into carrying the gospel to the Gentiles.

4. Dreams and visions give instruction.

Job 33:14-18 (NASB) says:

> *Indeed God speaks once, or twice, yet no one notices it. In a dream, a vision of the night, when sound sleep falls on men, while they slumber in their beds, Then He opens the ears of men, and seals their instruction, That He may turn man aside from his conduct, and keep man from pride; He keeps back his soul from the pit, and his life from passing over into Sheol.*

God speaks once, twice, and numerous times, and in a variety of different ways—including dreams and visions—so as to open people's ears and seal His instruction. The Lord's gracious and redemptive purpose is to turn men from their evil ways and prevent them from going to hell by leading them into knowledge of righteousness.

For years, Christians around the world have been praying for God to visit the Muslim people. As a general rule, Muslims hold a strong belief in the power of dreams. Not long ago, an international leader of Youth With a Mission reported that in Algeria (a primarily Muslim nation) some 10,000 Muslims had the same dream on the same night: Jesus appeared in all their dreams. As a result of this supernatural encounter, these Muslims came to faith in Christ.

Sometimes God gives dreams and visions to turn people from darkness and error to truth and light. His purpose is to deliver their souls from hell because, as Ezekiel 33:11 says, God takes "...*no pleasure in the death of the wicked, but rather that the wicked turn from his way and live*" (NASB), and He "...*desires all men to be saved and to come to the knowledge of the truth*" (1 Tim. 2:4 NASB). Part of God's last days' great purpose is to release conviction in the human spirit through revelatory graces.

5. In the spirit of revelation, God can deal with a man in a special way.

The prophetic has a way of cutting through our traditions and hard, outside "crust" to pierce our spirit. No matter what our tradition, theology, or doctrinal background, when God wants to get our attention, He can do it through prophetic expression.

God dealt with King Solomon in a particular way through a dream. First Kings 3:5 says: "*In Gibeon the Lord appeared to Solomon in a dream at night; and God said, 'Ask what you wish me to give you'*" (NASB). If God came to you with such an open-ended offer, what would you ask for? Out of all the possibilities Solomon could have chosen, he asked for wisdom to rule his people well. God was so pleased with Solomon's selfless request that He gave him not only wisdom, but riches and honor that were greater than those of any who came before or after him.

I believe that it is significant that God used a dream to communicate with Solomon in this instance. Notice that the verse says that "the Lord appeared to Solomon." Was this a theophany, which is a pre-incarnate appearance of Christ, the second Person of the Godhead? No one knows. At the very least, Solomon understood from his dream that he was being spoken to by God and not just an angelic being.

6. Prophetic activity predicts the future.

The Bible contains many examples of the prophetic predicting future events. For instance, in Daniel chapter 2, the King of Babylon dreams about future kingdoms that will arise after the Babylonian Empire is no more. Neither the king, nor any of his wise men, could understand the dream, but Daniel gives an interpretation, as the Spirit of God gives him the understanding to do so. The Babylonian Kingdom will be followed by empires built by the Medo-Persian, Greek, and Roman peoples. After these empires of men collapse, a divine Kingdom will come that will last forever.

The Book of Luke speaks of Zacharias, a priest who has a vision of an angel while he ministers in the Temple. The angel tells Zacharias that he and his wife, Elisabeth, who is barren, will have a son who will be named John.

Nine months later, Elisabeth does bear a son, who grows up to be known as John the Baptist and who, according to Jesus, is the greatest prophet to have ever walked the Earth.

Years ago, when our oldest son, Justin, was only a week old, the Lord awoke me at 2:00 A.M. and said, in a quiet, gentle voice, *"I have a surprise I want to show you."* I got up, went into the living room, and sat down on the couch. Across the room from me was our piano. As I gazed at the instrument, my eyes opened up into the spirit realm and I saw an open vision of a little girl sitting on a piano bench. Her long, dark hair hung down to her waist, and her skin had an ivory complexion. Even in that brief moment, I could feel her personality.

The Spirit's voice said, *"I'd like to introduce you to your daughter. Her name will be Grace Ann Elizabeth, and she will be tender and sensitive, and you will learn much through her."* To this day, I believe this vision was meant to prepare my wife and me for the one who was to come into our lives. Almost three years later, Grace Ann was born. With her long, dark hair, ivory complexion, and sensitive and tender spirit, she is the perfect image of the little girl I saw in my vision.

Today she is a beautiful, grown up young college lady with a love for God and the nations. I remember the open vision, but I cherish even more the fulfillment of it. That's what the supernatural is all about—seeing visions fulfilled!

7. Prophetic gifts give courage.

Paul was ministering in Corinth after having suffered hardship and persecution for the sake of the gospel in city after city. What lay ahead for him in Corinth? Paul was no different from us; in his lowest moments, he must have wondered at times whether all his hard work and sacrifice truly made any difference. In Paul's hour of need, the Lord brought him encouragement:

> *And the Lord said to Paul in the night by a vision, "Do not be afraid any longer, but go on speaking and do not be silent; for I am with you, and no man will attack you in order to harm you, for I have many*

people in this city." And he settled there a year and six months, teach-
ing the word of God among them (Acts 18:9-11 NASB).

Month after month and place after place, Paul had labored hard and
faithfully, often alone and against fierce opposition and hostility. How reas-
suring it must have been to hear that, in Corinth, the Lord had "many people." With these like-minded believers, Paul could work, worship, and
fellowship. Instead of being run out of town for preaching the gospel, as had
happened so often, Paul could settle down for a year-and-a-half of teaching
God's Word free from persecution. This period of rest and respite renewed
Paul's strength and gave him courage to continue the Lord's work.

Years later, Paul was sailing to Rome as an imperial prisoner who was to
be tried before the emperor. A violent, two-week-long storm at sea came
against Paul, his traveling companions, the ship's crew, and a contingent of
Roman soldiers who were guarding all the prisoners. Just when everyone else
had almost given up hope, Paul spoke to the entire company:

> *Yet now I urge you to keep up your courage, for there will be no loss of*
> *life among you, but only of the ship. For this very night an angel of the*
> *God to whom I belong and whom I serve stood before me, saying, "Do*
> *not be afraid, Paul; you must stand before Caesar; and behold, God has*
> *granted you all those who are sailing with you." Therefore, keep up*
> *your courage, men, for I believe God that it will turn out exactly as I*
> *have been told. But we must run aground on a certain island* (Acts
> 27:22-26 NASB).

This account says that Paul's words encouraged all on board and restored
their hope. In the end events transpired in precisely the manner that had been
foretold to Paul by the angel. The ship ran aground and was battered to
pieces by the waves, but everyone aboard made it safely to shore. As it happened, they had arrived on the island of Malta, where they spent three win-
ter months.

8. Dreams and visions are a major way
that God communicates to His prophets.

In Numbers 12:6, God says: *"Hear now My words: If there is a prophet among you, I, the Lord, shall make Myself known to him in a vision. I shall speak with him in a dream"* (NASB). There's not much else to be said, for prophets and other prophetic people, dreams and visions come with the territory. This is especially true with the seer prophets.

I remember years ago when Michal Ann and I were introduced to Bob Jones, a parabolic seer who lived at that time in the heartland of the United States and now resides in South Carolina. Bob seems to live in this revelatory realm. Most often, as a pattern now for many years, before someone would come to Bob's house for a ministry appointment, the Lord would show Bob that they would be coming beforehand in a vision or dream or in some other seer capacity. It has been stunning over the years to watch the significance of his many dreams and visions.

9. Revelatory graces draw us into worship.

Do you remember the story of Gideon? God raised up Gideon as a judge to deliver the Israelites from the continuous attacks of the Midianites. Gideon put out his fleece to verify that God had spoken, then went out and amassed an army of 32,000, which the Lord pared down to 300 men. Then, with their trumpets, torches, and clay pitchers, Gideon and his men surrounded the Midianite camp. The night before the battle, Gideon needed a little extra encouragement, so the Lord directed him to sneak into the enemy's camp. While there, he overheard two Midianites talking.

> *When Gideon came, behold, a man was relating a dream to his friend. And he said, "Behold, I had a dream; a loaf of barley bread was tumbling into the camp of Midian, and it came to the tent and struck it so that it fell, and turned it upside down so that the tent lay flat." His friend replied, "This is nothing less than the sword of Gideon the son of Joash, a man of Israel; God has given Midian and all the camp into his hand." When Gideon heard the account of the dream and its interpretation, he bowed in worship. He returned to the camp of Israel and*

said, "Arise, for the Lord has given the camp of Midian into your hands" (Judges 7:13-15 NASB).

Hearing God's plan come from the mouth of a pagan Midianite was all the confirmation Gideon needed. He returned to his own camp absolutely convinced and confident of victory. Notice what Gideon did before returning to camp, however: he bowed in worship. In humility and devotion Gideon acknowledged God as the Source of the revelation and the victory that was sure to come.

Gideon's revelatory experience served several purposes. First, it revealed a promise—that God had delivered the Midianites into Gideon's hands. Second, it predicted the future—victory for Gideon and his men. Third, it gave Gideon courage to follow through with God's command.

Fourth, it inspired Gideon to worship the Lord. That should be the effect of all revelatory graces upon our lives—they should draw us into worship. Whenever God speaks, He always does so in an incredibly personal fashion. He speaks to us out of symbols of the past; He knows our strengths, our weaknesses, and our failures, and He knows our destination. In the midst of it all, He comes to strengthen us with His power, enlighten us with His revelation, and encourage us with reminders of our destiny. Our response should be one of praise, humble surrender, and joyous worship.

10. Prophetic encounters cast new light and grant a new perspective.

God's prophetic revelatory graces can enlighten us with regard to past events, our current understanding, and even future incidents. Remember when Elisha and his servant were surrounded by the Syrians? Once God opened the servant's eyes to see the flaming chariots and their angelic occupants, his entire perspective of the situation changed. The revelatory grace God bestowed on him—as a result of Elisha's prayer—cast a whole new light on his circumstances.

In a healing dream, the Lord can pull something negative or hurtful out of our past and—by casting a new light or granting new perspective—give us a redemptive reinterpretation so that it is no longer a source of pain. Fresh light drives old darkness out. There is never a battle when new light shows up. The light of God always wins!

Basic Levels of Supernatural Visions

How do visions "happen"?

For me, they begin as what I would call mental pictures. After I was filled with the Holy Spirit in 1972, I began receiving "flashes" of light—mental images or pictures that lasted a second or less. At the time I did not know that they were legitimate "visions." I did not know what to call them. In those days there were no seminars or conferences and very little writing or teaching on the subject of visions, let alone on the subject of this book—*Shifting Shadows of Supernatural Experiences!* Through a slow process of growth, I gradually learned that these mental "snapshots" were visual insights from the Holy Spirit. The more I grew and matured in the visionary arena, the more sustained the images became.

A mental "snapshot" is a good way to describe how visions can happen. Think of how an instant camera works. The shutter opens, allowing light to enter through the lens, imprinting on the film the image that is in front of the lens. The film develops "instantly" so the image can be viewed and analyzed. In a vision, "light" from the Lord enters the "lens" of our spiritual eyes and imprints an image on the "film" of our heart and our mind. As the image "develops," we gain a better understanding of what it means. Most visions are internal in nature. An image is ingrained in our memory, and we can take it out, look at it, and study it any time we need.

Another way to understand how visions happen is to think of each believer in Christ as a house or a temple. First Corinthians 6:19 says that our bodies are temples of the Holy Spirit. As Christians, we have Jesus in the power of the Holy Spirit living in us; He dwells inside our "house." Houses generally have windows that let in light. Our eyes are the windows of our soul. Sometimes Jesus, who lives in our house, likes to look out of His windows and share with us what He sees. That is when a vision occurs—we see what Jesus sees when He looks out of the windows of His house.

Whether we see it internally or externally, as if on a large projection screen, is not of primary importance. Our first priority is to be sensitive to the Spirit's desire to let us see what He sees. Just look through the eyes of Jesus—He wants to share with you what He is seeing!

Supernatural visions are recorded throughout the Bible. Within the pages of Scripture we can identify at least 12 different types or levels of visionary supernatural experiences. In this section, we will examine five of these briefly, moving progressively from the simplest to the more profound.

1. Spiritual Perception

I speak the things which I have seen with My Father (John 8:38a NASB).

As the lowest level of supernatural vision, spiritual perception may or may not involve a literal "seeing." Perception is not limited to the visual. Spiritual perception is the realm of knowing, of *impression*. In this type of vision, a person may "see" something in his spirit while his mind sees no image. The Holy Spirit often reveals things to us by an *unction* or, to use a more familiar word, an anointing. Yet we may not be able to describe those things pictorially. Often, a hunch, a prompting, or a "gut feeling" we have is due to a perception in our inner self, as it receives nudges from the Holy Spirit.

Jesus walked by faith and always pleased His Father. (See John 8:29.) He discerned (saw) His Father's acts and acted accordingly: "*I speak the things which I have seen with My Father*" (John 8:38a NASB). He also knew (perceived the innermost heart of) all people: "*But Jesus, on His part, was not entrusting Himself to them, for He knew all men, and because He did not need anyone to testify concerning man, for He Himself knew what was in man*" (John 2:24-25 NASB).

It seems that in the life of Jesus, His spiritual eye perceived things that His mind did not always visualize. Such spiritual perceptions could be the operation of the gift of a word of wisdom, word of knowledge, discerning of spirits, the gift of faith, or even the gift of prophecy. Often, the higher the level of spiritual vision, the higher the dimension of spiritual sight occurs. I, like you, want to follow Jesus' example and "do what we see the Father doing."

2. Pictorial Vision

If there is a prophet among you, I, the Lord, shall make Myself known to him in a vision. I shall speak with him in a dream (Numbers 12:6b NASB).

In a pictorial vision an image is revealed and can be identified and described in terms of pictures. These are Holy Spirit visual aids! Symbols may or may not be involved. Often, the revelatory gifts come to us in the form of a pictorial vision that we see with our inner sight. However, a pictorial vision also may come in a picture that is superimposed over the subject. In other words we might see two things at once: the main scene in the natural, with the object of the pictorial vision placed over or around it. For example, I often see Scriptures written on people's foreheads.

This is a useful tool, as it depicts something they are deeply pondering or serves as medicine from the Lord to help them in their current or future situation. I often have to look up the verse and read it to them. This level of vision begins to enter both the internal and external arenas.

For another example, when praying for the sick, one may "see" an image of a bodily organ, a bone, or another body part flash in his or her mind. This indicates what to pray for or leads to dialogue with the person being ministered to. A pictorial vision is the type that is manifested when a Christian is praying for an individual and the Holy Spirit starts showing things in "snapshots." This person may say, "The Lord is showing me.... " or "I am seeing.... " or "Does this picture mean anything to you?" This happens because pictorial visions are presenting distinct pictures in his or her mind, and not only in the spirit, as is the case with spiritual perception.

Years ago, when I was pastoring a church in the Midwest, I "saw" an image of an inflamed stomach. I mentioned it from the platform, but no one came forth who was suffering from that particular ailment. But I could not get away from the vision. After a little while, one woman in the group went downstairs to the nursery in the basement to relieve her daughter who was tending the children there. When the young lady came up the stairs and through the back door of the sanctuary into the main meeting, a "knowing" went off on the inside of me. I knew she was the one. As it turned out, the daughter had an inflamed stomach, a pre-ulcerous condition. She came forward and the power of the Holy Spirit came upon her and the Lord healed her completely that night!

It all began while in worship with a momentary pictorial vision in my mind of the affected organ. That is very often how these visions work.

3. Panoramic Vision

I have also spoken to the prophets, and I gave numerous visions, and through the prophets I gave parables (Hosea 12:10 NASB).

A panoramic vision is one in which a person sees a pictorial vision, not in snapshot form, but in motion in his or her mind. This "motion picture" may last several seconds and may include words heard in the realm of the spirit.

A panorama is a picture that unfolds before the spectators in such a way as to give the impression of a continuous view. Acts 9:10-16 records two panoramic visions. First, Ananias receives a vision that he is to go and lay his hands on Saul (later to be called Paul) so that he may receive his sight back. The second vision is that of Saul himself who, although blind, had "... *seen in a vision a man named Ananias come in and lay his hands on him, so that he might regain his sight*" (Acts 9:12 NASB). In both cases, the Greek word for "vision" is *horama*, one of the roots for our English word "panorama." It is interesting that this is the term used often for cinema—it is panoramic. Both Ananias and Saul saw a "motion picture" vision of what was going to come about.

I remember when I received my call to the nations after receiving prayer from the healing evangelist Mahesh Chavda. As I was resting on the floor, I could see a list of nations in typed print roll before my eyes. It happened three times (I guess I needed to get the picture!). Over a period of years I have ministered in all the nations that "panned" before my eyes. It took 20 years, but God has been faithful to fulfill the vision He gave to me that glorious morning.

4. Simple Dreams (Sleeping Vision)

In the first year of Belshazzar king of Babylon Daniel saw a dream and visions in his mind as he lay on his bed; then he wrote the dream down and related the following summary of it (Daniel 7:1 NASB).

We looked at dreams and dream language earlier, but let's review them briefly for purposes of comparison. A dream is a visionary revelation from the Holy Spirit that one receives while asleep. Supernatural dreams can occur in any level of sleep: light rest, regular sleep, deep sleep, or even in a trance state. Any one of the revelation gifts, or any combination of them, may manifest in a dream. Symbols may or may not be present. In any given situation, an entire scenario may be revealed in the dream.

The Book of Job tells us:

Indeed God speaks once, or twice, yet no one notices it. In a dream, a vision of the night, when sound sleep falls on men, while they slumber in their beds, then He opens the ears of men, and seals their instruction (Job 33:14-16 NASB).

God wants to speak to us, but often during the day He can hardly get a word in edgewise. When we are asleep, however, our souls become more rested and more inclined to receive from Him. Then He can open our ears and give us instruction on various levels.

We need to be thankful to God for His persistence! After all, He often tries talking to us during the daytime but we do not listen. Rather than giving up, God waits until we are asleep, then releases His "secret service agents"—His gifts of revelation—to come upon us in our sleep. God comes in quietly at night and says, "*I want to talk to you.*" That is how supernatural dreams come about.

There is an ebb and flow in the life of the dreamer for sure. As I compose this to you, I am in one of those growth spurts again when I have more than one dream a night. But I have had other seasons also when it seems like the river had "done dried up"! Know what I mean?

But dreams do not happen because of the pizza or pickles or anything else we eat. They happen because of God's love. God wants us to watch with Him. He wants us to see and hear more than we want to see and hear. If He has trouble getting in through the front door, He will come in through the back door—through dreams. (For more on the subject of dreams, my wife, Michal Ann, and I have composed a full book called *Dream Language*.)

5. Audible Messages

And behold, a voice out of the heavens said, "This is My beloved Son, in whom I am well-pleased" (Matthew 3:17 NASB).

Often, visions include a voice speaking a message along with a visual image. Sometimes a message is declared apart from any visual pictures. Audible messages in the spiritual realm can involve people speaking words or objects making sounds. We can perceive such messages inside of us by our inner ears, or outside of us by our physical ears.

Voices or sounds we hear internally can indeed be messages from the Lord. That which we hear outside of us—a message from above and beyond the natural mind and ears—is called a supernatural audible message. Audible messages from the Lord come in many ways: from the Holy Spirit, Jesus, the Father, angels of the Lord of various realms, and numerous other sounds He uses.

Audible voices that are unfamiliar to us may bring doubt and confusion, or even fear. Deceiving or seducing spirits are usually the ones who behave mysteriously, as though they have something to hide. The word *occult* means "hidden." The enemy tries to hide, but we can flush satan and his cohorts out through the blood of Jesus. Just test the spirits to determine if they are from God.

God is not the author of doubt, confusion, or fear. When God releases His message to us, even through one of His angels, we should sense purity and holiness, a reverence to the Lord, and openness, because they have nothing to hide. The Spirit of God is not afraid to be tested. We should never fear offending God by testing the spirits. On the contrary, God is honored when we do so, because He told us in His Word to do so. (See First John 4:1-3.)

On the infamous morning of September 11, 2001, the voice of the Holy Spirit came to me in an external audible manner. He said, *"The hunters have just been released!"* I was familiar with this term from my history in prayer and carrying God's heart for the Jewish people. I then sensed an urgency to turn on the television. Sure enough—like millions of others—I saw the footage of the World Trade Towers being destroyed by terrorists. The Holy Spirit was giving a portion of God's interpretation to the events of our time by warning me, *"The hunters have just been released."* Indeed, we are living in days when the spirits of terror, antichrist, and anti-Semitism are increasing.

The Bible is full of examples where individuals heard God speak in an audible voice:

- God speaks from Heaven when Jesus is baptized—Matt. 3:17.
- God speaks to Peter, James, and John on the Mount of Transfiguration—Luke 9:28-36.
- An angel speaks to Philip—Acts 8:26.
- The Lord Jesus speaks to Saul on the road to Damascus—Acts 9:3-7.
- The Holy Spirit speaks to the prophets, teachers, and other believers at Antioch—Acts 13:1-3.

We should not be afraid of the possibility of hearing an audible voice from the Lord. Rest assured! Jesus said that His sheep know His voice. (See John 10:14.) He is a great teacher—the greatest teacher in all of history. He is *the* Teacher, and He wants us to hear His voice even more than we want to hear it!

Is There More, Lord?

Is there more, Lord? In a book like this? Are you kidding! That was the appetizer—remember? Now on to the next dish in our full-course meal. After all, we are seated at a banqueting table of His delights. The gifts of the Spirit are for today, and God is alive and well on planet Earth!

So if you are daring to go where you might not have been before, keep turning the pages with me on our journey of exploring the true from the false in spiritual experiences. Remember—keep it simple—always ask this question, "Does this experience bring me closer to Jesus?" If so, let's "keep on trucking," as we proceed to understand the categories and the diversity of our dreams.

CHAPTER 4

The Enchanting Shades of Dreams

BY JAMES GOLL

Wow! Are you ready for another round of potent Holy Ghost teaching, revelation, and impartation? I think I heard a, "Yes, sir!" or an "Amen" from somewhere! You really must be a hungry soul! Well, let's "load and shoot"— OK? In other words, let's get right to the task at hand. Let's push out deeper into the waters of dreams. It is such a vast subject— but let's dive right in and see what the Master has in store for us!

Dreams: A Living Language of Love

Dreams are as diverse as the languages we speak, the clothing we wear, and the food we eat. Dreams are a communicative expression of the creative heart of God. As the Master artistically paints each flower of the field, so dreams are individually tailor-made for you and me.

What are dreams made of? Are they spiritual gifts given for us to unwrap? Revelatory dreams naturally fall under the spiritual gift of prophecy. Yet they are too broad to be confined neatly and strictly just to one gift. Dreams may also be an impartation of the gift of discerning of spirits. Like the colors in a rainbow in overlapping shades, it's difficult to tell where one stops and another begins; similarly, dreams are definitely unique and creative expressions of spiritual gifts. There are no clear lines of demarcation between spiritual gifts. The word of wisdom blends into a word of knowledge. The gift of faith overlaps with the workings of miracles. Yes, dreams are spiritual gifts that intertwine with various enchanting shades.

Dream language is not a dead language but a dynamic, living language of love. The primary difference between dreams and other revelatory impartations is that we receive dreams first in our subconscious and only later become aware of them in our conscious minds. Because of the divine nature of revelation, we must depend on the Holy Spirit for understanding. Jesus said, *"When He, the Spirit of truth, comes, He will guide you into all the truth; for He will not speak on His own initiative, but whatever He hears, He will speak; and He will disclose to you what is to come"* (John 16:13 NASB).

As the Creator, God is incredibly diverse. He loves variety. Just one look at the natural world in all its abundant variety is enough to show the diversity of God's creative nature. This diversity is just as true for the spiritual realm as it is for the natural. Paul wrote:

> *Now there are varieties of gifts, but the same Spirit. And there are varieties of ministries, and the same Lord. There are varieties of effects, but the same God who works all things in all persons. But to each one is given the manifestation of the Spirit for the common good* (1 Corinthians 12:4-7 NASB).

There are diversities of spiritual giftings, but all come from the same Holy Spirit. Each of us, as believers, receives the manifestation of the Spirit, but in different grace packages and in a variety of ways. We are so different from one another. We think differently from each other and we perceive things in different ways. The Spirit of God tailors His impartations to match our individual callings. So, just as there are diversities of spiritual gifts, there are also diversities of dreams. The Holy Spirit matches our dreams to the way we think and perceive individually. In other words, He gives us dreams according to our sphere or realm of influence. It is part of His amazing nature.

Dreams According to Your Sphere

When the Holy Spirit gives you dreams and other types of supernatural encounters, He will do so according to the calling of God on your life. We receive according to our allotment or our sphere of influence. The Greek word is *metron*. Whether they are dreams about your home, your children, your workplace, your local church, city, or nation, you will receive dreams that relate to the sphere of influence you have in your life.

Because we each have different spheres of influence and callings, our revelations will differ from each other also—*not* conflicting or contradictory revelations, just different because of our different spheres. God never contradicts himself and neither does His revelation.

For example, if your calling is to evangelism, your dreams will probably tend to be evangelistic in nature. If yours is a pastoral sphere, you will receive dreams of sheep and tending to the flock. If your gifting includes prophetic ministry, your dreams will be highly revelatory in nature. If you are called to the marketplace, then His creative means of communicating with you will address that arena. If you are in the health care profession, then your dreams will often speak of nurture, healing, and releasing love. If you work in government, your dreams will deal with spheres of authority. Each revelation will demonstrate a different level of impact and anointing. It all depends on your sphere.

Measure of Rule

Just as we each have a sphere of revelation, we each also have a *measure of rule* or influence. Part of our creation mandate from God is to exercise dominion over the created order. We have a stewardship to rule in the Earth. The Holy Spirit determines our measure of rule according to the will of our heavenly Father, and it is different with each of us.

Our measure of delegated rule is determined by three elements: our measure of *gift*, our measure of *authority*, and our measure of *faith*. These three elements combined help to explain why some people seem to have a much greater sphere of influence than others. Some people have a sphere of influence that is global in scale. Most of us, however, operate on a smaller level, such as in our community or local congregation.

This does not mean that the ministries of people with smaller measures of rule are less important than larger ones. Don't fall into the comparison trap. Just because someone else's sphere may be larger than yours does not mean that God loves you or favors you any less than He does that other person. Remember, God never wastes anything. And He never acts without purpose.

The Lord determines our measure of rule according to His sovereign will and He gifts, He and equips us accordingly. Our measure of rule sets the boundaries for what God expects of us at any given time. In God's system of evaluation and reward, faithfulness is more important than volume. He promised that if we are faithful with a little, He will give us much. The key is being faithful with what He *has* given us. Large, small or in between, our measure of rule and how we exercise it are very important to God. They are crucial parts of His overall redemptive purpose for humanity.

Within our measure of rule we each have a measure of *gift*, which refers to the specific level or degree of grace gifting we have received from the Holy Spirit. This measure will always be sufficient for the sphere of influence God has given to us. We also each have a measure of *authority* that defines our functional position and sphere of influence. Inside that arena of authority we will be highly effective; outside of that position our effectiveness and impact will decrease. Paul recognized the scope of his sphere and was careful to stay inside it: *"But we will not boast beyond our measure, but within the measure of the sphere which God apportioned to us as a measure, to reach even as far as you"* (2 Cor. 10:13 NASB).

Finally, the measure of faith describes the degree of confidence with which we move in our gift with authority: *"For through the grace given to me I say to everyone among you not to think more highly of himself than he ought to think; but to think so as to have sound judgment, as God has allotted to each a measure of faith"* (Rom. 12:3 NASB). These three elements—gift, authority, and faith—make up our measure of rule, which determines how people will respond to us as servants of God.

You will receive revelation according to your measure of rule. Think of your measure of rule as a stewardship for which you are responsible to God. He will give you revelation in your field of stewardship. If your measure of rule, for example, extends over a small group, look for dreams (and interpretations) that will relate to that small group. Few start out with dreams or revelation that have global ramifications. God may very well give you such a dream, but if He does, it is typically an appetizer or preview for a future time. Before that revelation has application in your life, God will have to enlarge your measure of rule to match it.

Your measure of rule will determine how people respond to you as a servant of God. If you are faithful within your sphere, God will see to it that your gift makes room for you: *"A man's gift makes room for him and brings him before great men"* (Prov. 18:16 NASB). God never wastes His gifts. If you are faithful with what He has given you, watch out—the sky is the limit!

Categories of Dreams

One fundamental principle of understanding and walking in dream language is learning to distinguish between the two main categories of dreams: *intrinsic* or internal dreams, and *extrinsic* or external dreams. Intrinsic dreams are dreams of self-disclosure. This category encompasses the vast majority of our dreams. Believe it or not, most of your dreams are about you. Most of mine are about me. Never forget, though, that dream language is all about God. Yet He intricately gives us personal dreams of self-disclosure in order to help us in life's journey.

A small percentage of most believers' dreams fall into the extrinsic, or external, category, unless your sphere of influence indicates otherwise. These are dreams of outside events. They may involve you personally but will also have a wider scope. External dreams relate to your *metron* or sphere of influence. Sometimes these dreams will be used to call you to something but not fully to release or commission you into it yet. In this case, think of the dreams as being part of your learning curve, your training in your spiritual vocabulary. They are God's "teasers" to help you get farther down the road. He shows you a glimpse of what lies ahead in order to whet your appetite and inspire you to continue pressing forward. The most common purpose of external dreams is to draw us into intercession.

There are some prophetically gifted people who receive primarily external dreams rather than internal. This usually occurs after God has given them many internal dreams of self-disclosure to cleanse them of the many common-ground issues with the enemy. At the same time, however, God often gives a gift that is larger than our character. Why? To call our character up, to motivate us to greater growth and maturity, and to inspire us to reach for our fullest potential in Christ. God empowers us with a gift that will cause us to seek Him for the character to carry it.

Dreams From the Holy Spirit, Natural Self, and Demonic Realm

Another fundamental principle for operating in dream language is discerning the sources of our dreams. Essentially, dreams arise from three primary places. There are dreams from the Holy Spirit, dreams from the natural self, and dreams from the demonic realm. We will consider each of these in turn.

Dreams From the Holy Spirit

Dreams from the Holy Spirit are difficult to categorize because they come in virtually infinite variety and are tailored for each individual. Nevertheless, I want to discuss briefly 12 basic categories of dreams that we receive from the Holy Spirit.

1. Dreams of Destiny

Destiny dreams reveal part of the progressive calling of God regarding your life, guidance, and vocation. Generally, they relate to your sphere of influence. Sometimes they will be extrinsic dreams regarding God's redemptive plan for a city, region, or nation. At times destiny dreams are more personal, revealing the unfolding of your life in God's plan. They may relate only to the present, where you are right now, or they may deal with the past, present, and future of your life. Dream language moves in all three arenas.

A panoramic dream that seems to cover past, present, and future may be fulfilled over a short period of time. On the other hand, many years may pass before your destiny dream is completely fulfilled. This is why it is important to pay close attention to any words you hear in the dream, because they will be useful in interpreting the symbols in the dream. Dreams of destiny are inspiring and they charge our faith to soar to new levels!

2. Dreams of Edification

These are the "feel good" dreams. When you wake up from them, you absolutely feel great. You feel like you are on top of the world and ready for anything. Edifying dreams are inspirational in tone. They are filled with revelation and they produce hope. If you have been discouraged, you may receive a dream of edification that, even if you do not remember all the details, will instill in you a sense of hope and confidence, thus dispelling your discouragement.

Jacob's dream in the 28th chapter of Genesis is a good example. Fleeing from the wrath of his brother Esau and alone in the wilderness, Jacob was frightened and discouraged. He dreamed of a ladder reaching from Earth to Heaven with angels going up and down on it and God standing at the top. God promised to go with Jacob and prosper him. Not only did this dream encourage Jacob, it also changed the course of his life.

In the same way, dreams of edification can help change the course of *your* life.

3. Dreams of Exhortation

Sometimes called "courage dreams," dreams of exhortation often contain a strong sense of urgency. They challenge us to take action. While edification dreams produce hope, exhortational dreams produce faith. They impart inspiration and motivation to get up and do something for Jesus' sake. More than just giving simple advice, dreams of exhortation also reveal an accurate, detailed picture of what is going on behind the scenes, especially in the demonic realm. This revelation is for the purpose of challenging us to take action about what we have seen. Take courage and act!

4. Dreams of Comfort

Comfort dreams serve to heal our emotions and our memories. We can use them to reinterpret circumstances of our past with a heavenly lens, helping us to see things differently. In other words, comfort dreams give us a heavenly perspective on an earthly situation so that we can receive emotional healing.

A few months after my mother passed away, I had a dream in which I was back in the old country house where I grew up. I was seated at my place at the kitchen table, and my mother and father were at opposite ends of the table. Christian singer and songwriter Michael W. Smith was with them, and the three of them sang together Michael's song "Agnus Dei": "Alleluia! Alleluia! For the Lord God Almighty Reigns." This dream greatly comforted me and reassured me that my mother, as well as my father, was safely in the Presence of the Lord. Muse with me; just sing that sweet song of worship as it is being sung in Heaven!

Thus, comfort dreams can also release assurance. If edification dreams produce hope and exhortational dreams release faith, comfort dreams stir up love. They will help you love yourself better, love God better, and love others better as well.

5. Dreams of Correction

Corrective dreams reveal personal changes—character issues, heart issues, repentance issues—that we need to deal with in order to be able to move forward. These are *not* condemning dreams. The Holy Spirit never condemns. Rather, He comes in gentle love and releases a wooing to draw us to turn to Him and accept His correction. The Holy Spirit convicts and convinces us—but He never condemns.

Unlike a comfort dream, a corrective dream might unsettle us at first. They provoke us and stir us up; they even make us angry sometimes because our natural self does not always want to respond to the things of God. But God, in His infinite patience and loving-kindness, relentlessly pursues us. He wants to perfect us, so He sometimes uses dreams of correction.

6. Dreams of Direction

Directive dreams often contain a higher level of revelation and are obviously very prophetic in nature. Quite frequently they will convey a distinct sense of urgency. Their purpose is to give specific guidance, which may even include warnings of some kind. One example is the dream of the wise men in the second chapter of Matthew, whom God warned not to return to Herod. This prompted them to choose an alternate route home.

Sometimes, directive dreams will fill us with a desire for some spiritual quality or dimension that we do not yet possess and inspire us to begin pursuing it. Ultimately, dreams of direction serve to help us get farther down the road toward fulfilling our destiny and purpose, showing us signposts and helping us avoid pitfalls along the way.

7. Dreams of Instruction

These are primarily teaching dreams. Directive dreams give us direction; instructive dreams teach us. There is a fine line of distinction between the two. Scriptures are often highlighted in these dreams, and frequently you will hear a voice speaking to you. Sometimes instructive dreams will even be doctrinal in nature, but they will always contain insight with revelation.

In one dream that I call "A House That Is Built to Last," I was at a construction site, watching as a cement truck poured layer after layer of concrete into the foundation of a house. Two angels, symbolizing the jealousy of God, stood at the two front corners of the foundation, overseeing the construction. Because of shakings and Earthquakes that had occurred over the years, there was a great need for a strong and solid foundation.

As each layer of concrete set, words appeared in the foundation, similar to the handwriting on the wall that is recorded in the Book of Daniel. At the right front corner of the first layer appeared the words, "Jesus Christ, the Messiah of the Jew and the Gentile." The left corner read, "Apostles and prophets; fathers and mothers of the church ages." The Church is built on the foundation of the apostles and prophets, with Christ as the cornerstone.

As the second layer of concrete was poured, the word "Integrity" appeared on the right corner and the word "Humility" on the left. The activity of trucks releasing foundational concrete continued. Across the front of the third layer were the words, "Intimate worship from a pure heart." And, finally, the fourth layer of concrete bore the words, "God's heart for the poor and the desperate." Shooting out from those words was the phrase, "God's healing grace."

I believe this was an instructive dream with an apostolic nature to it. The dream released teaching insights into the proper way to build a strong house, whether a family home, a business, or a church. All of these qualities are necessary for the proper foundation.

Edifying dreams produce hope. Exhortational dreams instill faith. Comfort dreams stir up love. Instructive dreams impart teaching with wisdom.

8. Dreams of Cleansing

Some people call these "flushing" dreams, and with good reason. One of the most common images associated with the cleansing dream is that of being in the bathroom, on the toilet or taking a shower. These dreams deal with cleansing issues. To use scriptural terminology, we could call these dreams of sanctification. They are concerned with our purification process.

Cleansing dreams are used to wash us from the dust and dirt that we pick up by walking in the world. Christ is preparing a Bride in whom there will be no spot or wrinkle, not even on our garments. Sometimes our hearts and minds become tainted by our contact with the sin and evil in the world. Vile corruption attempts to put its grime on us. Sanctifying dreams can help with that process. Essentially, these dreams are all about applying the cleansing blood of Jesus to our lives.

9. Dreams Revealing the Heart

These are also known as dreams of self-disclosure or dreams of self-condition. The Scripture says, *"The heart is more deceitful than all else and is desperately sick; who can understand it?"* (Jer. 17:9 NASB). And Jesus said, *"For out of the abundance of the heart the mouth speaks"* (Matt. 12:34 NKJV).

Self-disclosure dreams show us where we presently stand with God. For example, let's say that you dream that you are in your car and you are stuck in a cul-de-sac. The car may represent your life or your ministry, and the cul-de-sac reveals that you are going around in circles or have almost reached a dead end. God doesn't want you to be at a dead end; He wants you back out on the highway of life.

When Abimelech took Abraham's wife, Sarah, into his harem, thinking she was Abraham's sister (which is what Abraham had told him), God appeared to Abimelech in a dream and warned him not to go any farther because Sarah was Abraham's wife. God told Abimelech to restore Sarah to Abraham or else he would die. The king did as he was instructed in the dream. (See Genesis 20:3.)

God gives us dreams of self-condition to show us where we are, to tell us what we need to do, and to reveal where He wants us to go.

10. Dreams of Spiritual Warfare

Spiritual warfare dreams are calls to prayer. They are intercessory-type dreams that reveal hindrances that are in the way and may include calls to worship and fasting. Their purpose is to inspire us to press through to victory to the cross of Christ, tearing down strongholds and overcoming every obstacle or barrier that stands in the way.

Sometimes dreams come in pairs and carry the same meaning to give additional insight. Recently, when I was diagnosed with a recurrence of non-Hodgkin's Lymphoma cancer, the Lord gave me two dreams that encouraged me to fight on to victory. In the first dream, the Holy Spirit said to me, *"You must call forth a courtroom hearing and bring before the judge three generational spirits: generational infirmity, generational witchcraft, and a generational thievery."*

In the second dream I was handed a revolver with a chamber for holding five rounds. Then I was handed five bullets of "effective grace" for loading the revolver. Each bullet had a Scripture reference on it:

- Jeremiah 30:17 (NASB): *"For I will restore you to health and I will heal you of your wounds,' declares the Lord...."*

- Proverbs 6:30-31 (NASB): *"Men do not despise a thief if he steals to satisfy himself when he is hungry; but when he is found, he must repay sevenfold; he must give all the substance of his house."*

- Leviticus 17:11 (NASB): *"For the life of the flesh is in the blood...."*

- Isaiah 54:17 (NASB): *"No weapon that is formed against you will prosper; and every tongue that accuses you in judgment you will condemn...."*

- Matthew 8:16-17 (NASB): *"When evening came, they brought to Him many who were demon-possessed; and He cast out the spirits with a word, and healed all who were ill. This was to fulfill what was spoken through Isaiah the prophet: 'He Himself took our infirmities and carried away our diseases.'"*

I believe the Lord gave me these Scriptures through a spiritual-warfare dream in order to arm me to be effective in the battle. I sent this dream out to our prayer shield and asked them to proclaim these five Scriptures over my life.

11. Dreams of Creativity

Creative dreams involve such things as designs, inventions, and new ways of doing things. They can charge our spirit self and help us become change makers, changing the culture of our homes, cities, and the lives of others and even the strongholds of our minds. God often uses creative dreams with artistic people to give them songs to sing, pictures to paint, or words to write. I have had dreams revealing the title of a new book along with a brilliant artistic cover. I call these "Holy Ghost cheat sheets," and I can use all of them He wants to give!

Some years ago I was preparing to go to Ohio for a week of ministry. It was at the height of the early prophetic movement, and the unusual amount of prophetic activity that was going on had raised expectations enormously high. Frankly, I had been moving in a level of revelation that was new to me at that time, and I was afraid that people were going to expect me to move at that level all the time. Pressure. Performance. Fear. As the day for my departure drew nearer, I was struggling with anxiety. I cried to the Lord for help, and He heard me!

The night before I left, I received two dreams or, rather, the same dream twice. An orchestra was playing, and a choir was singing. A banner unfurled in front of my eyes. Written on the banner were the words to a song. I realized that the orchestra was playing the melody and the choir was singing those words. That is when I woke up. Twice this occurred.

I flew to Cleveland, Ohio, and all that week, in every church sanctuary I ministered in, I searched for that banner. I really wanted to find that banner. I just knew it would be somewhere! I kept looking in the natural everywhere I went! The reason: I forgot the words that were printed on it! I kept looking for this sign from God, but place after place, it evaded me.

On the last night of the meetings I had a vision of a pair of shoes that I would be given to symbolically wear. On several occasions I have had visions of the shoes of an apostolic or prophetic leader as a clue to me of what particular anointing I was about to move in. This night I saw the shoes of my dear friend Mahesh Chavda. Having traveled with Mahesh and witnessed his meetings, I knew that in my last meeting the Holy Spirit would move in power, and people would be overwhelmed by the Holy Spirit all over the auditorium.

By the time of the last night's meeting, however, I was so physically depleted that I felt like I had nothing left to give to the people. When the time came for me to speak, I was introduced, but I still seemed to have nothing. Desperately I prayed, "Help me, Jesus!"

God is so faithful! As I stood up to speak, I received an open vision of— you guessed it—the unfurled banner from my dream. There it was, right in front of my spiritual eyes. I could see clearly the words written on it and immediately began to sing them a cappella: "How far will My love extend? How far will My arm reach? Will My blood cleanse when man sins, yet knowing? How far will the blood of My Son reach?"

As it turned out, this was a song of great comfort to this church, as they recently had removed a senior leader who had fallen into immorality and were currently without a permanent leader. They were dealing with a lot of disappointment, and the song of the Lord greatly encouraged them. God knew just what they needed and imparted it to me through a creative dream and vision. That night the anointing was so strong that no one could come closer than 6 feet from me without "falling out" in the Spirit. People were dropping by the power of God all over the sanctuary.

Was this a dream of comfort, a dream of cleansing, or a dream of creativity? Well, remember the illustration I shared previously about the colors of the rainbow? Where one color ends the other begins? Well, the answer is: it was all the above. It was a creative dream that brought cleansing and healing comfort! Dreams can do more than one thing at a time!

God is a Creator by nature, and He loves to give creative dreams to His children.

12. Dreams With Impartation

Impartational dreams are used to activate any of the various dimensions of the gifts of the Spirit. Many times it will be the gift of healing, both emotional healing and physical healing. In some cases an angel of the Lord may actually appear in your room and touch you, releasing one of Heaven's many power encounters.

My wife, Michal Ann, had a dream like this two weeks before she was scheduled to go to Mozambique. A number of people had been telling her that she was not well enough to go on this trip. In her dream, Aimee Semple McPherson, the apostle, evangelist, and founder of the Four Square Gospel Church, who moved mightily in signs and wonders, approached Michal Ann with a key card in her hand. She stuck it into her and pulled it back out. Upon awakening, Michal Ann felt the riveting Presence of the energy of God all over her. It was a dream of impartation. There was an impartation of faith not only for her own life but for the entire apostolic mission she was about to embark upon by leading a team to Mozambique. Yes, God knows exactly what you need and when you need it!

Dreams From the Natural Self

Some of our dreams are not supernatural in nature but come from our natural self. These "natural" dreams generally fall into one of three categories: body dreams, chemical dreams, or soulish dreams.

1. Body Dreams

Body dreams generally arise from and reflect some aspect of the physical condition of the person who is dreaming. For example, dreams of being pregnant are not uncommon. They often mean—you got it—the lady is pregnant! But even men have been known to have dreams of being pregnant. In their case, as well as in the case of women who dream this, there may indeed be a spiritual meaning behind the dream. A pregnancy dream may indicate that the person is "due" with the things and purposes of God. Something new is about to be birthed!

Most often, however, body dreams reflect physical realities. A person who is sick may dream of being sick. A person who feels as if he or she has the flu, well, he or she might have the flu! A person who is experiencing depression or grief may have dreams that reflect his or her state of mind. Somber and depressing dreams can also come from the enemy, so careful discernment is called for in distinguishing one from the other.

Just because body dreams are not necessarily spiritual does not mean that they are demonic. It is important to pay attention to body dreams because they can provide clues to changes we may need to make in our natural lives.

2. Chemical Dreams

These dreams, sometimes known as hormone dreams, usually come as a result of medications we are taking. Quite often, chemical dreams reveal the need for our bodies to go through some cleansing. I have had occasions when a chemical dream revealed to me that a medication I was taking, such as for sinus relief, was building up in my body too much. It was having a negative effect on me, and I needed cleansing.

Chemical dreams may also arise because of changing or abnormal hormone or chemical levels in the body. PMS, diabetes, hypoglycemia—these and similar conditions involving chemical imbalances can stimulate these type of natural dreams.

3. Soulish Dreams

The word "soulish" does not necessarily mean fleshly. As Christians, our souls are to be renewed in Christ—but honestly, we are all in various stages of being renewed. Soulish dreams may simply be our emotions expressing our needs or desires. They may speak to us about the need for sanctification in some area of our lives. One significant value of soulish dreams is that they can show us things about ourselves that we may otherwise fail to see when we are awake.

Dreams From the Demonic Realm

A third source of dreams that we must recognize is that of the demonic realm. Anything that God has and uses, the enemy seeks to counterfeit, including dreams. Demonic dreams tend to fall into any of three different types: dark dreams, dreams of fear and/or panic, and dreams of deception.

1. Dark Dreams

Dark dreams tend to be dark in two ways. First, they are dark in mood and tone; they are somber, depressing, melancholy dreams; dreams where everything is a little out of kilter, where something indefinable seems wrong or slightly off center. Second, dark dreams typically are literally dark with subdued or muted colors. Black, gray, and sickly green shades are in abundance. This lack of bright, vivid, and lively colors is one way of determining that a dream may come from a dark or even demonic source.

Dark dreams commonly conjure up dark emotions and often employ dark symbols, emblems that instill a sense of discomfort or unease. This is the type of dream that I referred to in the second chapter. Remember, I had a fair number of dark dreams before I was ever released into cleansing and later the power of extrinsic dreams. Of course, there are also dark chemical dreams that are brought on as a result of involvement with witchcraft and illegal drug use. Repent, turn to the Lord, and seek help if this is the case.

2. Dreams of Fear and/or Panic

Most nightmares, especially childhood nightmares, fall into this category. Dreams of fear and panic often arise from trauma, so simply rebuking the fear or the panic may not be enough. It may be necessary to ask the Holy Spirit to reveal the root of the frightening dreams so that repentance, cleansing, or healing can take place. My wife's early dreams of bears and tornadoes were of this nature. Learn to exercise your authority in Christ and ward off these haunting dreams in Jesus' name!

3. Dreams of Deception

Deceptive dreams are often the work of deceitful spirits, which the Scripture says will be particularly active in the last days: *"But the Spirit explicitly says that in later times some will fall away from the faith, paying attention to deceitful spirits and doctrines of demons"* (1 Tim. 4:1 NASB). These deceptive spirits seek to draw us away from the place of security to a place of insecurity.

The purpose of deceptive dreams is to create images and impressions in our minds that will turn us away from the true path of God's light into the darkness of error and heresy. Under the influence of deceptive dreams we can make mistakes in every area of life: doctrine, finances, sexuality, relationships, career choices, parenting; you name it. Whatever form they may take and whatever images they may convey, these disturbing revelations are from the dark side. Exercise careful discernment. Walking in the light of transparent relationships with other believers in the Body of Christ is ammunition that overcomes the deceptive spirit.

Keeping It Simple

In case you are starting to worry about information overload with all these categories of dreams, let me close by breaking all this down into simpler terms. According to authors Chuck Pierce and Rebecca Sytsema, all these categories we have discussed can be condensed into three basic dream types:

the simple message dream, the simple symbolic dream, and the complex symbolic dream. In their book *When God Speaks*, Chuck Pierce and Rebecca Sytsema explain it this way:

We find three types of dreams in the Bible:

1. **A simple message dream.** In Matthew 1–2, Joseph understood the dreams concerning Mary and Herod. There was no real need for interpretation. These dreams were direct, to the point, and self-interpreted.

2. **A simple symbolic dream.** Dreams can be filled with symbols. Oftentimes the symbolism is clear enough that the dreamer and others can understand it without any complicated interpretation. For instance, when Joseph had his dream in Genesis 37, he fully understood it, as did his brothers, to the point that they wanted to kill him, even though it had symbols of the sun, moon, and stars.

3. **The complex symbolic dream.** This type of dream needs interpretative skill from someone who has unusual ability in the gift of interpretation or from someone who knows how to seek God to find revelation. We find this type of dream in the life of Joseph, when he interprets Pharaoh's dream. In Daniel 2 and 4, we find good examples of this type of dream. In Daniel 8, we find a dream in which Daniel actually sought divine interpretation.[1]

If you are just beginning to walk in the realm of dream language and find all this talk on the various shades of dreams a bit overwhelming, be patient. It will take time and experience to become adept at identifying different dream types and categories and interpreting the messages you receive. Relax in the assurance that God will not move you along faster than you can handle. He will gently and lovingly guide you along the way in your very own diversity of dreams.

Dream a Little Dream with Me!

Yes, dream a little dream with me. In fact, let's dream some big dreams and watch them unfold right before our very eyes! His ways are amazing. He will lead you not only into revelation, but He will teach you how to understand what you just received! In fact, you can bank on that statement!

Are you still ready for more? If so, then you will love the next chapters on angels, trances, apparitions (you heard me right!) and other extraordinary spiritual experiences. Yes, they are all in the B-I-B-L-E and they are exactly right for you and me!

Endnote

1. Chuck Pierce and Rebecca Sytsema, *When God Speaks* (New York: Regal Books, 2005).

CHAPTER 5

Angelic Assignments

BY JAMES GOLL

As I mentioned in the previous chapter, angels definitely seem to have particular areas of stewardship. In essence, they have *assignments*. Their assignments fit within the context of their three primary functions. Here's a quick review:

1. Angels give service to God—worshiping God eternally. (See Psalm 148:2.)

2. Angels give service to people, especially believers. (See Hebrews 1:7,14.)

3. Angels perform God's Word. (See Psalm 103:20-21.)

Their assignment to worship God is their highest and grandest one, but it is far from being merely the "standard-issue" angelic assignment (and therefore the most mundane one). Angels define worship. They worshiped at the creation. They certainly worshiped at the birth of Jesus, the Messiah, showing up in the sky over the shepherd's field. They still worship now that the Church lives under the New Covenant; they will worship Him until the Second Coming of Jesus and beyond, throughout all eternity.

Nobody needs to pray that the angels will keep worshiping. It keeps happening without human cooperation. Our privilege is to participate to some degree in it, especially after we go to be with the Lord forever. The 24 elders cast down their crowns before Him, and the angels of God join with the people of God to declare, eternally, that He is worthy.

But while we're still here in this world, we do pray about a lot of other matters, and God assigns angels to perform His will. We don't pray only the sweeping prayers such as, "Thy kingdom come, thy will be done on Earth as it is in Heaven." We also pray, "Give us this day our daily bread" and "Lead us not into temptation." We pray very specific prayers, such as, "Lord, please heal this," "Father, help me forgive So-and-So," and "Holy Spirit, provide protection for my family on our trip."

Our prayers are often prayed in direct response to divine nudges. We don't just dream them up all by ourselves. Therefore, when we pray, we are releasing an invitation or request back to God. In essence, our best prayers originate with Him. And in response to our requests, He often assigns an angel or two to meet our need. This is the way it has worked since the beginning of time. Angels have always been waiting and ready to act according to God's command in response to human prayers. They were with the prophets of old and they visited priests of the Old Covenant. They helped Daniel in the lion's den. They released spectacular judgments on the Lord's behalf. They strengthened Jesus in the Garden of Gethsemane.

At other times He plants a word in our spirits and we give voice to it in a declarative manner. We might call that a *rhema* word or a gift of faith. We may actually say something like, "I call you forth, angels, to come and do this!" But it's not as if we originated the concept—God Himself did. Angels aren't at our beck and call; they are at His, and so are we. Therefore, a man or a woman who is in a relationship with God can sometimes tap into the heartbeat of Heaven and give voice to God's divine will for that moment in time.

Coming full circle, I don't want to leave the impression that all angelic assignments require human involvement, because they don't. A long time ago, God assigned His angels to perform certain functions above and beyond worshiping Him. We assume that many of them have stayed with their first assignments, with no human involvement whatsoever. For instance, He assigned "cherubim and the flaming sword" to guard the gates of Eden. (See Genesis 3:24 NASB.)

Angels do seem to "specialize" in particular duties. However, there is no rigid dividing line between different types of assignments. For example, when an angel brings someone a message, the word can provide guidance or protection or deliverance—or all three. As you will see in this chapter, we can say quite a bit about what God assigns angels to do, but our explanations come from the limited perspective of our little patch of the planet Earth, which is our "observation deck." For the most part, we can only stand in awe. God's angelic host is magnificent, and the Lord God is the most magnificent of all!

Ushering in God's Presence

Have you ever been in a worship gathering where you could tell that the spiritual "temperature" went up a notch? Something seemed extra-special about it. You may have identified it as what I call the "manifest Presence of God."

In the natural, this happens all the time—not the manifest Presence of God, but rather some natural "presence" riding into a room with a person. Even when your co-worker comes back from a vacation, he or she can bring a sense of relaxation along. Or the opposite can occur: your spouse can come home from work, bringing along all the tension of his or her difficult day. I believe that the angels, who spend so much of their time before the throne of God, can't help but bring His Presence to a place! Sometimes that Presence is a perceptible aroma or a feeling of electricity or a visible light. At other times, it's an awe-inspiring, even weighty feeling of pressure. God's holiness supercharges the atmosphere, and that affects His angels, who can't help but bring an extra wave of His holiness wherever they go.

I remember being in Kansas City in 1975 at the National Men's Shepherds Conference, which was held in the Municipal Auditorium. A lot of the "generals of the faith" were there, most of whom have now gone on to be with the Lord. I remember Ern Baxter delivering one of the greatest messages I've ever heard, called "Thy Kingdom Come." He had an unusual degree of authority on him, and he was declaring the government of God.

Something holy happened in worship, prophetic words were released, and a shift occurred. It wasn't just the generals of faith who were present—some "generals" of Heaven showed up too. In response to the holy Presence of God, every man took off his shoes in a unified response of humility. We just got on our faces. It was the least we could do. None of us had crowns on our heads that we could cast before God, but we had shoes on our feet. It was a true *kairos* moment, where Heaven and Earth met, a holy crossroads.

Angels were present, probably by the thousands, and we recognized that we were standing on holy ground. The climate shifted enormously, from one of familiarity with God to one of the fear of the Lord. Angels came to the Municipal Auditorium, carrying the golden light of Heaven to Earth.

We can assume that, whenever we feel God's Presence, angels are in the place, regardless of whether or not we can see them. Our response is always going to be worship—holy, holy, holy is the Lord of hosts!

Angelic *Direction*

Besides conveying God's Presence when they come, angels have specific jobs to do when they arrive.

I believe that the tasks God has assigned to angels fall into two major categories: *direction* and *protection*. Obviously, these categories overlap and mingle, just as they do with our natural human tasks When you drive your children someplace in the car, you are providing them with direction (by steering the car to a destination) and protection (by keeping them safe from traffic, weather, other potential hazards). But let's go ahead and take a look at each category, so we can better appreciate what angels do.

First, what are some of the ways that angels bring God's *direction* to us? Here are four of them. Angels:

- Deliver God's messages.
- Release dreams, revelation, and understanding.

- Give guidance.

- Impart strength.

In one way or another, all of these functions provide direction.

Angels Deliver God's Messages

What would we do without the services of God's angelic messengers? If you sit down and start turning the pages of your Bible, you will find story after story about angels bringing messages from God. They announce forthcoming events. They pronounce God's judgments. They bring encouragement. They "direct traffic," telling people what to do, how to do it, and when to do it. Here's a quick sampling of such angelic "instant messaging," from both the Old and New Testaments:

Joshua 5:13-15 (NASB). Joshua encountered a commanding angel who tells him how to take Jericho: *"Now it came about when Joshua was by Jericho, that he lifted up his eyes and looked, and behold, a man was standing opposite him with his sword drawn in his hand, and Joshua went to him and said to him, 'Are you for us or for our adversaries?' He said, 'No; rather I indeed come now as captain of the host of the Lord.' And Joshua fell on his face to the Earth, and bowed down, and said to him, 'What has my lord to say to his servant?' The captain of the Lord's host said to Joshua, 'Remove your sandals from your feet, for the place where you are standing is holy.' And Joshua did so."*

Judges 13:4-5. The angel of the Lord visited Manoah and his barren wife, telling them that she would bear a son and instructing them specifically about what to do: *"Now see to it that you drink no wine or other fermented drink and that you do not eat anything unclean, because you will conceive and give birth to a son. No razor may be used on his head, because the boy is to be a Nazirite, set apart to God from birth, and he will begin the deliverance of Israel from the hands of the Philistines."* The promised baby boy was Samson.

Luke 1:19-20 (NASB). An archangel brought a message to Zacharias. *"The angel answered and said to him, 'I am Gabriel, who stands in the presence of God, and I have been sent to speak to you and to bring you this good news. And behold, you shall be silent and unable to speak until the day when these things take* place, because you did not believe my words, which will be fulfilled in their proper time.'"

Luke 1:26. Gabriel brought a message to Mary. "*And coming in, he said to her, 'Greetings, favored one! The Lord is with you.' ...The angel said to her, 'Do not be afraid, Mary; for you have found favor with God. And behold, you will conceive in your womb and bear a son, and you shall name Him Jesus. He will be great and will be called the Son of the Most High; and the Lord God will give Him the throne of His father David; and He will reign over the house of Jacob forever, and His kingdom will have no end.... The Holy Spirit will come upon you, and the power of the Most High will overshadow you; and for that reason the holy Child shall be called the Son of God. And behold, even your relative Elizabeth has also conceived a son in her old age; and she who was called barren is now in her sixth month. For nothing will be impossible with God*" (Luke 1:28,30-33,35-37 NASB).

Luke 2:10. Angels filled the sky and a spokesman-angel announced Jesus' birth to the shepherds: "*Do not be afraid; for behold, I bring you good news of great joy which will be for all the people.*"

Matthew 1:20; Matthew 2:13,19. Angelic messengers spoke to Joseph in dreams to direct him to take Mary as his wife, to take Mary and the baby Jesus to Egypt for safety before Herod had all of the infants murdered, and to bring them back to Nazareth after Herod's death.

Matthew 28:1-7. An angel proclaimed the resurrection of Jesus. "*He is not here, for He has risen, just as He said. Come, see the place where He was lying. Go quickly and tell His disciples that He has risen from the dead; and behold, He is going ahead of you into Galilee, there you will see Him; behold, I have told you*" (Matt. 28:6-7 NASB).

Angels Release Dreams, Revelation, and Understanding

An angel in a dream told Joseph how to take care of Mary and Jesus. At other times, angels release revelational understanding without speaking in dreams. Here is a contemporary example, told by a man named Terry Law, in which a pastor who was named Roland Buck obtained a detailed under-standing of Law's past and future by means of angelic revelation:

> As a thirteen-year-old boy, I attended a camp meeting at Nanoose Bay in Vancouver Island, British Columbia. One night a speaker from the American Assemblies of God gave a stirring call for com-mitment and a challenge for missions, and the Holy Spirit began to move on me....
>
> [I stayed after] everyone else left for the night, and the lights were turned out. Midnight passed, 1:00 A.M. passed, and then around 2:00 A.M., the evangelist returned.
>
> His name was Dwight McLaughlin, and he had left his Bible on the pulpit. I was sitting on a bench in the shadows where he could not see me, but I could see him in the moonlight. I sat motionless, but he sensed someone was there and called out. When I answered, he felt his way to where I sat in a back corner.
>
> He said, "You know, the Lord must have sent me to you," and explained that he had awakened and felt impressed to go get his Bible. Then he asked if he could pray for me. When he laid his hand on me, warmth radiated through me. I started to tremble.
>
> He said, "Young man, I see a vision. God has called you, and He is going to send you around the world to preach the gospel. I see crowds of thousands and hundreds of thousands."
>
> ...Years later, in 1977, I was traveling with my music group Living Sound and came to minister at Roland Buck's church in Boise, Idaho. Roland and I were outside the church one night sitting in his car when he told me a story.
>
> He began by saying very quietly, "Terry, I talked with Gabriel last week."
>
> At the time, I knew no more about angels than the average Christian, perhaps less than some, and I said, "Gabriel who?"....

[Two years later, I returned to his church, and] as my co-evangelist, Gordon Calmeyer, and I were sitting at breakfast with Roland one morning, Gordon shocked me with a question for Roland about angels.

"Well, pastor," he said, "if these angels are talking to you all the time, and your church is a strong supporter of our ministry, why don't you ask the angels about us?"…Roland sat there with a slight smile and did not say anything. We went our separate ways and I forgot about the conversation.

Three months later I was asked to appear on a national Christian television program to introduce Roland…. Before the program went on the air, we were in a room backstage together, just the two of us.

He said, "Terry, do you remember when you were a thirteen-year-old and attended a camp meeting in Canada?"

I had never told another soul what happened that night.

Roland said, "Do you remember about 2:00 A.M., the camp evangelist"—and he actually named Dwight McLaughlin—"walked into the building? Do you remember that you were sitting there praying, and he walked over and laid hands on you?"

I said, "Roland, how do you know about that night?"

He looked at me and just smiled. I exclaimed. "Are you kidding me? The angels told you this?"

He nodded and said the angels had awakened McLaughlin because that was the night God had chosen for my ordination into ministry. "The angels told me a lot about you," he said. "They told me of times in your childhood when you went through great difficulties. You had to learn as a child to stand up against odds and overcome them. God was getting you ready for your ministry. He was building iron into your character…."[1]

Stories like this one make me wonder—how much of what we call prophetic revelation is actually handed to us by our fellow servants, the angels? The entire Book of the Revelation of Jesus Christ was communicated to John by His angel. Daniel had such profoundly disturbing experiences that only an angel could interpret them for him. (See Daniel 8:15-26; 9:20-27.) Quite likely, angels are helping you understand about angels as you read this book!

On October 4, 2004, I was in Colorado Springs, and I had a dream encounter that was about receiving interpretation. In the dream, I was with John Paul Jackson. (One seer was with another seer.) And John Paul turned to me and he said, "How do you do that?"

I smiled, saying "I have help!"

Then I turned and said, "He hands me scrolls, and I read them." When I turned, there was an angel by my side, handing me a scroll to read.

For a short time after that dream, maybe three or four days, I had sort of a holy buzz that was all around my head, some kind of supernatural capacity to understand and interpret revelation. I didn't tell a lot of people about this, but I could tell what God was speaking to people, and I could interpret it supernaturally. I have to believe that the scroll-bearing angel stepped out of my dream and into my waking life.

Angels Give God's Guidance

Besides releasing dreams, revelation, and understanding, angels give direct guidance. That's what happened to Philip before he met up with the Ethiopian eunuch: "*An angel of the Lord spoke to Philip saying, 'Get up and go south to the road that descends from Jerusalem to Gaza'*" (Acts 8:26 NASB). It was as if the angel handed him a set of directions.

That's also what happened when Abraham's servant went off in search of the right bride for Isaac. (See Genesis 24:7,40.) An angel "went before him" so that he would find the way to the right place at the right time when the right girl was right there.

Paul, when he was on board the storm-tossed ship, had an angel come to give him guidance for the crew and other passengers: *"This very night an angel of the God to whom I belong and whom I serve stood before me, saying, 'Do not be afraid, Paul; you must stand before Caesar; and behold, God has granted you all those who are sailing with you.' Therefore, keep up your courage, men, for I believe God that it will turn out exactly as I have been told. But we must run aground on a certain island"* (Acts 27:23-26 NASB).

Jumping back to the Old Testament, we see an angel confronting Balaam, literally directing traffic by redirecting his donkey—who opened his mouth and *spoke* to his master before the angel did:

> *Then the Lord opened the eyes of Balaam, and he saw the angel of the Lord standing in the way with his drawn sword in his hand; and he bowed all the way to the ground. The angel of the Lord said to him, "Why have you struck your donkey these three times? Behold, I have come out as an adversary, because your way was contrary to me. But the donkey saw me and turned aside from me these three times. If she had not turned aside from me, I would surely have killed you just now, and let her live."*

> *Balaam said to the angel of the Lord, "I have sinned, for I did not know that you were standing in the way against me. Now then, if it is displeasing to you, I will turn back."*

> *But the angel of the Lord said to Balaam, "Go with the men, but you shall speak only the word which I tell you." So Balaam went along with the leaders of Balak* (Numbers 22:31-35 NASB).

Talk about direct angelic guidance! Looks like it can get a little dangerous sometimes.

Angels Impart Strength

Sometimes angels come to impart encouragement and strength more than anything else.

In Genesis 16, we read about Sarai's Egyptian maid, Hagar, who was forced to become pregnant and then as a result was abused by Sarai, to the point that she ran away into the wilderness in distress. God sent an angel to comfort her:

> *But the Angel of the Lord found her by a spring of water in the wilder-ness on the road to Shur. And He said, "Hagar, Sarai's maid, where did you come from, and where are you intending to go?"*
>
> *And she said, "I am running away from my mistress Sarai."*
>
> *The Angel of the Lord said to her, "Go back to your mistress and [humbly] submit to her control." Also the Angel of the Lord said to her, "I will multiply your descendants exceedingly, so that they shall not be numbered for multitude." And the Angel of the Lord continued, "See now, you are with child and shall bear a son, and shall call his name Ishmael [God hears], because the Lord has heard and paid attention to your affliction. And he [Ishmael] will be as a wild ass among men; his hand will be against every man and every man's hand against him, and he will live to the east and on the borders of all his kinsmen.*
>
> *So she called the name of the Lord Who spoke to her, You are a God of seeing, for she said, "Have I [not] even here [in the wilderness] looked upon Him Who sees me [and lived]? Or have I here also seen [the future purposes or designs of] Him Who sees me?" Therefore the well was called Beer-lahai-roi [A well to the Living One Who sees me]; it is between Kadesh and Bered"* (Genesis 16:7-14 AMP).

Angels came to strengthen Jesus after His 40-day fast in the wilderness. (See Matthew 4:11; Mark 1:13.) Again, an angel came to His aid when he ago-nized in Gethsemane before He was crucified. (See Luke 22:43.)

During a time of distress, angels were used to impart God's strength to Daniel. (See Daniel 10:18.) As he and many others have discovered, one touch from an angel is enough to send a power surge through our mortal bodies.

After Elijah defeated the prophets of Baal, he ran into the wilderness, afraid and exhausted. There, an angel not only strengthened him with words, but also with supernatural food: *"He lay down and slept under a juniper tree; and behold, there was an angel touching him, and he said to him, 'Arise, eat.' Then he looked and behold, there was at his head a bread cake baked on hot stones, and a jar of water. So he ate and drank and lay down again. The angel of the Lord came again a second time and touched him and said, 'Arise, eat, because the journey is too great for you.' So he arose and ate and drank, and went in the strength of that food forty days and forty nights to Horeb, the mountain of God"* (1 Kings 19:5-8 NASB).

Thank you, Lord, for sending your angels to bring us divine strength and encouragement.

Angelic *Protection*

Next, we turn to the angelic assignments that can be loosely categorized as angelic *protection*. When angels come to protect the people God sends them to, sometimes they bring *deliverance* in their wings. At other times they bring some type of *healing*. And at the end of a saint's life on Earth, they provide a protective *escort* to Heaven. These are all aspects of protection.

Angels protect isolated individuals and they protect groups of people, families, and churches from harm. They protect soldiers on battlefields from injury; they protect the poor and disenfranchised from mistreatment and hunger; they stand watch night and day over households where people have called upon the blood of Jesus. We know about angelic protection from both Scripture and our personal experiences.

Angels Provide Protection

In Chapter 5, I mentioned "guardian angels." Matthew 18:10 is the verse from which we obtain our understanding of guardian angels for children. I see no reason why angels would not also be assigned to guard and protect adults as well. After all, grown-ups are His children too.

Psalm 91:11-12 (NASB) reads, *"For He will give His angels charge concerning you, to guard you in all your ways. They will bear you up in their hands, that you do not strike your foot against a stone."*

Most of us have heard many examples of angelic protection. The following story about a family working with Wycliffe Bible Translators in Bolivia gives an especially clear illustration. I have condensed an account that was written by the missionary mom. Her two sons, Doug and Dennis, who were seven and nine years old, were playing, and they had dug a shallow cave in a hillside of dried mud. Suddenly, it shifted and collapsed, trapping both boys. Their friend Mark ran for help.

Inside the cave, Doug had been slapped down on his chest. His face was smashed into the dirt, but a pocket of air helped him breathe.

"Dennis, can you hear me?" His voice seemed to make no sound at all, but he felt a slight movement beneath him. "Dennis," Doug went on. "I can't move. I can't breathe!" He felt another wiggle. An ant crawled onto his face, then another. The first sting came. It was on his eyelid. "Dennis, I can't talk…the air's going away."

The ants were all over him now, stinging. "Dennis, I think we're maybe going to die." He began to struggle. Dirt filled his mouth.

And then Douglas stopped talking. He even stopped struggling for air. For there, next to him, was an angel. He stood bright, strong.

"Dennis!" Doug called softly, his voice relaxed. "Dennis, there's an *angel* here. I can see him plain as anything. He's bright. He's trying to help us." Doug felt one oh-so-slight movement. "He's not doing anything. But Dennis…if we die now…it's not so bad…." Doug lost consciousness.

Mark reached the house, screaming for help. Men came with picks and shovels. Mark showed them where to dig.

Seconds later one of the shovels touched softness. Seconds again and Doug's back and legs were free. Strong arms pulled him from the Earth. Dennis's form appeared beneath him.

Neither boy was breathing. Their skin was blue. They lay on the red Earth, their bodies so terribly small….

Then Douglas moved. A moment later Dennis stirred…. "Mommy!" Douglas said as soon as he opened his eyes. "Do you know what I saw? An angel!"

"Shh, sweetheart. Don't try to talk yet."

[The next day, the doctor told us that] another two minutes, and the lack of oxygen would have damaged the boys' brains. But because they had not spent themselves struggling, the doctor said, they had just exactly enough oxygen to come through the experience without damage. And the reason they had not struggled, all of us knew, was the angel—the angel who kept them from being afraid.[2]

In his book, *Angels Around Us*, Douglas Connelly tells the story of a woman from his church:

A woman was in the critical care unit with a raging infection. She was not expected to survive. I was her pastor at the time, and as I stood by her bedside and talked to her, she would respond only with nods or whispers. Finally she said, "Who is the man standing in the corner, dressed in white? He's been standing there all night and all day today."

When I looked at the corner of the room, no one was there. I said, "What does he look like?"

"Can't you see him?" she replied. "He's all in white, and he is so strong. It's like he is standing guard. I'm almost afraid to speak in his presence."

I asked the nurse when I left the room if the patient had said anything about a man in her room. The nurse reassured me that the woman was just hallucinating. "Has she seen anything else that wasn't there?" I asked.

"Oh, no, she is very perceptive—except for the man in white!" As I walked out of the hospital I was convinced that what this dear child of God saw in her room was not a hallucination. It was a very real angel of God.[3]

This "man in white" had indeed come to guard her—or perhaps to wait until it was time to take her home to the Father. We'll look at that angelic assignment next.

Angels Escort Saints to Heaven

Many, many people have had experiences that seem to confirm that angels arrive at the time of the death of a saint of God specifically to escort that person's soul to the heavenly realm where they will dwell forever. Surely we can't get there on our own, so this must be true. What a comforting fact.

Not long ago, one of my aunts went home to be with the Lord. Her three daughters reported that she had an angelic encounter. An angel came into her bedroom and my Aunt Wilma was "caught up." They thought at first that maybe she was out of her mind, because she started talking about the things she was seeing. Her husband had passed on just a few months before, and she was looking for him. Then she saw someone else she knew, someone who had died already. Then, with the angel directing her on this side of death, she saw Jesus. She started declaring, "It's Jesus! I see Jesus. I see Jesus." At that, of course, her daughters realized that she was on the edge of death, so they agreed to bless their mother, and she was gone a little later. The angel came to carry her home.

We regularly quote a couple of Psalms that refer to the time of death. Psalm 116:15 (KJV) reads, "*Precious in the sight of the Lord is the death of his saints.*" Psalm 23:4 (NASB) is even more familiar to us: "*Even though I walk through the valley of the shadow of death, I fear no evil, for You are with me; Your rod and Your staff, they comfort me.*"

But the best biblical confirmation of the idea of angels carrying people home to God comes from the story about a beggar named Lazarus. Luke 15:22 literally reads, "*Now the poor man died and was carried away by the angels to Abraham's bosom,*" which means he was taken to paradise or Heaven. Angels took him there.

We don't know how it goes at the death of someone who doesn't belong to God. When the rich man in the story dies, no angels are mentioned. I don't know about you, but I know I'd much rather be assigned an angelic escort when I'm about to draw my final breath!

Angels are involved at the beginnings and the endings of our lives, with everything in between—and beyond!

Angels Bring Deliverance

Often angels deliver us from harm. Psalm 34:7 says, "*The angel of the Lord encamps around those who fear Him, and rescues them.*" The angel of the

Lord not only stands watch ("encamps"), but he reaches out to rescue those who are sinking.

When angels are assigned to a rescue operation, the assignment sometimes includes the destruction of enemies. Once, when the odds were impossibly steep against Hezekiah and the Israelites, God said, *"For I will defend this city to save it for My own sake and for My servant David's sake.' Then the angel of the Lord went out and struck 185,000 in the camp of the Assyrians; and when men arose early in the morning, behold, all of these were dead"* (Isa. 37:35-36; see also 2 Kings 19:24-25 NASB).

Angels are also helping when individual people are being delivered from evil spirits. Here's a current-day example:

> In [a] service where miracles were taking place, a young man who was about twenty-five years old came into the service crying. He had a wild and desperate look on his face. You could tell he had been drinking and was high on drugs. He said to me [the woman evangelist], "Please, please help me. Won't someone help me? I want to be delivered so badly. I'm tired of this life. I'm tired of this addiction. Help me. Help me!"

> The compassion of the Lord swept over the room. Filled with this compassion, we began to pray for the young man and to cast out evil spirits from him in Jesus' name. We anointed him with oil. Then we led him in the sinner's prayer, and immediately he began to shake his head. He was totally set free; when he stood up, his eyes were completely clear. This young man raised his hands in the air. Soon, he began to magnify and praise the Lord. God had totally transformed him in about fifteen minutes!

> Then a little twelve-year-old boy came over and said to him, "Can I tell you something? Do you know what I saw as the people were praying for you?"

> The man answered, "No."

"I saw when the demons left you, and they were standing around, trying to go back into you. But all the people were around you, praying. Then I saw an angel with a sword come and chase them away. They couldn't come back!"

The young man praised the Lord, and we were so happy that God had reached out and saved and delivered him. This man is now with good Christian people and is going to church.[4]

Angels Release Healing

Last, but certainly not least, angels are assigned to release healing. The obvious scriptural illustration of angels releasing healing is the story of the pool of Bethesda. (See John 5.) It's not that an angel shows up in the story itself, because Jesus himself stepped forward to release healing to a man who had been crippled for 38 years.

But you will remember how the story begins:

Now there is in Jerusalem a pool near the Sheep Gate. This pool in the Hebrew is called Bethesda, having five porches (alcoves, colonnades, doorways). In these lay a great number of sick folk—some blind, some crippled, and some paralyzed (shriveled up)—waiting for the bubbling up of the water. For an angel of the Lord went down at appointed seasons into the pool and moved and stirred up the water; whoever then first, after the stirring up of the water, stepped in was cured of whatever disease with which he was afflicted (John 5:2-4 AMP).

The sick people had what some might call a folk belief (but it was probably true) that when a particular angel came, you could tell because the water of the pool, which was otherwise perfectly smooth, would move. Then, and only then, the first person into the water would be healed. It must have happened often enough to draw all of those needy people to camp out next to the pool day after day after day in hopes of being the next candidate for healing. It must have been some angel's particular assignment to go, at God's bidding, to stir the waters and release His healing power.

In our day, an angel was involved in establishing the extensive healing ministry of William M. Branham, whose ministry triggered the 1946-1956 Latter Rain Movement. The account of Branham's angelic visitation on May 7, 1946, has been well documented:

> The angel said to Branham, "Fear not. I am sent from the Presence of Almighty God to tell you that your peculiar life and your misunderstood ways have been to indicate that God has sent you to take a gift of divine healing to the peoples of the world. If you will be sincere and get the people to believe you, nothing shall stand before your prayer...not even cancer!"
>
> The angel went on to tell William Branham that he would take the ministry of healing around the world and eventually pray for kings, princes, and monarchs. Brother Branham responded by saying, "How can this be since I am a poor man and I live among poor people and I have no education." The angel then continued the commission saying, "As the prophet Moses was given two signs to prove that he was sent from God, so will you be given two signs."
>
> For approximately 30 minutes the angel stood before Brother Branham, explaining the commission and the way the ministry would operate in the supernatural arena.[5]

The angel connected what was happening with what happened to Moses. The outworking of the experience connected Moses and Branham even more clearly, in that both angel-commissioned ministries were characterized by signs and wonders (including amazing healings) and deliverance.

Angels Worshiping, Watching, Working

After reading this chapter, it should be obvious to you that it's never just "me and Jesus." Angels are an essential part of the interchange between God and His people. Isn't it good to know that God has provided angels to watch over us and to give us their direction and protection?

God, what you did before, you can do again. So we welcome your angels to release your manifest Presence, to deliver your Word, to release revelation and understanding. Send angelic assistance to perform your words of healing and deliverance. May angels become our hedge of protection, as we serve you here on Earth, and may they usher us into your Presence when our time on Earth is finished. Amen, in the name of your Son Jesus.

Endnotes

1. Terry Law, *The Truth About Angels* (Lake Mary, FL: Creation House, 1994), 192-95.

2. Gloria Farah, "I've Got a Real, Live Angel," in *Angels in our Midst* (New York, Galilee/Doubleday, 2004), 46–48.

3. Douglas Connelly, *Angels Around Us* (Downers Grove, IL: InterVarsity, 1994), 105-106.

4. Mary K. Baxter, with Dr. L.L. Lowery, *A Divine Revelation of Angels* (New Kensington, PA: Whitaker House, 2003), 186-87.

5. As told by Paul Keith Davis in the E-Newsletter of WhiteDove Ministries dated November, 2005, http://www.whitedoveministries.org/content/NewsItem.phtml?art=292&c=0&id=30&style=, accessed December 8, 2006.

CHAPTER 6

Am I Dead or Not?

BY JULIA LOREN

Flying through darkness while your body remains lying in bed, speeding through tunnels, and meeting angels of light are part of the beautiful phenomena sometimes reported by the dying; these are referred to as near-death experiences (NDEs). One Gallup Poll taken in 1982 estimated that eight million people in America had experienced an NDE. Since then, others have doubled the statistic, making NDEs one of the most commonly reported "spiritual experiences" in North American society. No matter what spiritual belief system a person adheres to, the overwhelming majority of NDEs involve meeting angels of light, God, and Jesus. Not all individuals knocking on death's door are admitted. Those who are sent back to Earth have some amazing stories to tell indeed.

Surprisingly, only a select few experience a life-changing transformation as a result of their NDE. Over the past 20 years, medical researchers studying the phenomenon of near-death visions or experiences have uncovered why. It seems as if one key characteristic of a NDE needs to be present in order for a person to experience a dramatic difference in the way they live. That experience has to do with light. The properties of light and the energy released in the light serve to transform the personalities and resilience of ordinary people into extraordinary people, who, in some ways, find themselves healed by that light and radiating that light until the end of their days.

Mickey Robinson is one of those extraordinary persons who experienced a NDE after a severe accident. His story serves as an amazing example of one who has experienced a full-blown NDE. As a young man, Mickey discovered the adrenalin rush of sky diving and gave his life to the pursuit of the rush as a blast of air hit him in the face just as he leapt through the doors of an airplane at 12,000 feet, and experienced the sensation of free-falling, the sudden lift as the parachute opened, and the rapid descent to Earth.

Sky divers know that if your chute fails in this undeniably high-risk sport, complete death and total annihilation are the most likely outcomes. What they forget is that the plane itself harbors a whole host of other scenarios that can plague sky divers. Mickey's plane went down so fast, that no one could gain control of the aircraft. The crash left Mickey's body burned, his eyes blind, and his legs paralyzed. Unfortunately, his body didn't die upon impact and Mickey was left feeling the excruciating pain of hideous burns, broken bones, and a series of infections that doctors thought no one could survive. He lay in a hospital bed enduring rounds of doctors and nurses stripping the skin from his charred body and making sure the morphine flowed steadily. Days turned into weeks and weeks to months. But Mickey's young body held on to life. One day, however, his body finally began shutting down. Mickey lay closer to death than ever before. The end was certainly near.

Mickey tells the following story in his book, *Falling to Heaven*:[1]

> Walking into my hospital room, Dr. Jeric took one look at me and thought, No way! He'd seen soldiers in Vietnam die from less serious burns than mine. Still, he sat down by my bed and encouraged me to fight for life. When he was ready to leave, I stood to my feet and walked him down the hall.
>
> "Thank you for coming to see me," I said.
>
> But he didn't respond.

"How long do you think it'll be before I'm able to go home?

Once again, he didn't respond. That was odd. Didn't he hear me?

I stood there with him as the ICU doors began opening automatically. Then it happened. As if I were a ghost, the door swung right through me.

In the next second, my spirit was drawn back into my body like a rubber band being snapped. As I lay there trying to understand what just happened, I realized a part of me was hovering between this world and the next.

But why?

Two days later Mickey had his answer. The sensation of being out of his body was more than a hallucination created by a will to walk and talk normally again and induced by the ongoing doping of morphine. The out-of-body experience and his absence of pain are two of the most common traits of a NDE. What Mickey was experiencing was a precursor to death. Two days later, it would happen again and Mickey found himself experiencing a full-blown near-death experience.

...like a butterfly emerging from a cocoon, something strong and alive stepped out of my broken body. My legs sank down through the mattress as my spirit rose to its feet, sweeping through flesh as gently as wings sweep through air.

Instantly, I left behind tremendous pain and a burning fever to enter another realm—a realm not ruled by natural law. Gravity ceased and time stopped as eternity swung open before me like a garden gate.

Colors suddenly pulsated with brilliance, as if misted by a fine morning rain. Objects loomed into view with razor-sharp clarity, as if I were seeing them for the first time. I felt more purely alive than on the happiest day of my childhood. And when I looked down to see my mangled hand, it was perfect.

Instantly, I knew this was the real world. The eternal world….
Now I was swimming upward in waves of light and sound, bursting through the surface with an awareness far beyond logic or reasoning.

With relentless but gentle speed, I began traveling toward a pure white light, brighter than a thousand suns. I could gaze forever and ever into the wonderful light.

But then…I became aware of something moving behind me…

When Mickey found the light retreating and darkness overtaking him, he felt total emptiness, unending loneliness, a complete separation from light. It was like experiencing walking up to the brink of hell.

Shivering in terror, I watched the last eclipse of light disappearing. Then, like a drowning man gasping for air, my spirit screamed out the same words I'd prayed that night in intensive care: "God, I'm sorry! I want to live! Please give me another chance!"

These words came straight from my heart and just as they escaped my lips, I found myself standing in heaven.

Instantly, the darkness retreated and a living, breathing glory enfolded me….

Mickey caught a glimpse of Heaven, scenes from paradise, and scenes from the next seven years of his life before he was sent back to his demolished body lying in the hospital room. The visions sustained him through the next several years of recovery. Remarkably, the experience of seeing the light and being engulfed in a living, breathing glory, imparted a desire to live and triggered his optimistic, joyful personality into regaining the resiliency he would need to survive the following years of rehabilitation.

While the NDE imparted life-altering internal changes, his body launched into an accelerated healing process. Within a short while, his vision was restored and he started walking. The skin grafts took and the burns healed. He was transformed by the light and walked away form the NDE happier, healthier, without any fear of death, and aware of God's loving Presence throughout his life.

But one more thing also happened to Mickey during this experience. He walked away with an increasing ability to receive ongoing spiritual experiences and walk closely with the Lord Jesus Christ on this side of eternity.

Characteristics of an NDE

Dr. Melvin Morse, a pediatrician in Seattle, Washington, was introduced to the phenomenon of near-death visions by one of his young patients who survived a drowning incident. After three days in a coma, the girl sat up without any signs of brain damage. When Dr. Morse asked her what happened by the pool that caused her to fall in, she shocked the poor doctor by telling the story of what she saw in Heaven. She saw a man filled with bright light and love, met a guardian angel, toured Heaven, and was then given a choice to stay or return home. She chose to go home to her parents. The encounter with his patient led Dr. Morse to design a research project using solid scientific protocol that yielded amazing results, stunning both the science and religious communities with the outcomes.

His study involved 350 subjects who were drawn from major hospitals and had experienced childhood NDEs.[2] During the study he discovered nine commonly reported traits that characterized and defined an NDE. They include:

- a sense of being dead;
- peace and the absence of pain;
- an out-of-the-body experience;
- a feeling of going through a tunnel;
- meeting people who are filled with light;
- meeting one individual who was a being of light;
- experiencing a review of their life or a portion of their life;
- feeling a reluctance to return;
- and awakening with a personality transformed by the experience.

Many people only experience one or two of those traits, according to Dr. Morse. However, in rare cases, people have experienced all of the traits and entered into a full-blown NDE.

He noted that the entire population of research subjects who had experienced an NDE ranked higher on various assessments in several areas than the control subjects—those who had not experienced an NDE. They were happier, healthier, had no fear of death, and many reported an increase in spiritual experiences, particularly the ability to know the future, as if they had been sensitized to living in both the spiritual and real world at the same time.

While Dr. Morse separated out those who experienced various traits, he noticed that those who experienced just one of the traits of an NDE, such as having a sense of leaving their body, or traveling through a tunnel, or experiencing the absence of pain, came away with a fond memory of the NDE but did not find that it transformed their lives significantly. One particular group of people, however, experienced the greatest transformation. Those who reported some sort of encounter with a bright light or a being full of light were forever changed by the experience. His scientific mind led him to believe that somehow the light created a change in the electromagnetic field of a person's body. Spontaneous healing occurred as well as changes to their personalities if they encountered the light.

A tremendous amount of energy is released during the near-death experience. This energy is generated internally and probably reaches its peak when the person is bathed in light. Most NDEers are unable to describe this light, but what they are surely seeing is a blast of energy that powers their life....

This energy is funneled through the right temporal lobe which is altered by the experience. The temporal lobe, in turn, has a profound effect upon the various structures of the brain and the electromagnetic field that surrounds the body.

The person who has a near-death experience may look the same, but their electrochemical make-up is very different from what they used to be.[3]

He also debunked neurological findings about temporal lobe stimulation creating spiritual experiences. While the use of drugs or artificial probing of certain areas of the brain can spark a feeling of leaving one's body or other characteristics of an NDE, one particular trait, he claims, remains elusive. It seems that light cannot be artificially induced or generated from within the brain and is activated only at the point of death or during unique visions. Morse claims that those whose visions included an encounter with a loving light received the most impacting personality transformations. "The most powerful and lasting transformations were found in people who saw the light."[4]

Scientists and medical personnel try to offer rational explanations for the common traits accompanying an NDE. They say the traits occur from oxygen deprivation and pupil widening as the brain begins to die. Dr. Morse used to believe that as well; until he studied the experiences using traditional, scientific protocol, and research design.

One dissenting Dutch physician specializing in anesthesiology, believes that a person whose pupils are widely dilated not only sees bright light, but only clearly sees people upon whom the eyes are focused, while all other people are seen as bright and blurry forms. According to him, individuals who experience an NDE, interpret the bright and blurry images of out-of-focus people elsewhere in the room as "bright forms."

After studying the effects of oxygen poisoning and oxygen starvation, he learned that both tunnel and darkness experiences could be caused by oxygen starvation. Oxygen starvation does not cause all parts of the brain to fail at the same time. The brain stem, which generates consciousness, is the part of the brain most resistant to oxygen starvation. Therefore, oxygen starvation will cause vision to fail before causing a loss of consciousness.

"Darkness, tunnel, and light experiences are wondrous, seemingly paranormal experiences. Nonetheless, it is evident that they can be explained by the body's responses to oxygen starvation. The combination of tunnel and light experiences can only be explained by oxygen starvation, and nothing else. Other associated experiences, such as darkness and out-of-body experiences, can also be generated by other changes in body function induced by a wide range of different conditions. This explanation of tunnel-and-light experiences does not constitute conclusive proof that this is the only mechanism by which these experiences can arise. After all, this explanation does not preclude paranormal or immaterial explanations. But it is an alternative, provable physical explanation that accounts for all aspects of these experiences, as well as making it possible to predict when these experiences are likely to occur."[5]

While scientists probe for rational explanations and biological reasons behind NDE traits, they tend to believe that some form of our cultural archetypes remain with us and are involved in the NDE as it occurs. The reason why some people see angels, they believe, comes from their cultural expectations of seeing angels when they die. But what about after the NDE is long over?

How is it that some 12 percent of the population studied by Dr. Morse still report having regular contact with or visions of their guardian angels they met during their NDE? Why do more than 10 percent report seeing ghosts or apparitions? And a great number of them come away with the ability to foretell future events—some mundane events like knowing that the phone is about to ring and who is on the other end, but other more amazing events, such as being able to warn others away from impending danger.

Finally, why does each and every one of the subjects studied say they have no fear of death after an NDE? I believe it is because they know that the supernatural realm of Heaven is reached through the passage of death—a passage they no longer fear. The spiritual realm of God's creation is now almost as familiar as the natural realm of God's creation. Science remains stymied by immaterial explanations they can neither prove nor disprove. But the hearts of men and women remain captivated by the mysteries of the spiritual realm.

The Most Important Seconds of Your Life

Why would God allow a person to have a near-death experience? What is He trying to say ultimately about life and death? Did He whisk someone into His Presence because He wants him or her to do a certain job, or take a commission into ministry very seriously? Or did some cosmic accident occur in the bureaucracy of Heaven, causing God to say, "Oops, the angel of death picked up the wrong person. What are you doing here? Go back until your time has come."? I believe that God's heart longs for everyone to know Him and to accept His unconditional love. And He gives us every opportunity to accept or reject Him, even up until the moment of death.

Jill Austin, founder of Master Potter Ministry, had just walked onto the platform of a church in New Zealand when she received word that her mother had experienced an aneurism, lapsed into a coma, and now lay near death's door. As the scheduled speaker that night, Jill paused, wondering if she should go ahead and speak or cancel the meeting to focus on the crisis at hand.

Remembering that her mother, a medical doctor, stoically told her that should anything happen to her, Jill should continue with the work of the ministry, Jill went ahead and facilitated the meeting, holding her grief as best she could. Immediately afterward, she pulled out her cell phone and started calling a number of people back home in California asking them to go to the hospital to pray for her mother. An incredible Hispanic pastor from the inner city in East Los Angeles went to the hospital. Jill's mother had practiced medicine in the barrios for over 25 years working at the Los Angeles County Hospital. Jill waited until she knew the pastor had arrived, and then called her with specific directions about how they were to pray.

"I said we need to break the spirit of death, call forth life, and went into more detail about how to save her life," Jill explained. "Even while I'm telling her how to pray I began seeing something different. All of a sudden I'm having an open vision seeing Jesus coming for her. And I realized that it's her time. Jesus is coming for her. It's her time to go home. Now that is kind of startling because when you have a loved one you want to stand for life. So in the middle of the conversation I said, 'Lily, I see Jesus coming for her. So listen, this is what you are to do. Don't break the spirit of death. I want you to lean down into her ear and talk to her about accepting the Lord because she needs to know that Jesus is coming for her and she needs to go with Him.'

"She said, 'Jill I got it.'

"She prayed. And what I heard was that my mom came out of a coma, sat up in bed laughing and said, 'Now I know what Jill meant.' And she laughed her way into heaven."

Jill decided to take the next flight home and cancelled the rest of the New Zealand meetings. While in the airplane, she encountered a man who spoke to her about life and death, bringing comfort to her and insight into what the next few days and months would hold for Jill as she faced the traumatic aftermath of losing her mother.

"I wanted her to live," Jill said. "I'm over here ministering in over 60 meetings in the last 4 weeks and my mom died, the most significant person in my life; and I'm on the airplane going home, looking out the window crying with my Bible open on my lap. All of a sudden this man next to me taps on the Bible and says, 'I know the author of that book.'"

Jill had just been reading a Scripture in Ecclesiastes and thinking about the fact that her mother wanted to be cremated, and wanted no funeral. All of a sudden, as if the man were reading her thoughts, he said, "Oh but you must have a celebration to celebrate her life even if she has no funeral."

They launched into a most unusual conversation. "As he is giving me Scriptures, and I am looking them up, all of a sudden I am going to different places in the spirit. He was telling me about the spiritual warfare I was going to come home to and what would come to pass; preparing me for exactly what was to come," Jill said regarding the legal battles and sibling rivalry over matters of the will that plague some families after a parent dies.

By then, Jill knew that this was no ordinary man. He looked like a very conservative business man with a New Zealand accent. His words carried weight and brought in a realm of glory that took Jill away in the Spirit to see mini-visions of what was to come as he narrated the images playing across the screen in her mind. Eventually, they got to that one disconcerting question troubling Jill. She asked him if her mother was saved. Had she accepted Jesus before she died?

The man continued with more revelation, "There are a lot of people who are knowing and going Christians. They know the Lord and then they leave

Him. Man measures life in the passing of years. God measures life in the passage of seconds. The last three seconds are the most important in a person's life. When you watch someone as they are getting nearer the end of their life, do you notice if they are moving closer to God or are they moving farther away? Are they getting into the books, the Bible, reminiscing about old memories of Scriptures or things of the Spirit?"

According to Jill, as the man spoke, "The Lord reminded me of the books my mother had started to read before she died and the questions she asked, the Bible she started to read. And I could see this turning toward the Lord."

Her mother's laughter was not derisive—it was a laugh of joy knowing that the Jesus she had read about and heard about, was real...just as she hoped and believed He would be.

By the time the flight was over, Jill realized that her suspicion about the identity of this remarkably wise and deeply spiritual man was right and true. "When we got off the plane, the man was holding my hand, in a comforting way. But when we got near the baggage claim he disappeared...vanished into thin air." He was an angelic messenger sent by God.

Man measures life in the passing of years. God measures life in the passage of seconds. The last three seconds are the most important in a person's life. What transpires during the last three seconds for some is a moment of decision when they can choose to be embraced by the light and love of God. For others, those three seconds become a near-death experience, a forestalling of death for some purpose.

Loving on Borrowed Time

Dr. Morse and other researchers mention in their books and articles that those who were sent back to Earth by a being of light often reported that they were told they needed to return to Earth because they have a job to do. For many, that meant that they were simply to work in their chosen occupations, cherish their families, and live life to the fullest. There was no spectacular calling to the ministry or to become a wild-eyed prophet. They felt they were simply to become more focused and loving individuals. And the more loving they acted toward others, the more successful they felt their lives to be.

When Suzette Hattingh, a pleasant South African woman in her late forties, walks into a room, you immediately take notice of her. Something about the look in her eye and the way she carries herself, makes you realize that she is walking in an authority that far surpasses that of the ordinary Christian. She carries the Presence of God with her wherever she goes and it is that Presence that catches your eye and makes you wonder, "Who is this woman?"

Suzette Hattingh is an international evangelist who is based in Germany. For many years, she worked as an intercessor and an evangelist, preaching in huge crusades alongside Reinhard Bonnke in Africa and many other nations. God eventually called her to go with Reinhard Bonnke when he moved his headquarters to Germany in 1985. She started her own ministry, Voice in the City, in 1997. Voice in the City Ministry focuses on revealing Jesus throughout Europe while still conducting campaigns where she preaches to millions during campaigns in Asia and other countries of the world. Her words are accompanied by powerful signs and wonders and miraculous healings wherever she ministers. She is undeniably one who has been touched by God and who touches His heart in return, as they reap the harvest of salvation and healing together.

Prior to being called into the ministry, Suzette worked as a nurse. Oddly, it was her patients' near-death experiences that led her to take notice of the reality of the spiritual realm. According to her experiences with dying patients, not everyone who experiences a NDE sees Heaven. Some actually experience a glimpse of hell.

Bill Wise, a Southern California realtor, agrees that many have visions of hell. He once fell asleep on his living room floor and suddenly and shockingly discovered himself in hell. While he was not at death's door experiencing an NDE, the vision he experienced catapulted him into a season of soul-searching and longing for understanding. He says that his personal research uncovered about 1,400 stories of people who experienced some vision of hell during an NDE or vision.[6] Dr. Morse and medical researchers also report that a large number of people glimpse the darkness and despair of hell rather than the light and love of Heaven.

Suzette talked about patients she met who experienced both Heaven and hell during an interview with *Charisma* Magazine.[7] Their stories changed her life and most likely became the foundational experience that launched her into the ministry of an evangelist. She recounted:

"Dying patients started telling me about their near-death experiences. There was an old man, too weak to move, who suddenly sat up in his bed and cried out: 'I see the living God on His throne, and I am lost!' I did not even know what 'lost' meant. I was a very down-to-Earth person, and this terrified me."

Hattingh also remembers a man who was an elder in a church. In the moment of his death he cried out: "Please help me! My feet are sinking into this pit!" Then he died.

There was a third case, a lady with terminal cancer. "She was in pain and screamed at us and was very difficult. For some time she was moved to another hospital for treatment, and there she made peace with God. She returned a changed person, so kind. When she died I was on duty and sat by her bed," Hattingh said. "I thought she was gone already, but suddenly she came back, and smiled with open eyes.

"'Sister,' she said to me, 'do you hear the music? Look, the flowers! People with white clothes!' Then she turned around and said, 'Here they come to fetch me!'—and she was gone."

Hattingh says these experiences caused her to start seeking God again. On March 14, 1977, prompted further by repetitive nightmares dealing with condemnation, Hattingh finally prayed. "'God,' I said, 'if you are what these freaks say you are, do something!' A light fell on me, and I was born again."

For years after giving her life to God, she found herself burning bright in life and ministry yet eventually, overwork caused that light to dim. Just three years after both her parents passed away in different automobile accidents, she lay quite ill with exhaustion and heart problems. The effects took a toll on her body and she went to stay with friends in South Africa in hopes that she could regain her health and go back into the work of the ministry.

Instead, her health rapidly deteriorated and she realized that she was dying. Although she has had many of her own supernatural encounters and knew of the near-death experiences of others, she was about to enter into an encounter that would particularly transform her life and ministry.

During a telephone interview with Suzette in Frankfurt, Germany, she said this experience occurred in August, 1983, not long after her father passed away.[8]

> I went to stay with my dear friends Jimmy and Jessie Scott in South Africa because I was exhausted. As a workaholic, I had hidden myself in the work of God to get away from the pain of the death of my parents. I wasn't doing well and I was very sick. I knew from a pain in my chest that I was going to die that day. Jessie was going to call an ambulance. As I was lying on my bed, they prayed, "Please save her life for the ministry's sake." Then they went outside to continue interceding for my life in another room.

> At that moment in my room, it was dark and the next moment light surrounded me. Not a light like we know light. No shadows. The brightest light I ever saw but it did not hurt me. I saw the room exactly as it was but it was bright. I turned around at the door and looked at my body on the bed. When I turned around, both my mother and my father were standing there. They looked exactly like they did on Earth, except there was no burden on their faces. It was like a glow of softness coming out of them. My mother communicated with me—but not with words. She said, "You cannot come already, my child. You have to come back. You'll be better tomorrow."

> I woke up and found myself back in my bed. Jessie suddenly came in the room, turned on the light and said, "You will live! I am

going to make you some soup now." That was the turning point. I wasn't instantly, miraculously healed. But I was different.

That marked my life in such a way that I feel like we are not here to show our spirituality; we are here to show Jesus. Since then I realized I love on borrowed time.

Tunnels and Gates of Heaven

Scripture offers a great deal of information that supports the common traits of a typical near-death vision. Rita Bennet, CEO of Christian Renewal Association, believes that tunnels of light exist and offers her interpretation of Scripture for this experience. "It is possible that you and I will one day enter Heaven by walking or floating through a sparkling, blue-green jasper tunnel of light."

The clue lies in Revelation 21:17-18, which gives the thickness and dimensions of the wall surrounding the city. "My studies indicated that the wall's thickness would be about 216 feet, or 72 yards, close to the length of a football field. This seemed beyond belief to think that Heaven's wall is that thick...." She believes it is this wall that gives substance to the "tunnels" people zip through as they enter Heaven.

She is partly correct about jasper's color. Like many gemstones, jasper can take the appearance of a variety of colors. The most common jasper is a clear stone, extremely transparent. The transparent nature of the gemstone symbolically means that one is seen clearly or that one is overwhelmed by the light of glory. In biblical literature, jasper symbolizes water and the fullness of glory. The Revelation 21:11-19 passage Rita refers to illustrates the glory of the heavenly Jerusalem. A tunnel of jasper is likely to shine brilliantly with light as its clear properties refract the brilliant, blinding light of the glory of God. However, a blue-green version of the stone may also symbolize water and mean that one is immersed in the river or the sea of glory as one enters the gate of Heaven. A blue-green tunnel may be much darker than expected since light is not easily refracted in a tunnel.

Some people report soaring through a dark tunnel, while others report moving through a tunnel of light. Both experiences could be supported by Scripture according to the properties of jasper. Jasper could be a tunnel of darkness colored by the blue-green nature of the stone or it may be an extremely transparent stone—more able to refract a brilliant light. Those who experience leaving their bodies and traveling through a tunnel of light or a tunnel of darkness may just be moving through the gates of the New Jerusalem straight into Heaven, as Rita Bennet believes.

However, neither Dr. Morse's research nor Scripture support the idea that that those who recall moving through a dark tunnel actually discover a vision of hell awaiting on the other side or that those who move through a light tunnel experience Heaven. It seems that a tunnel is merely a tunnel. People move through both darkness and light to get to either Heaven or hell. What you are actually moving through and where it leads depend entirely on the purposes of God who is well in control of the experience and even directing it.

Encountering Beings of Light

What are these "beings of light" that people see during their NDEs? Some see only one person, hidden in the brilliance of light that obscures its facial features. Others see a number of people walking about as if the light not only flows from them internally, but it engulfs them externally. Many Scriptures talk about spiritual beings of light falling into one of two categories—a type of angel or God Himself. One, in particular, speaks of God: *"Who alone is immortal and who lives in unapproachable light…"* (1 Tim. 6:16).

One particular disciple of Jesus talked about Jesus as a being of light, as if he had personally experienced a remarkable revelation of that light. I believe that John, the disciple whom Jesus loved, saw and felt the impact of the light that emanated from Jesus well beyond the others' understanding. His revelation of the nature of Jesus as light and love far surpassed the other disciples' understanding.

In John 1:4-5 the apostle began his description of Jesus as light: "In Him was life, and that life was the light of men. The light shines in the darkness, but the darkness has not understood it." He knew that Jesus was different from all other men—that His light was special. Regarding John the Baptist, he wrote in John 1:8-9: *"He himself was not the light; he came only as a witness to the light. The true light that gives light to every man was coming into the world."*

He knew this because Jesus told him so. In John 8:12 Jesus says about himself, *"I am the light of the world."* And much later, John wrote in First John 1:5 *"This is the message we have heard from Him and declare to you: God is light; in Him there is no darkness at all."*

Yet John, more than any other writer of the gospels, also received a revelation about the nature of light that could only be imparted through supernatural visions. In Revelation 4: 5 he wrote, *"Before the throne, seven lamps were blazing. These are the seven spirits of God."* The seven-fold nature of God dwells in blazing light before the throne—the very blazing lights and beings of light that many report seeing as they move through a tunnel, fly up to Heaven and discover themselves in the Presence of God.

John also knew that Psalm 104:2 spoke of a God who *"wraps Himself in light as with a garment...."* And that this light was so powerful that it illuminated not just a localized area like a flashlight; it was more powerful than the sun and the moon. In Revelation 21:23, John wrote, *"The city does not need the sun or the moon to shine on it, for the glory of God gives it its light, and the Lamb is its lamp."*

Jesus is not the only light; the spiritual beings in His heavenly kingdom are also clothed in brilliant light. In the Old Testament, we read about one of Daniel's encounters with an angel, *"His body was like crysolite, his face like lightning, and his eyes like flaming torches..."* (Dan. 10:6). And in Matthew, we read a description of the angel of the Lord who rolled back the stone of the garden tomb and sat on it. His appearance reflects an extraordinary light. *"His appearance was like lightning, and his clothes were white as snow. The guards were so afraid of him that they shook and became like dead men"* (Matt. 28:3-4).

These angels must have been hanging around the throne. Beholding the light, they became like the One they beheld. Saturated in the light of God, they came as messengers to Earth, still shining in all His glory. For the throne itself is so electromagnetically charged that it releases "...*flashes of lightning, rumblings, and peals of thunder*" (Rev. 4:5). Imagine lightning flashing against all the multicolored jewels in the throne room; it would seem like a giant light show. All of these images of God as light, angelic beings of light, rainbows of light flashing, are contained in the stories of those who have experienced NDEs. What is most interesting about their stories is that many of those who tell them are not Christians and have little or no Judeo-Christian faith background or knowledge of biblical descriptions of Heaven's throne room.

No wonder that when individuals encounter pure light, come face-to-face with the origin and Creator of electromagnetic energy, they are forever transformed, as Dr. Morse's research reveals. No wonder Jesus could perform miracles. The nature of His being, comprised of powerful light, or electromagnetic energy, altered everyone He came in contract with—if He chose to release that light. Sometimes He walked incognito, healed only one person rather than the whole crowd, or healed and delivered whole crowds, walked on water, turned water into wine. Light, love, power, and glory combined in Jesus, enabling Him to do extraordinary things.

His power and His light have been released to not only those who experience an NDE, or visions where an individual encounters the light, but also to those who feel every molecule exploding in their bodies, as Jesus comes closer. Those who are forever transformed are changed not because of the vision, but because they met God and the power contained in His brilliant light.

The Purpose of Life

Not everyone walks away from an NDE having met Jesus and recognizing Him as God. In fact, most walk away with more questions about God than ever before. Some turn to the New Age spiritualistic practices and theories as they look for answers. Others walk away content with their newfound discovery of an afterlife, but focused more on living this life than what lies beyond in "a galaxy far, far away." And that seems to be the point of their experience. The majority of those who experience a near-death vision of Heaven and encounter the God who is the light of the world, come away with two key insights:

1. The first is the message that you are created for a purpose. Whatever the job you were created to do, whoever the people you are called to love, you'd best get on with it! Our time here on Earth is short. As Suzette Hattingh says, we love on borrowed time.

2. The second is that there is a God in Heaven who sits on a throne surrounded by angels and that Heaven is full of loved ones who have passed before us. What do you do with this knowledge? Jesus says, *I am the way and the truth and the life. No one comes to the Father except through me*" (John 14:6). He also says that He is *"the gate of heaven"* (see John 10:7) He knocks on the door of your heart, and if you open it to Him, He will come in and develop a friendship with you that will last throughout all eternity. But you must open the door on this side of eternity in order to pass through to the other side. Why wait until the last three seconds of your life? You never know when those last moments will be. And there are no guarantees that an NDE will buy you some decision-making time.

Do you want to be with Jesus, or do you want to live in the absence of light, the dark void that Mickey Robinson felt for a split second and knew was but a taste of the alternative? Open the door of your heart, take a moment to pray now in your own words and invite Jesus to come in, and surrender your life to Him. And as you die to yourself, you will find your life transformed by His light, and you will receive an uplift of joy, as His love floods your heart. If you have no words of your own, pray this simple prayer: *Lord Jesus, light of the world, God who is all loving, I invite you to come into my heart. Open the eyes of my understanding. Forgive me of all of my sins and reveal yourself to me so that I might know you today and for all eternity. You are Lord of Lords and King of Kings. I believe that Jesus Christ is the Son of the Living God. There is no other way to the Father or into eternity but through you. I surrender my life into your loving hands.*

Endnotes

1. Mickey Robinson, *Falling to Heaven* (Cedar Rapids, IA: Arrow Publications, 2003), 94-95.

2. More published his research in the book *Transformed by the Light* and in various pediatric medical journals.

3. Melvin Morse, M.D. with Paul Perry, *Transformed by the Light: The Powerful Effect of Near Death Experiences on People's Lives* (New York: Villard Books, 1992), 147-148.

4. Morse, *Transformed by the Light*, 197.

5. G.M. Woerlee, *Darkness, Tunnels, and Light*, http://www.csicop. org/q/csicop/neardeath.

6. Bill Wise, *23 Minutes in Hell*. This information is excerpted from a testimony Bill gave in Kansas City.

7. "She Dared to Claim a Continent," Tomas Dixon, *Charisma* Magazine, October 2002.

8. Phone interview with Suzette Hattingh in Germany, June 2006.

9. Rita Bennet, author of *To Heaven and Back*, this quote was excerpted from her column in *The Edmonds Beacon*, August 25, 2005.

CHAPTER 7

A Walk on the Wilder Side of Supernatural Visions

BY JAMES GOLL

Having passed through the corridors of *Common Experiences of Visions and Dreams*, we now head farther down the hallway to find another entrance way into another vast room. The name over this doorway is a bit startling at first. It reads, *A Walk on the Wilder Side*. As I peer through the opening, I can see four separate doors with names written on each passageway.

On the first door we find these words imprinted, *Walk on the Wilder Side!* This makes me wonder what in the world is behind that door! The door right across from it reads, *Beam Me Up—Open Heavens, Sounds of Heaven and Visiting Heaven*. Oh my, I think we just got over our head for sure! Door number three intrigues me, as it jumps right out at me, *Ecstasy, Peeps, Mutters, and Prophecy*. But if you're brave enough, rest assured, if you have not been stretched yet, you will be as you enter this room which bears the name, *In the Body or Out?*

Whew! We are in for one wild ride as we continue on our progressive journey from the *Common* to a *Walk on the Wilder Side!* So here we go—but this is not "Ready or not, here we come." It is, "Yes, we are ready for more from our dear Lord!"

Trance

It happened when I returned to Jerusalem and was praying in the temple, that I fell into a trance (Acts 22:17 NASB).

Because it is so easily misunderstood today and is linked in so many people's minds with New Age and the occult, we must be very careful in dealing with the subject of trances. But let's move ahead with a brief overview of these ecstatic experiences.

A trance is more or less a stunned state wherein a person's body is overwhelmed by the Spirit of God and his mind can be arrested and subjected to visions or revelations God desires to impart. The New Testament Greek word for trance is *ekstasis*, from which our English word "ecstasy" is derived. Basically, a trance is a supernaturally incited excitement of the physical body. Often, a person in a trance is stupefied—held, arrested, and placed in a supernormal (above normal or other-than-normal) state of mind. *Vine's Expository Dictionary of New Testament Words* defines a trance as "a condition in which ordinary consciousness and the perception of natural circumstances were withheld, and the soul was susceptible only to the vision imparted by God."[1] *Vine's* continues by giving us a second definition by stating, "An ecstasy is a condition in which a person is so transported out of his natural state that he falls into a trance, a supernatural state wherein he may see visions in the spirit."[2]

Webster's Dictionary describes this state in the following manner, "Ecstasy; a being put out of place; distraction, especially one resulting from great religious fervor; great joy, rapture; a feeling of delight that arrests the whole mind."[3] The Greek word for trance is ek-stas-is, from which we get the word "ecstasy." A displacement of the mind, bewilderment, "ecstasy"; hence to be amazed, amazement, astonishment.[4]

Dr. David Blomgren in his balanced prophetic book, *Prophetic Gatherings in the Church*, gives us the following definition: "A trance is a visional state in which revelation is received. This rapturous state is one in which a prophet would perceptively be no longer limited to natural consciousness and volition. He is 'in the Spirit' where full consciousness may be temporarily transcended."[5]

My final composite definition of a trance is a rapturous state whereby one is caught up into the spiritual realm so as to only receive those things that the Holy Spirit speaks.

A More Detailed Look

Below are eight biblical examples that could be said to describe various forms of a trance-like state:

- Amazement—Mark 16:8.

- Astonishment—Mark 5:42.

- Falling as dead—Rev. 1:17 (*ekstasis* not used here, but the condition of falling as if dead aptly describes a trance-like state).

- A great quaking—Dan. 10:7.

- A trembling or a shaking—Job 4:14.

- A sudden power—Ezek. 8:1.

- The hand of the Lord—Ezek. 1:3.

- A deep sleep from the Lord—Job 33:15 and Dan. 8:18.

Let's unwrap a couple of these other scriptural examples in a fuller manner. First, let's take a peek at Peter's pivotal trance experience as recorded in Acts 10:9-16 (NASB):

> *On the next day, as they were on their way and approaching the city, Peter went up on the housetop about the sixth hour to pray. But he became hungry and was desiring to eat; but while they were making preparations, he fell into a trance; and he saw the sky opened up, and an object like a great sheet coming down, lowered by four corners to the ground, and there were in it all kinds of four-footed animals and crawling creatures of the Earth and birds of the air. A voice came to him, "Get up, Peter, kill and eat!" But Peter said, "By no means, Lord, for*

I have never eaten anything unholy and unclean." Again a voice came to him a second time, "What God has cleansed, no longer consider unholy." This happened three times, and immediately the object was taken up into the sky.

Do we really realize what happened here? The entire history of the Church was changed by the experience of one trance! An entirely different way of interpreting Scripture was given! Gentiles came to faith in Christ Jesus and the Body of the Messiah was no longer viewed as being exclusively a Jewish entity! Salvation came to the Gentiles! What a paradigm shift! "Do not call unclean what I call clean!" That is absolutely amazing! Now let's thank the Lord for all of these spiritual experiences!

Let's take one more specific peek into the experience of a trance in the life of Balaam, a gentle prophet, as recorded in Numbers 24:4 (KJV):

He hath said, which heard the words of God, which saw the vision of the Almighty, falling into a trance, having his eyes open.

Balaam is overcome by God's Spirit and he cannot even curse, but only bless Israel. (Would that this would happen again today!) This proclamation, while in a trance state, was done while his eyes were wide open. Mercy! I guess God had a point to make and he induced a full-blown spiritual experience of a trance state so that Balaam could only speak those things which God intended.

Well, He did that one before—let's see that one happen again and again! Up, up, and away. Here we go soaring into expressions of our dear Lord's love! My, what a wonderful, creative, beautiful, and approachable Lord!

Out-of-Body Experience

He stretched out the form of a hand and caught me by a lock of my head; and the Spirit lifted me up between Earth and heaven and brought me in the visions of God to Jerusalem (Ezekiel 8:3a NASB).

An out-of-body experience is the actual projecting forth of a person's spirit from his or her body. When God inspires such an experience, He puts a special faith, anointing, and/or protection around the person's spirit so that he or she can perform in the arena where the Lord is leading.

In an out-of-body experience, a person's spirit literally leaves his or her physical body and begins to travel in the spiritual dimension by the Spirit of the Lord. Once out there, the surrounding environment appears different than it does naturally, because now the spiritual eyes, not the natural eyes, are seeing. The Lord directs the eyes to see what He wants them to see in exactly the way He wants them to see it.

Ezekiel is the prime biblical example of a person who had out-of-body experiences:

- "The Spirit lifted me up..." (Ezek. 3:14 NASB).

- "He...caught me by a lock of my head; and the Spirit lifted me up between Earth and heaven ..." (Ezek. 8:1-3 NASB).

- "The Spirit lifted me up and brought me..." (Ezek. 11:1-2 NASB).

- "The hand of the Lord was upon me, and He brought me out by the Spirit of the Lord and set me down in the middle of the valley..." (Ezek. 37:1-4 NASB).

- "And the Spirit lifted me up and brought me into the inner court" (Ezek. 43:5-6 NASB).

Paul also apparently had an out-of-body experience. Most scholars believe Paul was referring to himself when he wrote:

> *I know a man in Christ who fourteen years ago — whether in the body I do not know, or out of the body I do not know, God knows—such a man was caught up to the third heaven. And I know how such a man— whether in the body or apart from the body I do not know, God knows—was caught up into Paradise and heard inexpressible words, which a man is not permitted to speak* (2 Corinthians 12:2-4 NASB).

Look at the way Paul speaks of this holy, wonderful realm. He does not make a big deal out of it. Whether he was in or out of his body is not the issue.

The issue is what he heard and learned while he had this experience. What was the message and what was its fruit?

As with the trance, this is a visionary experience that we must approach very carefully because of its occultic associations in the minds of many people. Counterfeits of all true Holy Spirit-inspired experiences do exist. Outwardly, there may seem to be little difference, but internally the difference is great both in fruit and purpose. We are *never* to *will* ourselves into such an experience! This type of experience is *only* to be God-induced and God-initiated!

This is *not* self-projection or some rendition of astral projection. It is *not* "willing" to project ourselves forth; that is of the occult, and of witchcraft. God, by His initiative and through the Holy Spirit can, if He desires, lift us up into a spiritual realm, but we are not to project *ourselves* forth into anything.

When spirits, sorcerers, and yogis practice this without the Holy Spirit and seem to prosper by it, it is because they are not a threat to satan. They are already deceived. Whether they realize it or not, they are already in league with him and are not his enemies.

Do not let the enemy steal what God has ordained. Do not be afraid of these unusual ways of the Holy Spirit, but always be sure not to enter into some type of self-induced activity.

Translation

> *When they came up out of the water, the Spirit of the Lord snatched Philip away; and the eunuch no longer saw him, but went on his way rejoicing* (Acts 8:39 NASB).

Translation (supernatural transportation or translocation) is more properly defined as an actual physical experience, not just a vision. But when this unusual experience does occur, the individual could be shown various things of the supernatural visionary sort, as he or she is being transported. Out of all of these levels of activity mentioned, I have not yet experienced this one. I have friends who have incredible stories of such events. As for me, I am asking the Lord that I might experience all that He has available for me and desires for my life.

Here are a few biblical examples:

After Jesus was tempted by the devil in the wilderness, He was transported to another place. (See Matthew 4:3-5.) Philip the evangelist was translated after he shared the gospel with the Ethiopian eunuch. (See Acts 8:39.) Peter was translated out of prison, but while it was happening, he did not realize it. As far as he was concerned, he was having a vision, or a dream. Although there is no way to know for sure, this could have been some form of a translation. (See Acts 12:8-9.)

Of all of these types of experiences, I have encountered them all except this one. But I have friends who have experienced this, as well. One friend of mine had his car advance more than two hours further down the road on one of their mission experiences. Years ago, Bob Jones and his wife experienced his truck being picked up and translated hours ahead of their arrival time. Another prophet friend of mine was late to meet his scheduled flight, and before he knew it, he arrived at the airport with moments to spare in order for him to make his next ministry trip right on time. I guess it must have been important for him to get there!

Now, when I read the Word of God, I ask that I can experience everything that is in the Word of God. I don't just read it as I might read a history book; I read it at times more like a menu list. I say, "I want this one!" I encourage you to do the same!

Heavenly Visitation

> *I know a man in Christ who fourteen years ago—whether in the body I do not know, or out of the body I do not know, God knows—such a man was caught up to the third heaven* (2 Corinthians 12:2 NASB).

The Bible refers to three heavens:

1. The lowest heaven, the atmospheric sky which encircles the Earth. (See Matthew 16:1-3.)

2. The second heaven, the stellar heaven that is called outer space, where the sun, moon, stars, and planets reside. (See Genesis 1:16-17.)

3. The third heaven, which is the highest one, and the center around which all realms revolve, is paradise, the abode of God and His angels and saints. (See Psalm 11:4.)

A heavenly visitation is like an out-of-body experience, except that the person's spirit leaves the Earth realm, passes through the second heaven, and goes to the third heaven. This can occur while the person is praying, while in a trance or a deep sleep from the Lord, or at death.

Some biblical examples include:

*   *Moses*. During his 40 days of fasting on Mount Sinai, Moses "saw" the Tabernacle in Heaven and was given the "blueprint" for building an earthly version. This may possibly have been a heavenly visitation; we cannot tell for sure. At the very least, it was an open-Heaven experience. (See Exodus 24:18; 25:1,8-9 and Hebrews 8:5.)

*   *Paul*. Again, the apostle was "caught up to the third heaven," where he heard unspeakable words and had a true experience of paradise. Paul seems to have immediately been caught up into this realm. (See 2 Corinthians 12:2-4.)

*   *Enoch*. According to Genesis, Enoch "walked with God" and God took him. He was caught up into Heaven without dying and never returned to Earth. (See Hebrews 11:5.)

In the same way that a person can visit the third heaven by having an out-of-body experience, he or she can also visit the various regions of hell. If he is a sinner, he approaches hell by descending—in death or a near-death experience or in a supernatural vision—and is shown where he is destined to spend eternity unless he repents and accepts Jesus Christ as his personal Lord and Savior. Then he is brought back to Earth into his body by the mercy of God.

If a person is a Christian, the Spirit of the Lord may bring him or her to hell in such an experience, as well, for the purpose of revealing the suffering torments of the damned. They are then sent back to their bodies in order to testify and warn non-Christians to repent and to receive Jesus as their Lord. These experiences are also used as tools of encouragement to the Body of Christ to let them know that the unseen world is real. God is a rewarder of those who diligently seek Him. (See Hebrews 11:6.) Heaven and hell are real! Every person is an eternal being and his or her final destination is what matters!

I believe heavenly visitations have occurred not only in the Bible, but throughout history, and that such experiences will increase as true apostolic ministry emerges in these last days. Join me and express your desire that you might step into all that our Father God has prepared for you.

The Significance of These Experiences

My mother said I was a very curious child when I was growing up. Apparently, I constantly asked many "why and what" questions. Therefore, I still tend to ask questions like, "What is the meaning of all these bizarre experiences?" I would encourage you to do the same in your relationship with the Holy Spirit.

With this thought in mind, here are some clear, straight-to-the-point answers from my perspective to the "what and why" questions we each need to ask concerning these types of spiritual experiences. Why does God grant these wild experiences anyway?

1. It is an honor for God to grant these kinds of audiences before or in His great Presence.

2. The more subjective the experience, the greater the possibility of pure revelation.

3. Our own thoughts are out of the process, and reception in the spirit realm is in clearer focus.

So, let's thank the Lord for granting us even the opportunity for such a thing to occur!

To close this chapter, let's consider the exhortational statement from the second chapter of Acts, when the Holy Spirit was poured out upon the infant church. The disciples of Jesus became so filled with the Holy Spirit that they were accused of being "drunk with new wine!" Peter stood with the other eleven and declared, *"These men are not drunk, as you suppose"* (Acts 2:15 NASB).

Just imagine, the disciples were so filled with God that the world misunderstood what was really going on. Sound unusual to you? Not really to me! It was that way back then, and it is that way again today!

There Are Not Mad, as You Suppose!

There are several scriptural references which mention the prophets as being madmen or fools. However, a closer study shows that these designations are the contentions of the prophets' critics who assert this of them in mockery. Critics arose in those days and they still arise in ours. But for closing out this stretching chapter on the "Wilder Side" of things, let's look for a moment at the "names" onlookers called those who had extraordinary supernatural experiences in the past. Know this—if you too have taken a ride on the wilder side of things—you are in good company!

Second Kings 9:11 states, "When Jehu went out to his fellow officers, one of them asked him, 'Is everything all right? Why did this madman come to you?' 'You know the man and the sort of things he says,' Jehu replied."

Jehu receives a powerful prophetic word that was given to him by a young prophet. (See 2 Kings 9:1-10). The prophetic word states that Jehu will be king and destroy Jezebel. Some called the young man, *"This mad fellow."*

Jeremiah 29:26 (NASB) gives us another example, where he indicates that everyone who prophesies is called a madman.

Hosea 9:7 gives us another account, "The days of punishment are coming, the days of reckoning are at hand. Let Israel know this. Because your sins are so many and your hostility so great, the prophet is considered a fool, the inspired man a maniac."

This piercing Scripture describes the view of most toward the *"prophet"* and the *"inspired man."* They are said to be *"a fool"* and *"demented."* These vessels are not fools and demented. They are truly inspired, God-breathed-upon men and women. These are among those in the Hall of Fame of Faith in Hebrews chapter 11 where it states that these people were *"men of whom the world was not worthy."* These are not drunk, or mad, as you suppose! These are inspired men and women of God.

May the Lord grant light, revelation, and understanding to us regarding these and other wonderful and unusual ways in which a supernatural God works with natural men and women.

So let's continue in our "ride on the wild side" and "take the roof off the house" by gazing into this subject: *Beam Me Up—Open Heavens, Sounds of Heaven, and Visiting Heaven.*

Endnotes

1. *Vine's Expository Dictionary of New Testament Words.*

2. *Vine's Expository Dictionary of New Testament Words.*

3. *Webster's Dictionary.*

4. James Goll, *Revival Breakthrough Study Guide* (Franklin, TN: Ministry to the Nations, 2000).

5. David Blomgren, *Prophetic Gatherings in the Church.*

CHAPTER 8

Beam Me Up!

BY JULIA LOREN

Heaven. Just the word stirs up rich images of angels and music, jewels refracting light, and hundreds of thousands of individuals surrounding the throne and worshiping God. But is Heaven limited to the biblical descriptions? Or is it much bigger? In the past several years, many people have talked about moments when they were caught up into Heaven and received amazing visions, talked with angels and Jesus, received prophetic words for individuals and churches or even nations. Some of them now offer conferences and workshops that encourage people to seek the Lord for greater insights into the revelatory realms of Heaven.

It seems as if certain segments of the Charismatic church believe that God actually desires our company—not just here on Earth but in Heaven! They also believe that, as Christians, we have a right to explore our inheritance and, like in the old "Star Trek" movie series, Heaven can send down its transporter of light and beam us up into Heaven.

Those who experience such visions of walking in heavenly realms are accessing the promise of God in John 1:51, "*Truly, truly I say to you, you shall see the heavens open.*" What are the "heavens" that Jesus is talking about here?

Is it the same Heaven John saw open up and lift him up into visions that he later wrote about in the Book of the Revelation? According to the testimonies of others who enter into "throne room" experiences and experience "open heavens," people are having amazing, life-changing encounters with God in Heaven as well as on Earth. You only need to stand in the right location, posturing your heart and mind, in order to catch the "transporter beam" and be lifted up. And you, too, can receive visions similar to the Apostles John, Peter, Paul, and others.

God's abode is Heaven itself—it is referred to as the third heaven in Second Corinthians 12:1-4, when Paul notes his experience as being caught up into the third heaven. Whether his experience took place in the body (translating him into Heaven) or out of the body (as a form of vision), he didn't know, but he described it as paradise. God, having given all authority in Heaven and on Earth to Jesus Christ, can dispatch revelatory experiences and angels at will throughout all of the heavens and Earth. He may also catch up believers into the third heaven and enable them to see and experience the throne room of God and walk in His Kingdom in Heaven. Those who have authentic "throne room" experiences undeniably come away with a much greater revelation of who Jesus really is and what He is saying to the Church at present.

I've attended several meetings that are designed to bring people into an experiential awareness of Heaven. Several dozen Christians lay on the floor, as worship music lulled them into a relaxed state of mind. As they focused their attention on Jesus, worshiping Him, moving away from the cares of their days and into His Presence, many felt themselves rising into new spiritual heights. It was as if Earth lay far below and the gates of Heaven had swung open. Some met angels who escorted them into the throne room of God. A few discovered themselves face to face with Jesus. After about 30 minutes, the worship came to an end and they sat up, one by one, and came forward to speak about what they had seen and heard and felt. For the most part, their encounters involved hearing the tenderness of Christ speak to them about the concerns of their hearts: concerns about family members, church matters, and desires to serve God in significant ways. A few received spiritual gifts.

During this meeting, while others ventured into the throne room, I found myself wandering through one of the rooms of the library of Heaven. The Father sat with His eyes cast downward as He focused on the book that lay open before Him. His broad, wooden desk was covered in a scattering of papers strewn between the piles of books. He held a long quill in His hand. Shutting the book he was reading, He deliberately opened the front cover, leaned forward and signed the book, as I stood watching, silently. As if noticing me for the first time, He looked up, smiled, and said, "I like this book. In fact, I like all of your books," he added, sweeping His hand toward a pile of books on His desk, then nodding toward the piles of books that were stacked up on the floor.

Then, He held the pen out to me as a gift to take back to Earth. As I took the pen in my hand, still standing speechless before Him, a rather tall angel appeared on my left side. The Lord let me know that this angel had arrived to give me sword-fighting lessons, and then He vanished immediately from the room, as the angel took over. The angel raised his arm, which appeared to have feathers extending from it—a stereotypical angel dressed in white, with a sash binding his waist, and a sword raised high above his head. I lifted my arm, pen in hand, and extended it alongside his. He swayed his arm toward the left and my raised arm followed. Then he swayed his arm to the right, gently pushing mine. We got into sync and he waved his sword, while I waved my pen gently, powerfully. I laughed because it seemed like delightful child's play. However, I knew this vision was very serious, so serious, in fact, that much of it lies beyond my comprehension even today.

However, I left feeling a little miffed at the vision, and I thought, at the time, that it was merely a figment of my imagination. Exercising my sanctified imagination, I simply intuited what I already knew to be my destiny as a writer. In the aftermath, I realized that the experience served to catapult me out of a state of frustration of being locked into a series of jobs that drained my time and energy and into an intention to pursue writing more seriously. But I didn't consider it a valid trip to Heaven, a beam-me-up-Jesus encounter where Heaven's sights and sounds and tastes and smells were more real than the floor that I was lying on at the time.

I thought that God took that moment to speak to me personally; He was honoring my decision to spend time entering into His Presence and drawing closer to Him, and meeting Him there. It was a valid experience, yet it somehow seemed inferior to me—when I compared it to others' descriptions of their visions. However, I think our comparisons make God feel nauseated.

Many people immaturely debate about whose experience is greater—one who went to Heaven in their imagination or one who was beamed up suddenly and shockingly in the form of an open vision, a vision so real that reality fades away, those who were translated in bodily form. In the process, it leaves people feeling like they received an inferior encounter. Some even try to exaggerate their encounter and make it seem more than it was in an attempt to elevate themselves as more "spiritual" or "prophetic."

In the year following my trip to Heaven's library, I realized that I was wrong about my analysis of the experience. I knew it was rooted in my imagination rather than in an actual out-of-the-body, beamed-up-to-Heaven experience. Yet neither is inferior or superior to the other. Sanctified imagination moves us into authentic encounter. We need to take care not to grieve the Holy Spirit—to value the insights God gives us with regard to ourselves and His Kingdom—and not to compartmentalize spiritual experiences into degrees of superiority. The true imagination intuits the realities of God's Kingdom and brings them into the domain of our lives.

Back-Door Revelation and Throne-Room Revelation

My imagination set me free to pursue what God had intended for me all along; and the experience served to bring me into alignment with God's plan for my life. Subsequent experiences and open visions increased my understanding of what I was to write. What remains hidden from my eyes as far as the contents of books, ledgers, and the contents of written materials locked away in hidden vaults that I have seen in subsequent visions, are slowly being opened to me. Immediately after that experience, God's vision and timing came together. Doors that had previously been shut opened, enabling me to write and publish.

In fact, this *Shifting Shadows* series of books and my *Glimpses of Jesus* series are a direct result of that visit to the library room of Heaven. The fruit of that vision attests to the fact that it was a God-ordained encounter. I call it a back-door prophetic revelation—an encounter that comes through the back door of our defenses and gives us an *aha!* of personal revelation. It makes us more aware of ourselves, unblocks inner obstacles, and unleashes a desire to fulfill our purpose as well as to understand the nature of God more fully.

Others have experienced visits to Heaven that seem much more profound. But the question of who had the greater experience—one who went to Heaven in his or her imagination, or one who was suddenly beamed upward and into the council chambers or throne rooms of God—should never be an issue. They are both valid experiences. However, what makes them profoundly different is not the intensity of the vision of Heaven; it is the calling, the message, the revelation received, and the understanding of what one is called to do with that encounter. It is the difference between receiving back-door prophetic revelation and throne-room prophetic revelation. The responsibility of receiving revelation and knowing what to do with it is a huge weight to carry.

Back-door prophetic revelation is revelation that slips in behind our defenses. God gives us heavenly encounters that speak about the issues of our hearts. My encounter in the library of Heaven and others' experiences in the throne room during meetings where people spend time in God's presence seeking Him for revelation, are examples of God speaking to each one of us about the callings, gifts, and concerns on our hearts, drawing out of us what He knows we need. This kind of revelation may be initiated as we spend time in His Presence during worship and it may feel like we initiated it and received it largely through our sanctified imagination.

Throne-room prophetic revelation speaks more about the issues on God's heart. God initiates the encounter, senses are heightened beyond imagination, and you know that you are actually out of your body and in another dimension—the realm of Heaven. The insights received here often have to do with

God's heart toward an individual's calling, as well as the future of the Church and nations. The one who receives that level of revelation has a tremendous responsibility to not only share the burden of God's heart, but to discern how to express His heart and His message to the Church and even to the nations.

My vision of writing books was all about me—back-door prophetic revelation that I was being invited to respond to or not. For all I knew, God was showing me a pile of romance novels that I was going to write. I just knew that I had to respond to the gifts that God had placed within me and that it was time. I was left feeling that novels or non-fiction, whatever I chose to write, was up to me. God the Father just loves the fact that I was created to write and speak and was going to help me become fulfilled in that calling.

If God had dramatically lifted me into Heaven and opened some of the library books, and I discovered that I am to co-labor with Him in writing a specific message that He revealed to me, I would have received a direct mandate from the throne room. I would have received throne-room prophetic revelation. What I wrote following that vision would be exactly what I heard in Heaven. It would no longer be about me and the desires of my heart. It would be about Him and the concerns and desires of His heart.

Both personal revelation and corporate revelation are very important to God. Neither is inferior to the other. One is not of lesser importance than the other. However, not many people receive authentic throne-room revelation.

According to prophetic minister Shawn Boltz, "Unlike common prophetic experiences and revelations, throne-room encounters have an eternal quality about them. These types of experiences can not be forgotten, even down to the smallest detail. They are written upon our hearts; these experiences are glimpses of our eternal reality and will not go away because they are forever. Whereas, a revelation or vision may fade in our minds once it has fulfilled its course."[1]

Whether one calls it a third-heaven visit or a throne-room encounter, everyone who has experienced this has accessed the encounter through a vision, a visitation, a near-death experience, an out-of-the-body experience, or was translated to Heaven in his or her body.

Let's look at some of the throne-room revelations others have received.

Throne-Room Encounters

A number of people in prophetic ministry today have seen visions of Heaven, and claim to have been transported in dramatic ways into the throne room, council chambers, and long corridors of Heaven. While I would love to include all of their stories, I only have room for a few. But believe me, the number of people who have experienced throne-room encounters is increasing every day. God is dispensing fresh revelation straight from the throne rather than descending into a person's awareness through a dream, an open vision on Earth, or during a moment when the person is spending time in prayer actively envisioning Heaven in their sanctified imagination. God is calling individuals to: *"Come up here, and I will show you what must take place after this"* (Rev. 4:1). And immediately, they find themselves *"…in the Spirit, and there before me was a throne in heaven with someone sitting on it"* (Rev. 4:2). What follows are a few stories of those who were "beamed up" to God's throne room.

Anna Roundtree

Anna Roundtree, the wife of a retired Episcopal priest, considers herself an unlikely candidate to receive throne-room revelation. Now in her early 70s, Anna began experiencing visions of Heaven while she was in her 60s. She has since written two books containing the revelations she received—*The Heavens Opened and The Priestly Bride*. Her husband, Albert, conducted detailed research into Scripture and adds scriptural references in the books, giving further credence to the reality of what she saw by validating them through descriptions that are contained in the Word of God. During a telephone interview with her, she gave away a few hints as to what it is like to receive throne-room revelation and how she was able to write down exactly what she saw:

Ever since I was a Christian, anyone with a prophetic gift said I was going to see into Heaven, and I thought they were loopy. There are so many visions. Both books were written by going through the visions and I mark what I believe the Lord would have in the book. He indicates which ones He wants in the books.

"The visions are more like experiences," she explained. "It isn't that I am seeing something outside of myself; I am really in it, taken there, experiencing it. I am actually walking through them. When the heavens first opened for me, I was able to get up from the experience and write it down. It wasn't long. Then I asked the Lord that if he was going to give me more of these, I wanted to be able to write down exactly what He said or the angels said. So He granted that to me, and it's like I am in it and look down onto a page and I write what has been said, but sometimes it's only a few words. I am going through the experience, but also, simultaneously, I am writing it down."

The most remarkable thing about Anna's vision was that she was able to be in two places at once—in Heaven experiencing a vision, and on Earth writing it down. But it wasn't always so. As she beheld increasing revelation, she learned how to function in both worlds at the same time. Learning how to live in the spiritual realm takes practice. It's like swimming in another atmosphere. The more you dwell in that atmosphere, the more familiar it becomes, and you discover new ways of moving, thinking, transcending the limitations of gravity, and floating in the Presence of God. Anna talked about how she learned to interact within the vision as she first began experiencing them.

"Al and I were praying and while we prayed, my eyes were closed. I saw this angel standing before me in the spiritual realm, and he said, '*Come forward.*' I didn't know I could get up and out of my body. I got up and followed this angel and there were two others parting a curtain. I had this big argument with myself. I thought this cannot be a visitation; this just can't be, because a visitation is when Jesus comes. The angel said, '*Stop. Come forward.*' It was very matter of fact. Another set of blue curtains opened and it was lighter behind that, and a third released a blazing light behind it. A voice said, '*What would you have?*' I realized then that I was, standing before the throne of God and I didn't know what else to do. So, I continued to pray aloud with my husband.

"I would pray and the angel would say, *'Done. Proceed.'* I thought, 'Here I am, standing before God who is saying it will be done.' I was stunned. I got to the end of what my husband and I always prayed and the angel said, *'Step forward.'* Out of the light, two huge hands of light came down on my head and all sorts of power and electricity flowed into me. He lifted his hand and the angel started lifting me backward."

The vision released the beginning of a series of visions. Like many people who receive a vision, or a throne-room experience in which they are lifted into Heaven to meet the Lord, Anna thought it was a once-in-a-lifetime experience.

"I thought I am only going to have one shot at this and I want to have it all. But the Lord said, *'The way is open before you now and if you have forgotten to ask me something you can ask me again.'* It was then that I realized I could come anytime."

At one point during this revelatory season, Anna walked in Heaven, talked with angels, and met the Lord. During one encounter, when an angel invited her to meet the Lord, the angel "… smiled at me and spoke quietly, 'The Creator of the Universe desires your company. Don't keep Him waiting.'"[2] That simple statement unlocked in Anna an ability to come boldly before the Lord and meet Him face to face. This same invitation resounds loudly from Heaven in the lives of all who would venture into the realms of Heaven. Many prophetic ministers believe that God is waiting for us to come to Him. The way has been opened. The heavens are opened. We need only draw near to Him and He will draw near to us. (See James 4:8.)

But why Anna? Why was she chosen to receive this series of revelations? She wondered that herself and asked the Lord about it.

"My Father continued, 'You will tell of what you have seen and heard. You will reveal my heart and give hope by revealing "home" to others. Your words will be like letters from home to those in the field. When a soldier is on the battlefield, a letter from home, telling of the people and places of home gives a soldier great hope. He keeps going because he longs for home and realizes that he is greatly loved. Hope, Anna, is a gift to mankind. Without hope, they languish.'"

"Why have you chosen me?"

"Because you are simple Anna, and know little. Before the foundations of the world, I called you, not because you are wise and intelligent, but because I delight in you. My Son delights in you. The Holy Spirit delights in you. And I have brought you to myself this day to ask for your help."[3]

Throne-room revelation comes to those the Lord delights in, the humble of heart, the contrite, the ones who will be obedient to do what the Lord desires in such a way that it glorifies Him, rather than calling attention to oneself. Throne-room revelation is not restricted to those with international prophetic ministries. It is available to you and to me. And those experiences are not limited to a prophetic nature and perspective either.

Many who have related stories of a near-death experience report that they, too, have been lifted out of their earthly bodies and into Heaven—seeing the light and glory of God, hearing His voice, and encountering the supernatural realm of God. These encounters cause us to understand that we need not wait until death to know that we know that God exists. The Creator of the universe desires your company. How long will you keep Him waiting? You enter His courts through praise and thanksgiving. You come into His Presence through prayer and worship. For Anna, the visions began as she practiced her daily discipline of prayer. How long will you tarry there in that place of prayer? How much do you desire the company of the Creator of the universe?

Larry Randolph

Larry Randolph is another prophetic minister who speaks with humor and humility about the revelatory encounters of his life. As individuals struggle to speak of their encounters, listeners are drawn into the awareness of how difficult it is for one person to adequately describe what it is like to be in the glory, see the hugeness of God, and how it feels to experience Him so personally. Here, Larry describes the shock and awe of being flung into the

Presence of God. He also implies that just one encounter with God in the realm beyond reason, will unlock the meaning of one's destiny and purpose in life.

"I was hurled in the vision through time and space, where I landed on my hands and knees on an enormous marble courtyard. Now completely over-taken with the awe of my encounter, I fell prostrate on the surface of the gigantic floor, shaking with reverent fear. I realized that I was in the court-yard of Heaven, lying face down before the throne of Almighty God. Even more astonishing, there was no sound except what I can only describe as the sound of golden silence described in Revelation 8:1. The atmosphere was so thick with God's glory that nothing needed to be said, other than to acknowl-edge that the omnipotent God is seated on His throne, ruling in the affairs of men and angels.... From that day forward, I intuitively knew the value of my calling and the meaning of my destiny."[4]

John Sandford

John Sandford, co-founder of Elijah House with his wife, Paula, has been in the prophetic and healing ministry for decades, and they serve as mentors to many well-known prophetic voices of our day. Prophets tend to live in the space between Heaven and Earth—a realm of the spirit that seems foreign to many believers. As a result, traveling in the spirit and visiting Heaven have been common experiences for him. Being a self-described "practical prophet," John realized that little was to be gained by spending more time in Heaven than on Earth, and he sought to find a balance in his mysticism—a balance that would bring more Heaven to Earth, than him to Heaven. He offers his nuggets of wisdom here:

"I learned to travel in the spirit at will and also had the power to come up into the heavens at any time. I've visited Him many times. While it is a won-derful thing to do, I am a very practical mystical person and saw no virtue in it for the sanctification of others or for intercession, so I quit it. It was fun. The grass in Heaven is like spring. It's alive and it welcomes you. You can go into the river and it flows right through; you can breathe in it. It refreshes you and so on. But what virtue was that for anyone else? If you talk about it to others, it can cause an estrangement. If God calls us to go up and see something, we will. But we won't do it just because we can do it."[5]

You Can Come, Too

Ian Clayton, a prophetic minister in New Zealand, believes that, as sons and daughters of the King, we have a right to explore the realm of Heaven and to walk back into the realms of Earth bearing God's Presence, revelation, and power. The realms of Heaven Clayton walks in include glimpses of the Garden of Eden, the throne room of God, and areas of His Kingdom that few have seen and even fewer have words to describe.

Much of his ministry today focuses on revealing the inheritance Christians have as sons and daughters of the King. He also brings people into the mystery of the supernatural, mentoring them along until people access the realms of Heaven for themselves and visionary experiences become supernatural. Clayton believes anyone can be taught to access greater intimacy with Christ—literally on Earth as it is in Heaven. Clayton demystifies the experience by explaining that accessing Heaven can be a learned experience:

"Entering the realm of the Kingdom is a learned experience. The spirit-man can go with Jesus and walk with God because the Holy Spirit resides in your body. I surrender to the glory of God and then I walk with Him. He initiates it. I follow by my desire to be with the Father in His Kingdom. As children, we have a right to be with God the Father in Heaven. As a son, he gives me a right to discover the realm of Heaven. My single desire is to encounter and know Him as a friend, to know all that He does and all that He is about. Every time I walk into the realms of Heaven, it always leads to a deeper love and encounter with God."[6]

So how does one enter into greater experiences of the Kingdom of God? How does that shift occur from imaginative prayer encounters to feeling as if we are beamed up to Heaven with our eyes wide open, as the awesomeness of God encounters us?

According to prophetic minister Shawn Boltz, who has had many of his own throne-room encounters, "There is one primary distinction that sets apart a vessel for Throne Room Encounters; those who hunger for the reality of heavenly encounters are pursuing it so that they might share in the burning desire of Jesus for His reward. They don't want to just have a manifestation of gifting or an encounter so that they can know future events, but they have a longing to know Jesus the way He longs to be known."[7] Boltz, like many others, believes that the increase in revelation is about to be released *en masse*, rather than restricted to individuals scattered here and there around the world.

"God is about to visit a generation with a manifestation of the Throne Room Presence. More and more people are experiencing this reality than ever before. This is especially true because we are approaching a generation that truly lives with a manifestation of Heaven on Earth. The goal is to bring the greatest agreement and communion that has ever been seen in any generation between His desires in Heaven and our walk on Earth. Are you ready to see Heaven?"

Endnotes

1. Shawn Bolz, *Throne Room Encounters*, June 2004.

2. Anna Roundtree, *The Heavens Opened* (Lake Mary, FL: Charisma House Publishers, 1999), 7.

3. Anna Roundtree *The Heavens Opened*, 92.

4. Larry Randolph, *Spirit Talk: Hearing the Voice of God* (Wilksboro, NC: Morning Star Publications, 2005), 38.

5. Based on a personal interview with John Sandford.

6. Based on a personal interview with Ian Clayton.

7. Shawn Bolz, *Throne Room Encounters*, June 2004, 2004-07-22.

CHAPTER 9

Ecstasy, Peeps, Mutters, and Prophecies

BY JULIA LOREN

The Presence of God filled the room as thousands stood worshiping, their faces upturned to Heaven, some with hands stretched up or out as if welcoming more of Him. Their daily worries, cares, and ailments fell by the wayside as they focused on the King of kings and Lord of lords. Their hearts had become captivated by the Lover of their souls. A few dared come closer still, worshiping more intentionally—pushing aside every thought or distraction until all their worship centered on God, who seemed vibrantly alive and present, not only filling the room but enveloping their hearts so completely that some fell to the ground and lay motionless, as if they were in a trance. Others remained standing in spiritual ecstasy, tears silently flowing as love released the wounds in their souls, a healing beyond words brought about by the Comforter, the Holy Spirit, washing through them. It is a scene that is replayed countless times during conferences and in Spirit-filled churches around the world.

Draw near to me and I will draw near to you, the Lord promises us all. (See James 4:8.) A few of us venture closer still. It is not enough to catch a glimpse of His Presence, feel a momentary rush of love or peace or joy. The Creator of the universe desires your company. How close will you come?

As individuals and groups of people enter into a sense that God's Presence is manifesting tangibly, it becomes easier to draw closer to Him. Many enter into a state of suspended reality during worship or prayer, feeling a sense of oneness with God and entering a trance-like state where the cares of Earth grow strangely still and Heaven seems only a heartbeat away. It is here where God often meets with people in an extraordinary way.

What is this spooky state of mental suspension that is called a trance? A trance is simply a state of suspended reality. It is not a vision but often serves as a precursor to a vision. It must be God-initiated, however, for it to become a valid spiritual experience. A trance that is induced by practicing deliberate disassociation or detachment is fraught with peril, as the demonic spirits of this age seek any opening in a person's life in hopes of destroying personalities and warping lives. It is spiritually and emotionally dangerous to try to induce trance states. But if God draws you into a place of worldly transcendence, it could be the beginning of a wonderful spiritual encounter.

People describe trance states as being states of mental suspension, a place either without thought, devoid of feeling, or the opposite—rich with imagery and filling one with a sense of rapture and ecstasy. Others say it feels like being lifted up to Heaven—becoming wide awake in the Spirit. Yet, the opposite is also true as others claim to fall into a deep sleep or feel sedated in their bodies while being wide awake in their spiritual understanding.

The Bible contains numerous instances of people undergoing trance-like experiences such as Samuel's. After Samuel was awakened out of a sleep, he entered into a revelatory state where he heard the voice of God speaking to him. Trance-like states also seem to put people into deep sleeps as well. Genesis 15:12 describes a "deep sleep" that fell upon Abram as a precursor to revelation. Daniel also received visionary revelation while in a "deep sleep." Other trance states serve as precursors to out-of-body experiences, such as Paul's account of being "caught up to the third heaven." In such a state he did not know whether he was "in the body" or "out of the body." (See 2 Corinthians 12:2.)

There are occasionally times when I awake in the morning only to find myself immediately sprinkled with some spiritual anesthesia that lulls me into a trance-like state. I lie in a place where I feel mentally alert but I am focused only on the things of the Spirit unfolding—hearing or seeing into the spiritual realm of angels on assignment standing beside my bed, speaking to me about someone or some event that is about to occur. I suppose if I awoke out of a deep sleep to see an angel standing before me, the shock would be so great that I would let loose a piercing scream or perhaps think I had just died in my sleep and was on my way to Heaven; and so, God in mercy keeps me somewhat sedated.

This type of trance is simply a state of suspended reality wherein my thoughts, feelings, and emotions seem alert, yet a bit sedated in order for my spirit to grasp the revelation at hand. For whatever reason, a trance state may seem like a form of spiritual anesthesia that enables us to see in the spirit without "freaking out" in the flesh.

Trances often precede a vision or spiritual encounter but sometimes a trance is simply a conditioned response to worship or prayer. When I sense God's Presence saturating me during worship, it is as if I am stepping into an atmosphere of God's Presence that seems thick with revelatory anointing. I stand in place as both my earthly and spiritual senses are suspended. Seeing nothing at first, but knowing that I am in a trance state, I simply ask God for more revelation.

The things that happen to me in a trance state vary. On rare occasions, my spirit rockets to Heaven, leaving my body standing still or lying on the ground, motionless as the trance state moves immediately into a vision. More usually, however, I am aware of nothing but a deep peace that feels like I have spent hours in focused, contemplative prayer. It is as if my brain finally stops the endless chatter and shuts off abruptly. Hazy images take shape in my imagination during these times.

I have learned to test these images and the spirit behind them during the initial moment of a trance state. Are they a type of dissociation—a blocking out of any unpleasant feelings or thoughts, a running away from pain, or perhaps just a checking out of reality that tries to tighten its grip by releasing these hazy images that are begging for attention? Am I just soulishly trying to tune into nothing but the Presence of God in order to drown out my day rather than focus on worshiping Him to make His day? We all dissociate from time to time, "space out," or take a mental break. When that break becomes more frequently practiced in order to escape from reality, dissociative states can become dangerous.

Worship is not meant to become a pleasant escape. It is designed to bring us closer to God who calls us into the depths of reality—a reality where He works His grace of healing in our hearts and makes us whole, or lifts us into His perspective, or enables us to glimpse Him in all of His majesty and glory. Worship is not a time to stand in a state of ecstatic nothingness. We worship in spirit and in truth—actively, not passively. When I realize that I am using worship as an escape, to just tune out the world, I realize that worship has become all about me and nothing about Him.

So, I invite the Presence of the Lord to soak me in His love and feel His deep peace and love filling me to the point where I can release it back to Him. At other times, I ask God to move me beyond whatever shadowy images beg for attention and into the purity of His revelation. It is here, in this place of worship, that He speaks most clearly a word about some issue of concern to me, a person dear to my heart, a problem in my life that needs addressing, or releases words of affirmation, such as *my dearly beloved…my beautiful one…I loved what you gave in secret the other day*. It is also here, in this place of worship, where visions unfold and I see or intuit the realities of how His Kingdom invades our lives and we glimpse His plans and purposes unfolding.

The heart of God touches our hearts in the place of worship. We need only turn inward and listen. And in this turning inward, we may enter a trance-like state, fully focused on the loving Presence of God, listening for His voice, waiting on Him, and watching for Him.

It takes practice to know how to respond to God when His Presence draws near. Seeing or hearing nothing in a trance state means that you need to push through into greater revelation like Samuel did as a young boy when he heard his name called but did not know how to respond. The prophet Samuel, as a small boy lying asleep on his mat, heard a voice calling his name.

He rose and went to the lead priest's side, thinking the priest had just summoned him. After being called out of his sleep three times, the priest realized that the boy was being called by the Lord and told Samuel to stay in bed the next time he heard his name called and ask the Lord to keep speaking to him. "Speak, Lord, your servant is listening," is the cry of one who knows that God is initiating an experience and doesn't want to miss out.

The Danger of Self induced Trances

George Otis, a man who has extensively studied and written about the spiritual realm and why evil resides in certain places, recognizes that not all revelation comes from God when it is received in a particular trance state that he calls "microsleep."

He writes, "Christian intercessors are also vulnerable to brief lapses of awareness known as microsleeps. These episodes, triggered by extreme fatigue, can occur in prayer meetings, in the middle of conversations, even while driving. Although microsleeps are brief, lasting no more than a few seconds, they are rich in hypnagogic imagery—fleeting, undefined forms that serve as building blocks for hallucinations. The danger in these episodes, as UCLA professor Ronald Siegel points out, is that 'the fatigued brain can embroider these ambiguous forms with specific features.' Without adequate rest or a grounding support system (wise leaders and loving friends) long-haul intercessors can fall prey to false, even demonically inspired impressions."[1]

Microsleeps and dissociative states are two types of self-induced trances that can lead to soulishly inspired or demonic revelation. If you are just "spacing out," or disassociating because you don't want to face some issue or person, you are entering a type of trance that is called a "dissociative state." Clearly, dissociative individuals, with fragmented personalities, fall into a number of categories of mental illness from schizoid to identity disorders to delusional disorders.

Those who focus on intercession, or spend late night hours in prayer in a desire to gain a breakthrough in some area of their lives, can fall prey to microsleeps. The hazy images that result during these times need to be questioned. "Is this you, God, or is this me?" God is not the author of con-fusion. In Him there are no shifting shadows. Purity of revelation tiptoes in during the most mysterious moments; it does so rarely on demand.

There is a clear difference between mystics and the mentally ill. Accountable relationships and increasing knowledge about Scripture are increasingly important to our spiritual well-being, as we enter into ongoing spiritual encounters. We need to bounce our experiences off of others in order to increase in discernment as to what may be God-initiated, self-initiated, or demonically inspired revelation. Even those who know the Word of God can fall prey to demonic inspiration and fall into the realm of the evil one, as they enter into a dissociative state, or a trance state at will.

There are also clear differences between mystics and psychics. Those in occultic or New Age religions deliberately practice dissociative techniques that are designed to bring them to a point where they can passively invite spirits to enter in and take them on out-of-body excursions, listen for guid-ance from the spirit world, or tune into the presence of ecstatic nothingness. It is a dangerous place that invites the demonic to infiltrate. Christians with a bent toward mysticism deliberately practice the Presence of God, not the presence of nothingness. Nor do Christians deliberately invite demonic enti-ties to take possession of their spirit, soul, and body. Visions and miracles are to be initiated by God, not by self.

Trance Mediums and Psychic Healers

Trance mediums and psychic healers willingly enter into a trance state in order to make room for a spirit to move in and speak and act through them. Nicknamed "the sleeping prophet" in the press, Edgar Cayce was born in Hopkinsville, Kentucky, in 1877, a time when religious revival meetings swept through the area.[2] Raised as a Christian with a deep interest in reading the Bible, his dream as a child was to become a medical missionary. By the age of six he told his parents he could see visions and occasionally talk to rel-atives who had died. At the age of 13, he had a vision that transformed his life. In the vision, a beautiful woman appeared before him and asked what he

158

wanted most in life. He replied that more than anything, he wanted to help others—especially sick children.

Shortly after that, Cayce received every struggling schoolboy's dream (apart from a beautiful woman's appearance); he could sleep on his schoolbooks and acquire a photographic memory of their entire contents. Eventually, he discovered that he could sleep on any book, paper, or document and repeat every word, even though the contents were beyond the scope of his limited education. This gift gradually faded as Cayce left school to assist his uncle on the family farm. He continued attending church, married, and fathered two children; he worked steadily as a photographer, and eventually became a popular Sunday school teacher who could make the Bible come alive to his listeners.

Later in life, Cayce attended a hypnotist's show and, after repeated attempts to use hypnosis to cure his long struggle with laryngitis, he discovered that while in a hypnotic state, he received information that would cure him. After he regained his speech, he recognized a newfound ability to enter a hypnotic state and give medical readings—diagnosing and giving prescriptive cures for those with a variety of illnesses. For most of his adult life, he was able to put himself into a sleep state and answer virtually any question posed to him in what became initially known as "psychic readings." Initially, the information dealt with medical problems and solutions. Eventually, he branched out into such topics as meditation, dream interpretation, and predicting future events.

He drifted from his Christian faith, as his "life readings" began to reflect many of the themes and terminology inherent in Theosophy, such as past lives, the person's potential and purpose in the present, the lost continent of Atlantis and its influence on other cultures, and higher levels of consciousness or the latent power of the mind to tap into the "collective" spiritual realm.

Both his healing gift and predictions stunned and amazed the nation. He claimed to predict the beginning and end of both World War I and World War II, the lifting of the Depression in 1933, and the coming holocaust in Europe. Still, his other predictions are reflected in today's world events as distinct possibilities—namely, that China would become a cradle of Christianity, that Russia would be a leader in freedom, and from Russia would come "the hope of the world" (a type of the anti-Christ), and the possibility of World War III arising in the Middle East.

In 1944, he collapsed from exhaustion and died soon afterward.

To this day, many believe the source of his power was rooted in the authentic power of Christ. A closer look at his childhood experiences reveals otherwise. Early childhood experiences of visions, conversations with dead relatives, and a beautiful spirit-woman do not present a revelation of Jesus Christ or a calling to glorify Jesus. Instead, the experiences reveal a successful demonic attempt to seduce him into a spiritual realm that was distinctly not in keeping with his biblical upbringing and sway him away from the religious revival of his youth.

Had someone taught him in church that he was not to consult the dead, something about the difference between angels, demons, and familiar spirits; that spirits are to be tested; and that Jesus Christ is the only legal source of authentic power and vision, perhaps Cayce could have been one of the most authentic Christian prophets of the last century. The demonic had clearly intervened to make sure that Cayce would not come into the fullness of his calling as a true prophet and become their worst enemy.

Instead of releasing authentic gifts of healing—not through trances, but in full conscious awareness of the Presence and power of the Holy Spirit, he fell into deception and became controlled by occult powers. The more Cayce gave himself over to the dissociative trance state, the more he found himself under the control of demonic spirits who sought to influence listeners into new ways of thinking that were rooted in Eastern religions and Theosophical foundations. One of the marks of demonic power is to bind people into new ways of thinking, thereby taking away their freedom.

Rather than being remembered as a true prophet, Cayce may just go down in history as the greatest false prophet the U.S. has seen to date—a prophet operating from demonic spirits whose mission was to shift the shadows of darkness over the light of the power of Christ and establish revelation derived from occult sources into the mainstream of the nation.

Michel Nostradamus, a 16th century French physician, is also one of the most famous of "prophets" still making headlines in today's tabloids.[3] During a plague that swept Europe, he gained a reputation as a gifted healer. Ironically, it was a plague that took the lives of his first wife and daughter. Devastated by the loss, he focused more on astrology and began to fall into trances and see his first visions. Most of his visions were written in poetic form of four-line verses, in groups of 100. Many readers believed the writing was deliberately obscure in order to allegedly prevent persecution.

Those who study his verses believe that Nostradamus predicted the rise of Hitler and World War II, the fall of New York's twin towers on September 11, 2001, and numerous world events before and between. Tabloid newspapers continue to reprint doctored translations of his poetic prophecies, attributing his predictions of specific events usually after the fact. Many find the words of Nostradamus so cryptic that they could mean almost anything. One thing all readers can agree on—the revelatory poetics are all about doom and gloom.

The visions he wrote about and historic accounts of his personal life (which I will not go into here), reflected not only the depressed state of the prophet but a budding psychosis that was evidenced in his fractured relationships and in the whisperings and mutterings of obscure speech.

Isaiah, an Old Testament prophet, speaks about this process of psychological disintegration in prophets who give themselves willingly to the darkness of occult power rather than seeking the authentic power of God—a power who speaks clearly to all, with revelations based on the Word of God, which imparts the light of dawn.

When men tell you to consult mediums and spiritists, who whisper and mutter, should not a people inquire of their God? Why consult the dead on behalf of the living? To the law and to the testimony! If they do not speak according to this word, they have no light of dawn. Distressed and hungry, they will roam throughout the land; when they are famished; they will become enraged and, looking upward, will curse their king and their God. Then they will look toward the Earth

and see only distress and darkness and fearful gloom, and they will be
thrust into utter darkness (Isaiah 8:19-22).

Popular mediums, such as JZ Knight, who channels a demonic spirit called Ramtha (among others), and individuals who invite spirit guides to speak to and through them, are common in our culture. Psychic healers whose bodies are taken over by spirits who conduct operations and prescribe potions for healing are also common· overseas. They all seem to fall into a trance state as a precursor to the spirit entity emerging.

John of God, a Brazilian psychic healer, is what is called an "unconscious medium." At the age of 16, the "entity" of King Solomon entered his body, and performed a miraculous healing, leading João to become an itinerant healer wandering Brazil until he took residence in his casa in the plateaus and became known as "John of God." Today, he channels over 30 spirit entities, doctors, and notables who can enter his body and treat ailments such as cancer, AIDS, blindness, asthma, drug addiction, alcohol abuse, tumors, physical problems of any kind, debilitating psychological problems, or spiritual desperation. Desperate people from all over the world flock to his compound seeking miracles of healing.

"The 'incorporating' happens in an instant, without warning. As João prepares to operate, his body suddenly jerks. He is said to take on the personality and even the eye color of the entity who inhabits him.

About the surgeries, he said: 'I don't do that. God and the spirits do that.' He says even looking at the videotapes of the surgeries makes him queasy. He says he doesn't even remember the experience. 'I am unconscious,' he told "Primetime Live's" John Quiñones. He likened his state to being asleep."[4]

Even the Bible speaks of mediums and spiritists who abounded in both the Old Testament and the New, challenging the power of God and calling attention away in hopes of luring people to follow the demonic rather than to step into a relationship with God.

Saul, devastated in heart and spirit, longed for a word from the prophet Samuel who had anointed him king in the first place. The problem: Samuel was dead. God didn't seem to be speaking with Saul in his hour of need. No other prophets nearby held any words of comfort for Saul. He felt alone, abandoned, and afraid of the days to come. In the absence of any other prophets in the area, he sought out a medium, hoping she would channel the spirit of Samuel. She dwelt in a cave, hiding her profession because Saul had condemned mediums and spiritists to death. So, she was dubious at first to grant Saul an audience, but she went ahead and did so because she did not recognize that it was Saul who stood before her.

She sat back, closed her eyes, spoke a few unintelligible words of incantation, calling out to the spirit of Samuel, hoping that his familiar spirit would show up, a spirit that could, at best, imitate Samuel's voice and know intimate details of Samuel's life. Suddenly, she felt the presence of another in the cave. Out of the darkness, a figure emerged. She gasped and cried out in shock. It wasn't the familiar spirit of Samuel. It was Samuel himself, raised from the dead. Then she realized Saul was her client and she became very afraid.

The power of mediums, psychics, and psychic healers is real. The source, however, is demonic. Rather than experiencing the love and light and peace that comes to Christians during worship and having God initiate spiritual experiences, they experience the opposite, becoming slaves to the dark lord and his familiar spirits.

Discerning the Origins of Revelation

What is the difference between the origins of psychic power, and how can you tell if someone is accessing the power of God, the power of their soul, or demonic power?

Many Christians believe that Adam, the original man, had unlimited cognitive and paranormal abilities. Given his direct access to God and his capacity to manage a vast garden and name all of the animals, they reason that he must have commanded an unlimited memory, be able to see remote places and events mentally, and teleport himself to other places, among other powers.

163

After the Fall, and Adam was booted out of the Garden, many believe that those mental powers were removed from humans or they lapsed into dormancy. Fallen angels and creatures like demons, however, retained the ability to counterfeit miracles and power.

Christian author Watchman Nee wrote in *The Latent Power of the Soul* that he believed that many of Adam's original capabilities remain buried deep in our minds. As generations passed, Adam's spiritual and cognitive power became a latent force in our lives. Yet it is not a power to be tapped into. According to Nee, "The work of the devil nowadays is to stir up man's soul [in order] to release this latent power within it as a deception for spiritual power."[5]

Nee believes that God invites us to call on the power of the Holy Spirit rather than draw upon our own soul power. The enemy, satan, hopes to substitute realities that call for man to rely on soul power as a deceptive alternative to the power of the Holy Spirit.

The draw toward power, then, is a draw toward one of two sources of power—either God's power or satan's power. The mind of man is, therefore, neutral until it is swayed into exercising and developing the power of one's soul through demonic influence or reaching out for the power of the Holy Spirit. The trance state is a neutral state of suspended mental activity, a moment of nothingness that can be filled by either God's pure revelation or demonic inspiration. It is not to be entertained or self-induced. God's revelatory encounters must be initiated by Him, not by us.

Displays of power come from both kingdoms—one offers false power, a counterfeit to the true or authentic power of God. For every paranormal New Age activity in this world there is a corresponding authentic activity found in the Kingdom of God that makes satan's power look like flashy magic tricks that are conducted by a jealous adolescent. Until authentic power, displayed through God's prophets, healers, and new creation power brokers, infuses society, people will continue to turn toward the only source of power they see—occult and paranormal power displayed through television and in New Age circles.

As the days grow darker, we need to shift through the shadows of deception and determine the source of the power that is speaking to us. There are spiritual realms and dynamics operating as surely as there are natural laws of physics. Invisible to the naked eye, most of us can only observe their effects. The source of revelation fueling authentic prophets and demonic trance mediums and unconscious healers falls into spiritual realms of revelation that were originally established by God.

Testing the Spirits

Johanna Michaelson trained to become a full trance medium as a young woman under the moniker of Pachita, a psychic healer, and she knows first-hand about how fickle the dark spirits are—healing one moment, destroying lives the next. She later moved out of the demonic circles and became a Christian. Her book, *The Beautiful Side of Evil*, is a classic that exposes the spirits behind the healers and encourages Christians to really test the spirit behind a spiritual encounter, according to First Thessalonians 5:19-20, which tells us not to quench the Holy Spirit, but to examine everything carefully. God has given us the ability to examine the Scriptures daily (see Acts 17:11) and make a careful search concerning what the Holy Spirit speaks to them. (See 1 Peter 1:10-11.) It is not enough to welcome a God encounter—we must seek to understand the source of the encounter, discern whether precedence has been set in Scripture, and finally, to unpack the meaning of the encounter or spiritual experience so that we can fully understand what God wants us to understand. According to Johanna, this pleases God.

She writes, "The only one who is insecure about testing the gifts is one who doesn't know the Scriptures, for they tell us such practice proves the genuine and pleases God. Unless the Church recognizes this and repents before the Lord, seeking to bring restoration and purity to the Body which is now polluted by counterfeits and false doctrines, how will we survive these days?

"As it is, occultists feel right at home in our meetings, for they see the whooping down of the Spirit, shaking hands 'uncontrollably' in techniques that smack of aura manipulation, falling into trance-like states, and crying out 'words of knowledge' just as the clairvoyants do in certain spiritualist centers. They see us demanding God's immediate performance as do white magicians who also use the name of God and Jesus and the Holy Spirit in their rituals.... They see us being bounced off the floor by an unseen force, even as I frequently saw happen to Pachita when she was possessed. They hear a deafening confusion of babbling tongues, each one screaming louder than the next, as though the Lord were deaf. They see us indiscriminately laying on hands for healing, even as they do, with no call whatever to confession and repentance of sin" (James 5:14-17).[6]

I agree in part with Johanna. We must call people to confession and repentance. But we must also encourage people to come to meetings where the Presence and power of the Lord Jesus Christ resides and His kindness sweeps them into His embrace—for it is His kindness that leads them to repentance. We owe them a God-encounter that will enable them to see the difference between God's powerfully loving Presence and the false gods and demonic spirits that they worship. Occultists should come to Charismatic and Pentecostal meetings. It is there where they will meet the King of kings and Lord of lords, get delivered of their enslavement to the enemy, and find healing for their souls.

During such meetings, where the Presence of God seems to come in power, it is imperative to discern what God is doing individually and to recognize that we are all in need of healing and that some are in need of deliverance. Some manifestations that occur during meetings, such as what Johanna described, are simply soulish hurts emerging in loud cries and screams, as God's Presence touches the deepest wounds of an individual's life. Other manifestations appear as symbolic or prophetic acts and intercessions where the movements of the person have meaning in themselves. Some manifest demons and are in need of deliverance. Some fall into trances where they see authentic, God-initiated visions. Others fall into dissociative states that they think are God-initiated trances.

Unfortunately, most churches that welcome the manifest Presence of God have too few people who are trained to discern what is happening with others. God is bigger than us all and His ways are not our ways. Healing and deliverance of His people remains foremost on His heart. It may look messy to us, but His Presence and power eventually sorts us all out.

Standing in the Light of Christ

Why should we care about psychics and mediums who peep and mutter or the marks of God's authentic revelation and marks of the demonic? As we move toward the close of this age, Scripture reveals that the shifting shadows of supernatural power will increasingly clash. The darkness will grow darker. But will the light grow brighter? You are the light of the world. The light of Jesus Christ should be glowing ever brighter within you.

How close do you want to come to the bonfire of God's love? Entering into worship is the first step. It is there, in that place where your heart touches the fire of His love, that you may just find yourself igniting with passionate love or standing in awe of the vision unfolding before you.

We have no need to fear the shifting shadows of supernatural experiences when we know that God is initiating the encounter, for He is the Light, and in Him there are no shadows of darkness.

Endnotes

1. George Otis, *The Twilight Labyrinth* (Grand Rapids, MI: Chosen Books, 1997), 252.

2. While many books have been written documenting Cayce's life, this information was derived from the online encyclopedia Wikipedia at http://en.wikipedia.org/wiki/Edgar_Cayce.

3. While many books have been written about Nostradamas, this information was derived from the Nostradamas Society of America's Website: http://www.nostradamususa.com/html/biography.html.

4. "Is 'John of God' a Healer or a Charlatan?: Searching for Hope and Health in a Remote Brazilian Village," February 10, 2005, ABC News Internet Ventures, "PrimeTime."

5. Watchman Nee, *The Latent Power of the Soul* (New York: Christian Fellowship Publications, 1972), 44, 19-20.

6. Johanna Michaelson, *The Beautiful Side of Evil* (Eugene, OR: Harvest House Publishers, 1982), 191.

CHAPTER 10

In the Body, or Out?

BY JULIA LOREN

The hand of the Lord lifted me from my bed and, as I drifted slowly toward the ceiling, I realized that this was not a dream. I was awake, immobile but alert. With a sudden rush, my spirit broke through the ceiling; an unseen force pulled me through the night sky, and the wind generated by my own propulsion roared past my face. In a mere second I traveled what would normally be a 40-minute drive to church. Passing through the ceiling of the church, I hovered in an upper corner looking down on a circle of women; their backs were turned toward me, and they were obviously engaged in prayer. Some wept. Others stretched out their hands as if they were focusing their intercessions on a specific woman who was present in the room.

Eventually I realized that these were the women on the leadership team of the church who were praying through some sort of crisis. Lingering there for a moment in my vantage point from the ceiling, as the women moved around praying, I could see their faces and could tell their names, but I heard nothing of what they said. Suddenly, I felt a yank and found myself sitting up in bed, startled by my midnight journey.

The following Sunday I went to church and saw a friend, one of the women whose faces I had seen in that prayer meeting. Tentatively, I approached her and asked if there had been a special prayer meeting held a few nights ago. She said that there had been; they had come together to pray for one of the pastor's wives who had been diagnosed with late-stage cancer. I rattled off a list of names and asked her if those particular women were present in the room. Again she confirmed what I had witnessed during my spirit journey.

Why had God allowed me to glimpse that particular event? During that season in my life I experienced a number of supernatural events. It was as if God was giving me a foretaste of what was to come. Prophetic dreams and visions, angelic visitations, and accurate words of knowledge flowed into and through my life, as if the manifest Presence of God had moved into my little apartment and taken up residency. I walked for several months, more conscious of the atmosphere of Heaven than the restrictions of Earth. Joy and peace and light radiated from me.

I said nothing to anyone about what was happening to me while I was in the middle of that season, partly because I had no words to explain it and partly because no one would understand it if I had tried to tell them. However, everyone who knew me knew I was different. Those who didn't know me were drawn to the light and peace and revelation that were coming from me. Fully alive in the Presence of God, I felt no need to talk about what I was experiencing; I just enjoyed dwelling with Him continually. It seemed pretty natural that I could walk with Him, talk with Him, and, why not fly with Him to see what He sees. I came to understand the experience was given to me just because Jesus delighted in being with me and sharing His realm with me, showing me His heart and His viewpoint. It was part of the package of being in an intimate relationship with Him.

What I found most astounding wasn't the fact that I had somehow left my body and attended an actual meeting, but the fact that at the time of my "arrival," the meeting had already come to an end. I had gone to bed around midnight and immediately traveled in my spirit just before drifting off to sleep. The meeting had already ended by then. I had gone backward in time to witness the event!

God is no respecter of the constructs of time that have been created by man. The Bible reveals out-of-body experiences that take people into the future and translations that move a person rapidly from one place to another in the present. Why not move a person to glimpse something in the recent past or in the near future? God's ways are not our ways.

Scientific Research Explanations

Out-of-body experiences (OBEs) are as old as humankind.

Various researchers, conducting both formal and informal polls and studies, reveal that 5 to 10 percent of the population has at one time or another experienced a sense of their spirits leaving their bodies. Some hover in the room near their physical bodies and later discover that the experiences were generated as a result of being under anesthesia or having a near-death experience. Others move beyond the limitations of time and space, as if their spirit journeys elsewhere, leaving their bodies far behind. Out-of-body experiences are one of the most common spiritual experiences that are felt by people, irrespective of their faith backgrounds. We are all spiritual beings.

It seems that OBEs can occur to anyone in almost any circumstance—while resting, sleeping, or dreaming. Surveys reveal that the majority of OBEs occur when people are in bed, ill, or resting, or on some form of anesthesia or medication. But they can occur during almost any kind of activity. I've had the experience of turning a corner while walking only to discover that my spirit suddenly took a flying leap upward and into a vision. Motorcyclists have reported that while riding at high speed, they have suddenly found themselves floating above their machines, looking down on their own bodies still driving along. Pilots of high-flying airplanes have also found themselves apparently outside their aircraft, struggling to get in. People engaged in intercessory prayer have reported traveling in the spirit to another location and seeing and hearing the same things simultaneously.

OBEs are brief sensations that occur when a person feels as if his or her mind separates from his or her body. During OBEs people sense that they are floating above their own bodies. No one knows what causes OBEs, but some people believe that OBEs are religious or spiritual events. Interestingly, many people who have come close to death report that they have had an OBE.

Scientific researchers have been trying to unlock the mystery behind this phenomenon for years, giving rise to a variety of neuro-theological explanations.

Researchers from the University Hospitals of Geneva and Lausanne (Switzerland) have found that OBEs can be produced by direct electrical stimulation of a specific part of the brain. Dr. Olaf Blanke and his colleagues worked with a 43-year-old female patient who suffered from right temporal lobe epilepsy. In order to identify the location where the seizures occurred, the researchers implanted electrodes on the brain under the patient's dura. While the patient was awake, the researchers could pass electrical current through the electrodes to identify the function of the brain area under each electrode.

Electrical stimulation of the angular gyrus on the right side of the patient's brain produced unusual sensations. Weak stimulation caused the patient to feel as if she was "sinking into the bed" or "falling from a height." Stronger electrical stimulation caused the patient to have an OBE. For example, the patient said, "I see myself lying in bed, from above, but I only see my legs and lower trunk." Stimulation of the angular gyrus at other times caused the woman to have feelings of "lightness" and of "floating" two meters above the bed.

The angular gyrus is located near the vestibular (balance) area of the cerebral cortex. It is likely that electrical stimulation of the angular gyrus interrupts the ability of the brain to make sense of information related to balance and touch. This interruption may result in OBEs. Blood flow changes within the angular gyrus may alter brain activity during "near death experiences." This may result in OBEs reported by people who survive such events.[1]

While many scientists try to make believe that we are merely biological beings, and they denounce faith as mere primitive thinking, other scientists and intellectuals dissent.

Belief and faith, believers argue, are larger than the sum of their brain parts: "The brain is the hardware through which religion is experienced," said Daniel Batson, a University of Kansas psychologist who studies the effect of religion on people. "To say the brain produces religion is like saying a piano produces music."[2]

At the Fuller Theological Seminary's school of psychology, Warren Brown, a cognitive neuropsychologist, said, "Sitting where I'm sitting and dealing with experts in theology and Christian religious practice, I just look at what these people know about religiousness and think they are not very sophisticated. They are sophisticated neuroscientists, but they are not scholars in the area of what is involved in various forms of religiousness." At the heart of the critique of the new brain research is what one theologian at St. Louis University called the "nothing-butism" of some scientists—the notion that all phenomena could be understood by reducing them to basic units that could be measured.

And finally, believers say, if God existed and created the universe, wouldn't it make sense that he would install machinery in our brains that would make it possible to have mystical experiences?[3]

Spiritual Explanation

What is going on spiritually that causes this sensation of a person's spirit leaving their body? Your spirit, according to the Bible, is the breath of God in you. (See Genesis 2:7.) It is your life breath. Many believe that if your spirit were to leave your body, you would die. Instead, the sensation of your spirit leaving your body is either a type of vision or it is a supernatural experience of being spiritually and physically transported in such a way that it transcends the laws of physics as we currently understand them. The Bible doesn't offer a clear explanation. In fact, most descriptions of spiritual encounters and visions seem deliberately obscure. Even the normally blunt apostle Paul only offers us this description of an OBE in Second Corinthians 12:2: "*I know a man in Christ who fourteen years ago was caught up to the third heaven. Whether it was in the body or out of the body I do not know—God knows."*

This passage also alludes to the fact that our spirit can function outside of the body. Theologians twist themselves up in a tripartite debate regarding whether humans can be divided into three parts—the physical body, the soul (comprised of the mind, the will, and the emotions) and spirit—or two (just body and spirit), or perhaps we're all just bags of old, dry bones. The standard belief taught in many churches is that God made humankind as tripartite beings. God created our bodies, gave us a soul, and breathed life into us. In other words, His life breath in you is your spirit.

According to prophetic minister Patricia King, the founder of Extreme Prophetic, just as our daydreams take our thoughts beyond the confines of our bodies, our spirits may also function beyond the body.

In her book *Spiritual Revolution*, Patricia describes an OBE that she is experiencing to her friend Linda, even as they talked. During this OBE, she traveled to Vancouver and prayed for a friend to be healed. And the friend was healed. She writes, "During the entire Ephesians 1:3 spiritual encounter and while symbolically depositing a healing blessing, I was aware of my natural surroundings. I even continued to talk to Linda during this time…. My spirit was not removed from my body, but I was experiencing something in my spirit that my body was not engaged in."[4]

Many people involved with the counterfeit spirituality inherent in New Age and occult churches believe that they can learn to travel at will, to "project their astral body" or spirit. Practicing a form of dissociation and entering into a relaxed state often bring about the desired results—their spirit does feel as if it is leaving their body and moving beyond the limitations of space and time. Moving through the heavenly realms in a state of what they call "astral projection," they are open to the demonic influences that helped initiate the OBE and they are open to their attack, as well. There is little protection from the demonic for those who willingly align themselves with darkness or seek to empower their soul as a substitute for God. Satan copies everything in his attempts to entice people away from knowing the Lord of lords and experiencing the realm of the King of kings.

John Sandford, co-founder of Elijah House with his wife Paula, has been in the prophetic and healing ministry for decades, and he and Paula serve as mentors to many well-known prophetic voices of our day. John has learned much as he has reflected on the variety of experiences he has encountered through the years. He offers this word of caution to many who would venture into the spiritual realms uninvited:

"When the prophets are in the spirit the Lord can take them on trips. Philip, in the Apocrypha, is one example. And there is an account of Habbakuk, who is caught up and taken to give his meal to Daniel in the den. In the Old Testament, Gehazzi running after Naaman was seen by Elisha who said, 'Did not my spirit go with you?' So a prophet can travel when the Lord calls. He can also do it at will but should not do it unless the Lord calls him.

"Again satan copies everything. Satan's copy is astral projection. He can project his spirit or his body. What we did, at the invitation of the Holy Spirit, was not astral projection; it's the Holy Spirit saying, 'Come, I want to show you something. He has called me and I feel myself traveling and I see the person. And later I ask them what's happening? And I say, *yeah I know because I was there*."[5]

Patricia King and John Sandford are among the many Charismatic ministers who believe that not only can our spirit function outside of our body, travel to a distant place and release healing, but our spirit can travel to a distant place and catch of glimpse of what is to come.

Come, I Will Show You!

Out-of-body experiences are a form of vision that releases to us a glimpse of what is on God's heart. Carried away to see a city that is to come, God gives us an experience to enable us to know His purposes in a situation. In Revelation 21:9-10, an angel carried Paul away: "*One of the seven angels who had the seven bowls full of the seven last plagues came and said to me, 'Come, I will show you....' And he carried me away in the Spirit to a mountain great and high, and showed me....*"

Flying between cities during a short mission trip to Brazil, I sat back in my airline seat, listening to my Mp3 player lull me into a worshipful state. Others on this mission trip filled the seats around me. My headphone barely drowned out their voices, laughter, and excitement over what they were experiencing in Brazil. I listened to them comment about the doe-eyed inno- cent faces of the Brazilians, their endlessly tanned skin, the result of an artist's pigmentation born of blended races, and their openness to the Holy Spirit. Others spoke of the miracles of healing and variety of medical issues they were witnessing. Excitement ran high. I tried to block them out and use the plane ride as a time to worship and pray silently for the meetings yet to come.

For a moment I felt a little turbulence on the airplane and realized my seat was shaking. My cheeks felt mysteriously wet as if it were raining inside the aircraft. The Presence of God flooded into me and I realized that I was leaving the plane. My spirit shot out into the sky and sped ahead to the city of our destination. Breaking into a room full of people, I noticed a row of young adults standing in worship, as the power of God ministered to them, moving one girl to loud tears. A tall young man danced and hopped as if his feet were burning, another rocked forward, praying out loud in tongues.

The whole room erupted in loud cries as people experienced inner heal- ing and deliverance. It was loud and hot. I heard and felt it all, but my atten- tion was drawn to the row of young adults. This was their moment; the moment that would catapult them into their destinies.

Then suddenly, I once again became aware of the plane's turbulence shaking my seat. My cheeks were even wetter. My body was hot. I opened my eyes to find the woman seated next to me staring at me. Apparently, the tur- bulence was not being generated by the plane. I had been shaking in my seat. The woman asked if I was all right. She realized that I had just had some sort of God encounter and she wisely refrained from questioning me further.

The next day, a group of us boarded a bus that took us to a storefront church on a busy street in a small and dusty town somewhere in the middle of Brazil. Inside, the standing-room-only crowd waited in eager expectation. And God did not disappoint them. Moving in response to their faith, He came in power to the same crowd I had already visited. I stood beside a row of young adults, their faces exactly as I had seen while "on the airplane" and their manifestations exactly as I had already witnessed. I knew, at that moment, how I was to pray for them and facilitate their breakthroughs, and I enlisted a few other ministry team members to assist me in this ministry.

Such encounters are meant to be normal experiences for believers. The Bible is full of stories about supernatural experiences of being and seeing. The experiences always accelerate the purposes of God in individuals' lives and in the lives of nations. If an experience or encounter with God serves only to titillate the one who receives it, I would question whether it was actually initiated by God. The fruit of the experience and how the person uses that experience speak more about the origins of the experience.

Both the soul and satan can create supernatural experiences and seek the glory and accolades that come about in the aftermath. A valid, God-initiated spiritual experience, however, always results in an acceleration of the purposes of God in the lives of others—not in the life of the one who received the experience. OBEs, visions, dreams, and visitations that are written about in the Bible are recorded not to give glory to the spirituality of a man, but to give glory to a supernatural God who desires to move Heaven to Earth and release a revelation of His love and power and plans for all of humanity.

Corporate Experience of Out-of-Body Visions

Sometimes groups of people who have prayed together for years suddenly enter into a unity of the Holy Spirit during their intercessions. Rather than each one praying out the particular concerns on their hearts for family members, their local church, or a host of other topics that flood the mind on any given day, they step into a corporate vision of the heart of God for that moment in time. These are special occasions in which they discover that they are all experiencing the same burden for prayer.

Some describe these experiences as going through the same gateway of intimacy that leads to a heavenly encounter, where they see the same vision of Jesus or Heaven simultaneously. Others feel as if their spirits are being transported to another place on Earth.

Patricia King talks about meeting a group of intercessors who had met every week for a year. During one particular meeting, "They were all led unexpectedly by the Spirit into a prison in China. Their natural bodies were in the USA, but in the spirit they were in China. They found themselves in a prison cell with a Christian man who had been imprisoned for his faith. They all saw each other there. They ministered to him and then all came out of the vision at the same time."[6] The leader of the meeting had them all write out what they saw prior to the discussion of the experience. As they read their reports out loud, their stories all matched.

John and Paula Sandford also talk about corporate visions they have experienced through the years. John writes, "Paula and I have taken many trips in the spirit. We're aware of what's happening in our body but know that in our spirit we are traveling. A group of four of us were in intercession one day and, traveling in the spirit to Heaven, we saw the same during that visit and talked about it afterwards."[7]

Many prayer visions have been experienced by groups in recent years, as they all see and hear the same thing simultaneously. I believe that a spirit of unity bound them to one another and carried them into the realm of Heaven where they saw and heard alike. The intimacy born of corporate unity often leads to corporate revelation. In an atmosphere where no one is fighting to be heard and no one is vying for some phantom reward for the one who got the best revelation in prayer, a spirit of unity prevails. And this unity enables them to all walk through the gateway of intimacy together, into the prayer garden of God, where He meets with them all at once or takes them on a journey to see what He sees and participate with Him in the work that He is doing around the world.

Translations and Bi-location

Shamans around the world have developed their powers and demonic alliances so radically that they are reported to not only experience their spirit venturing to other locations, but their bodies tagging along as well. While in the Vanuatu Islands on a short-term mission trip, I listened to Australian missionaries talk about shamans in the Solomon Islands who suddenly appeared in a place that would have taken them hours to reach on foot. The missionaries also witnessed shamans' forms shifting into animals whose glowing eyes watched them at night. Mere fear and superstition?

Missionaries have amazing tales to tell. At times, their experiences rival those of the most advanced shaman, as the power of God rises up to meet the challenge of demonic influence over a culture. Most missionary experiences cannot be substantiated by the testimony of two or three witnesses, because they are alone in the jungles and deserts of the world, facing demonic spirituality that defies our Western world view. They also face extreme circumstances that call for extreme measures. In order to advance the Kingdom of God, they need the power of God. And God comes through.

Stories of missionaries who have been translated from one location to another have been talked about for decades. Their extreme circumstances call for miracles of transport across flooded rivers and through jungles. John Crowder writes about some of these cases of missionaries who have been supernaturally transported from one place to another in his book, *The New Mystics*.

"Translations alone have been a common occurrence in recent decades. Many people are carried out of their bodies *spiritually* to minister in other places, or to see events before they happen. But even their physical bodies are carried off at times. Christian missionary H.B. Garlock was walking toward a flooded river in Africa, without any way to cross. He was suddenly on the other side of the river, with his own sweat being the only dampness in his clothes. Another minister, David J. DuPlessis was also transported while ministering in Africa. He was needed very urgently for ministry while he was walking towards his destination. DuPlessis was walking with some friends, but was suddenly jolted to the place he was headed. It was about 20 minutes before his friends ever arrived and caught up with him."[8]

Not only have there been recent cases of missionaries who are mysteriously and quickly transported across bodies of water, there have also been reports of people transported across vast distances to accomplish some task for the Lord. It seems as if angels are not the only messengers who can travel beyond the laws of physics and transcend atmospheres, time, and distance in a flash.

Prophetic minister John Paul Jackson relates the following story of a man whom God transported to his bedside to pray for him:

> God also transported someone to pray for me. In 1990, I was on a 21-day ministry trip through Europe, but after speaking in Geneva, Switzerland, I doubled over in pain from what doctors later told me was pancreatitis. Lying on my bed in excruciating pain that night, I told God that if He didn't heal me, I would cancel the rest of my trip and check into a hospital.
>
> Around 2:30 A.M., I sensed someone standing beside my bed. To my right was an elderly man with weathered skin and thick, knotted fingers. First, I thought I was hallucinating; then I thought it was an angel. As the old man reached out his hand towards me, he said, "I have come to pray for you." Placing his hand on top of mine, which rested on my stomach, he began to pray. I felt heat leave his hands and enter into mine. It felt thick like honey and was glowing hot. Heat unrolled like a scroll down my legs and out my feet and up my abdomen and out my head. As it steadily unrolled, the searing pain left my body. Then, we looked at each other and he disappeared before my eyes.
>
> I jumped out of bed and began dancing around the room, thanking God for healing me and sending His angel. That's when He said it wasn't an angel. Nor was it the devil. A vision appeared to me of a man with outstretched hands and tears running down his face telling God, "I just want to be used by you, but I'm an old man in a small village. People think I'm crazy. Can you use me?" And God said to me, "I took him from an obscure village in Mexico, used him and sent him back."
>
> God does supernatural things like that. It's not a big deal to God. We make it a big deal because it violates physical laws. It seems out

of the ordinary to us, but not to God. What is abnormal to us is normal to God.[9]

One of the more bizarre stories making the rounds of Charismatic circles in recent years is the story of Jeff Jansen, a man of whom it can definitely be said, "Whether in the body or out of the body, I do not know." Some believe he was transported from his home in Tennessee to a conference in Cincinnati where he was seen by at least 40 people and interacted with several. Others believe he experienced a supernatural experience of bi-location, the ability to be in two places at once. More practical mystics believe the person seen at the Cincinnati conference was the man's angel. Still another well-known prophetic minister believes it was the Lord who took the man's appearance and ministered in a form that others' could receive at the conference.

According to Jeff, he was expected to attend the Thursday evening session of the "Engaging the Revelatory Realms of Heaven" conference held at the Passion and Fire Worship Center in Cincinnati, but couldn't make it because of a prior commitment that involved having dinner with a couple in Nashville. Jeff, who has a prophetic ministry, was well known to many people—pastors and leaders who would be attending the conference.

After dinner they returned with the other couple to Jeff's house and decided to take communion together. "I felt the Presence of God come on me and I felt this fire come on me. Something I've never felt before. I remember telling the people that there is something going on, it's really strange. I feel like I'm here but not here somehow," Jeff explained.

"I went to bed for several hours and got up at 2:00 A.M. to get ready to drive to the conference in Cincinnati. When I got there, the conference had already started, so I signed in, put on my name tag, and went through the whole day. At the end of the day, the host pastors saw me and said, 'Hey, I thought you weren't coming until this morning but I saw you here last night.' I told them I had just arrived, that I got up at 2:00 A.M. to drive to the conference and I was going to the hotel to rest. They didn't believe me and said, 'What are you talking about? We saw you here last night.'

Jeff insisted that he wasn't there on Thursday night and told them that he was in Nashville with his wife and another couple. "The host pastor said, 'Don't you remember our conversation? You signed your name in the book. I put your name tag on you and you prayed for me that night.' I came to find out that there were over 40 people who I spoke to, ministered to, or touched on Thursday night. It was a supernatural event. The big buzz about the thing was that people started speculating that it was my angel who showed up. I didn't know what it was. I was just as confused as everyone else. I do know this—it was not me."[10]

What are we to make of these experiences? Are they translations? Or are they a phenomenon known as bi-location? Could it be that your guardian angel could take on your human likeness and make personal appearances without your knowledge? Or is it Jesus taking the appearance of another and walking around ministering to others in such a way that they can receive Him? Or, was it a familiar spirit or a demonic spirit shape shifting into the form of a human?

The outcome or fruit of the experience and the sense of God's Presence during Jeff's experience reveals that the source was God, indeed. The one who looked like Jeff ministered prophetically to several people at the conference. The prophetic words released a revelation of what God intended to do in Cincinnati—a revelation that glorified God and released encouragement to those who had been praying and working towards seeing a greater release of God's Presence in their city. Satan is incapable of glorifying God. Nor does he have a vested interest in raising the faith of believers and encouraging them. His nature is to undermine the things of God, not to bless them. Jeff's experience may not be easily defined as an experience of bi-location or his angel speaking to those at the conference that night. But the fruit of the experience speaks volumes about its source.

Many of us who have experienced the supernatural and revelatory realms of God agree with Jeff when he says this, "In Malachi 3:16-18, it says He is getting ready to reveal his precious and peculiar treasures, his signet rings. We're in a brand-new season of glory." And stranger things than this will amaze us in the days to come.

I believe it is almost impossible for us to understand the mechanics of such experiences, and it is foolish for us to attempt to classify spiritual experiences according to our natural understanding. God's ways are not our ways and His thoughts are not our thoughts. (See Isaiah 55:8-9.) Mystery still abounds, but God desires to increase our understanding in the days to come. He does have a purpose in releasing experiences and encounters with God. It is a purpose that continually leads us to embrace mystery:

> *My purpose is that they may be encouraged in heart and united in love, so that they may have the full riches of complete understanding, in order that they may know the mystery of God, namely, Christ, in whom are hidden all the treasures of wisdom and knowledge* (Colossians 2:2-3).

Demonic Counterparts

We can embrace mystery and still be aware of the counterfeits and demonic influences that seek to twist the gospel into a darker domain. In fact, it is important that we learn to discern what is of God and what is not—that which may be clearly an experience that is born of our soulish desires or one that is clearly demonic. One person who has walked on both sides of the fence, dividing demonic counterfeit experiences and those that are authentically of God is author Johanna Michaelson who writes of her experiences as a personal assistant to a psychic surgeon in Mexico in her book, *The Beautiful Side of Evil*.

During a meeting when she would become a full-trance medium, she writes about how she was trained to release her spirit into a self-induced OBE. This was her first experience with it:

"The now familiar procedures were followed. I went to level and waited. Suddenly I felt myself sinking deeper and deeper. I felt something deep within me wrench away; my body seemed to fade. I looked down and could see my empty shell sitting straight in a chair—hands floating palms up. I was aware of being far away in a new space beyond where I had been before. I had passed through a deep darkness, but now everything was filled with a pure white light. I now fully understood that my essence, my spirit, did not have to be tied down to a sack of flesh beneath me. It had been given me for a while to facilitate the work which lay ahead, to help fulfill my karma and purify my spirit so it could rejoin God. But I, I was eternal, an inseparable part of the Living Force.... I was filled with ecstasy; there was no time, no sorrow, no pain, only vibrating, unbearable joy and light and peace beyond anything I had yet experienced. I looked down. A silent, incandescent figure stood by my body waiting...waiting...yet not possessing me."[11]

She "returned" to her body when earthly voices called her back into her body and her consciousness. Johanna claims that it is not only dangerous to initiate trances and OBEs, but that many in the Church who profess to be Christians are also practicing the occult counterfeits of spiritual experiences:

"Today we are seeing many signs and wonders. They may even be done in the name of Jesus and "to the glory of God above." But which Jesus? Which Father? To use His name does not guarantee its source, for many today have so redefined Him that what they call "Jesus" in no way resembles the Bible, and so they lead the undiscerning into the worship of 'other gods whom you have not yet known.'

> *For if one comes and preaches another Jesus whom we have not preached, or you receive a different spirit which you have not received, or a different gospel which you have not accepted, you bear this beautifully* (2 Corinthians 11:4).

"Incidentally, Paul said this to a church 'not lacking in any gift' (1 Cor. 1:7), a church that was sincere in its devotion to the Lord. (See 1 Corinthians 1:4-8.) Yet their gifting and sincerity alone, Paul says, does not preclude the possibility of their being tricked and deceived and led astray because of their lack of discernment and their unscriptural emphasis on experience."[12]

Lack of discernment and an unscriptural emphasis on experience beyond the confines of Scripture are major stumbling blocks for the majority of Charismatic and Pentecostal Christians who are open to the supernatural and revelatory realms of God. I find it interesting that the spiritual gift of discernment is lumped into the very same Scripture passage as miraculous powers, prophecy, and tongues, in First Corinthians 12:10 where apostle Paul writes,

"...to another miraculous powers, to another prophecy, to another distinguishing between spirits, to another speaking in different kinds of tongues, and to still another the interpretation of tongues."

When it comes to gifts of miraculous powers and prophecy, we need mature elders in every church who are equipped with the gift of discernment to watch over the flock. We also need apostolic voices who will release guidelines for discernment in the years to come, as the sense of God's Presence and power increases throughout the world—growing alongside the "tares" of this world, evidenced in soulishly and demonically induced counterfeit expressions of power. Right now, we are sadly equipped with too few apostolic leaders who are respected enough to speak the truth in love about issues of discernment and correction. And we have too few humble church leaders who are open to correction from apostolic leaders, regardless of their denominational preferences, networks, or alliances.

Where Do You Fly From Here?

So what if your spirit flies from Canada to Washington or from Tennessee to Cincinnati? What difference does it make? Once the sensation ceases, the adrenalin rush subsides and the experience recedes; once the cares of the day resume their relentless intrusions, you are always left with one simple question: What the heck do you do with that experience? In other words, where do you fly from here?

First, discern the source. James Goll offers us an amazing checklist for increasing discernment later in this book.

Second, determine the meaning. Perhaps the meaning increased a revelation of the nature of God to you personally. Maybe the meaning involves a revelation of something in you God is trying to expose and heal, or something He wants to release through you. Or perhaps the meaning is a spiritual gift that you are meant to unwrap for another. It takes time to fully understand a God encounter. Take the time to pray about the meaning and invite others to share their interpretation with you.

And finally, if in doubt, toss it out.

According to prophetic minister Graham Cooke, "If you don't understand something, you are under no compulsion to do something about it. You need to pray, 'Lord, I am putting this back in your hands. Help me understand what it means.' Until He manifests himself in it, I'm choosing not to do something with it. Sometimes, it's just the enemy trying to get us off track. Either I receive confirmation or reassurance. I am allowed both. Gideon's fleece wasn't about knowing the will of God; he had that. It was about reassurance."

Endnotes

1. http://faculty.washington.edu/chudler/obe.html, September 27, 2002.

2. Tracing the Synapses of Our Spirituality: Researchers Examine Relationship Between Brain and Religion.

3. Shankar Vedantam, *Washington Post*, Sunday, June 17, 2001.

4. Patricia King, *Spiritual Revolution* (Shippensburg, PA: Destiny Image Publishers, 2006), 76.

5. Based on a personal interview with John and Paula Sandford.

6. Patricia King, *Spiritual Revolution* (Shippensburg, PA: Destiny Image Publishers, 2006), 77-78.

7. Based on a personal interview with John and Paula Sandford.

8. John Crowder, *The New Mystics*. (Shippensburg, PA: Destiny Image Publishers, 2006), 180-181.

9. "Naturally Supernatural," John Paul Jackson, http://streamsministries.com/blogger/2000_08_01_archive.html, August 4, 2000.

10. Johanna Michaelson, *The Beautiful Side of Evil*, 103.

11. Michaelson, *The Beautiful Side of Evil*, 174-175.

12. Roland and Heidi Baker, *Always Enough: God's Miraculous Provision Among the Poorest Children on Earth* (Grand Rapids, MI: Chosen Books, 2002), 176-177.

CHAPTER 11

Miracles

BY JULIA LOREN

While most spiritual experiences happen within us, miracles are events that happen externally. They happen to us. They are materialistic events that transcend the laws of physics and supersede nature. Both the Old and New Testaments speak of miracles, signs, and wonders. They are used to validate the words of God and the all-surpassing love and power of Jesus Christ. While some thrill to the stories, others despise them as mere myths that are enhanced by primitive thinking. Countless books have been written through the years seeking to discredit the accounts of miraculous events in the Bible or to disprove them through scientific analysis.

People will always believe what they want to believe. In the words of a physician friend of mine, "People will believe in miracles of healing if they want to or not. Even if you provide documentation that testifies to the authenticity of a miracle, it won't sway the opinions of a skeptic. Either you choose to believe or not."

In our rationally minded culture, choosing to believe is getting harder and harder as people make fantastic, unsubstantiated claims to miracles of healing, supernatural provision, and encountering events that transcend the laws of nature. For most of us, seeing is believing. We must see them or experience them for ourselves before we will believe that God is alive and powerful and the Creator of the universe still holds the laws of the universe in His hands. Or, in the very least, we need some affidavit of authenticity through witnesses and medical documentation that verify the miracle as a genuine event that lies beyond the ability of modern science to produce.

Many stories of miracles, however, cannot be substantiated. They are personal accounts that no one witnessed. Perhaps they were fabricated to draw attention to an individual or an individual's ministry. Or, perhaps, they were not. The one who experienced the miracle may have decided to risk the skeptic's ridicule in order to use the story to raise your faith level, leaving you with a choice to believe or not. The stories included in this chapter are meant to draw your attention to the glory of the all-surpassing power of God and to raise your level of faith to believe that you, too, will see the impossible one day, perhaps, even in your own life.

For me "of little faith," seeing makes it easier for me to believe. It's easy to doubt or criticize the stories I hear; it's harder to criticize those I have seen. For me to believe a story that has been passed from one person to another, usually through the Internet or word of mouth, I must at least know that the source of the story is a credible witness. It's so easy for individuals to fabricate stories if you know they cannot be substantiated. And stories get embellished and distorted and changed as they pass from one person's mouth to another's ear.

For that reason, I am only including stories of those who are credible and minister with integrity, those who have no need to fabricate stories in order to advance their ministries. Their stories are well-documented. The stories I include here have been witnessed either by myself or by others, and they have been in print (not that you can believe everything you read, either). They are not sensationalized; they are simply stated.

Most of us tend to rest in the safety of our homes and refrain from risk-taking behaviors, such as sky diving and walking on water. When we throw a dinner party or invite others over for lunch, we make sure we have enough food. Starvation is usually optional in North America. If you cannot afford groceries, food banks and homeless shelters will serve something for you. In North America, those who go hungry are usually addicts and the mentally ill on the street who forget to eat, children who are neglected, or the elderly who are homebound and forgotten. In developing countries, hunger is a daily battle that is facing millions. But on many occasions, the supernatural provision of God breaks through or the sovereign multiplication of food comes at unexpected moments, especially overseas. When the Holy Spirit multiplies the food and feeds the masses, the masses turn to follow Him.

In North America simple sickness is curable with any number of pharmaceuticals (or at least the symptoms can be greatly reduced). Overseas, simple sickness often means a death sentence for both young and old. Whenever God reveals the power to heal, people's hearts will be won. When Jesus shows up and heals the chief, the people follow his lead. Plagues are stopped by the prayers of the faithful few, blind eyes see and deaf ears hear. And sometimes, usually in third world countries, even the dead are raised to life! Miracles happen and faith to see the impossible increases all the more.

Missionaries often find their faith stretched as their material resources run out. And so they pray in faith, appealing to God's compassionate love, and they see results. Their faith, initially rooted in desperation, blossoms into something quite beyond ours. They discover that if they pray, God will respond. If they step out of the boat, God will catch them. The tenuous belief in the Jesus talked about in the Bible that launched them onto the mission field in the first place becomes, for many, an encounter with the powerful reality of the Jesus who walks alongside them in miraculous ways.

Jesus releases His signs and wonders that turn the hearts of unbelievers toward Him and increases the faith of us all. Miracles happen and faith to see the impossible not only increases but becomes the normal way of life for third world Christians. And their faith positions them to receive more as the supernatural becomes a natural way of life.

What follows are just a few of the miracles that others are witnessing on the mission field.

Transcending Nature

In Joshua 10:12-15 God listens to a man and grants his request that the sun stand still for more than 24 hours, providing enough light on the battlefield for the nation of Israel to avenge itself. *The sun stopped in the middle of the sky and delayed going down about a full day.* As their enemies fled, the Lord rained down large hailstones, killing more of them than those who were killed by the swords of the Israelites. (See Joshua 10:11.) It was the opposite of an eclipse. Total sunshine peppered by a hailstorm wiped out the retreating enemy.

In another incident where God not only stopped the sun but sent it backward, the Lord listened to another man, Isaiah, as he asked the Lord to provide a sign that King Hezekiah would be healed. In Second Kings 20:9-11. Hezekiah is given a choice: should God send the sun forward or backward? Hezekiah says it is too easy to send the sun forward. And he watches the shadows on the stairwell retreat ten steps as time moves backward.

In the Old Testament we see God listening to the prayers of men and transcending the laws of nature in response to their faith. In the New Testament, however, we see Jesus moving in His own authority, as God transcends the laws of nature. Jesus stood up in a boat and spoke to the wind and the waves; He calmed the storm and took authority over nature's wrath. (See Mark 4:35-41.) Later, He walked against a headwind across the lake to the boat containing His disciples. Peter yells out, "Lord, if it's you, tell me to come to you on the water!" Jesus says, "Come." And so Peter crawls over the gunwale of their fishing boat, tentatively steps onto the water, and since it feels solid to him, decides to venture out a few steps—until fear sets in. Immediately, Jesus reaches out His hand and catches him. Later, Jesus chides Peter about the incident, "O you of little faith, why did you doubt?"

Peter is the epitome of the Church, and he symbolizes those of us who are in the Church. Was Peter doubting Jesus by saying, *"Lord if it's really you"*? Or was Peter doubting whether he, too, could summon up his authority as a believer in Jesus Christ and walk on water, raise the dead, heal the sick, cast out demons, and see many, many more miracles that were not recorded? Whatever doubts Peter had, we all have them. When we witness a miracle or hear about one, we all tend to ask, "*Lord, is it really you?*" And we all suffer from various degrees of unbelief and doubt if we try to pray for the healing of another or ask for a miracle, thinking, "*If I pray will I see results?*" When we step out of the boat of our comfort zone in fear and trembling, we wonder, "*Will He catch me if I fail?*"

In Imparatriz, Brazil, on September 8, 2005, former Vineyard Christian Fellowship pastor and Global Awakening Associate Minister Gary Oates stood preaching before a crowd of more than 3,000 people in the large Assemblies of God church. The church looked like a miniature football stadium with giant openings in the walls on several levels of the building to allow air to flow. Not a cloud hovered in the starry night sky when we arrived at the church. Only the sliver of a new moon blinked its greeting from Heaven, giving no hint of what was in store. It was the dry season. Dust blew through the streets, piling up alongside the road, and walls in houses that were topped with broken glass and barbed wire served to keep out intruders. The city and the people were hot, thirsty, and afraid of each other.

Gary preached about Elijah, the sound of the abundance of rain, and about praying persistently for the rain of God's healing Presence. Elijah, Gary explained, prayed seven times for rain, each time looking up to see if a cloud the size of a man's hand would sweep in and shower down an abundance of rain upon the people, breaking the drought. At the end of his story we heard the sound of the abundance of rain carried on the wind. Suddenly, a squall blew in through the windows, circulating rapidly counter-clockwise within the vast building. Palm trees bent and swayed, dancing ecstatically with the wind outside. The tangible Presence of God swept through the church, and the people rose to their feet cheering. Gary stood on the platform; his arms were raised high overhead for about ten minutes, as long as the rain and wind lasted.

God had completely suspended the laws of nature. Not only did rain come out of season and on a night of a new moon rather than a full moon as they had traditionally seen in the area, His Spirit wind blew in, as well. A woman stepped out from the pastor's office where a group of intercessors had gathered to pray. She and her family had been missionaries with New Tribes

Mission in the area for more than 21 years. Just before dropping to her knees she said, "This never happens. This is a genuine miracle."

The rain continued pummeling the street but the palm trees finally stilled. Only a light wind blew outside. Eventually, it died down and the audience grew quiet, wondering. Oates invited people to receive the healing Presence of the Lord, saying the Lord was present to heal. Indeed, He had just illustrated His message with signs and wonders. Hundreds of people received instant healings. Hundreds more received Jesus and entered into salvation that night.

Do you believe the story? I do. I was there, along with a team of North Americans who can verify this account. The moment I realized that I was witnessing a miracle was when the missionary fell to her knees acknowledging that in more than 21 years of living the area, this had never happened. The sheer numbers of people receiving instant healing became an undeniable miraculous event that has become indelibly etched in my memory.

You Give Them Something to Eat

People walked miles to listen to Jesus. Most forgot to pack their water bottles and stuff backpacks full of snacks and sandwiches. Perhaps they didn't think they would linger long, but His words strangely warmed their hearts and they stayed. Something about what He said and the way He spoke raised their faith. And then the miracles started happening. No one wanted to leave. But the disciples started getting hungry and urged Jesus on at least one occasion to send the masses away for a lunch break.

Jesus replied, "They don't need to go away. You give them something to eat" (Matt. 14:16).

His disciples rounded up five loaves of bread and two fish. Then they turned around to count the crowd. At least 5,000 men, along with countless women and children, surrounded them. Suddenly, it dawned on them that they had witnessed Jesus turning water into wine. Why not turn this meager lunch into a sit-down feast for thousands? They broke the bread and fish and kept moving down the line, passing out a chunk of each until everyone had something to eat. Behind them, some people moved along, catching the smaller chunks of bread, gathering them into baskets for left-overs. Within hours everyone knew they were witnessing a miracle of supernatural provision.

Not only did Jesus feed them all, there were leftovers; at least a basketful for each disciple to eat. It was as if Jesus was saying to them, "You feed the masses, and I will feed you. Don't worry about what you will eat, for I know what you have need of. Just ask. Believe. Start ignoring what you see in the natural in order to receive what is supernatural."

Jesus multiplied food for the masses twice in Matthew's account. Still, the disciples didn't get it. "Where will we get enough bread to feed such a crowd?" they asked Jesus as freshly healed, formerly lame people danced all around them and the formerly deaf people giggled and laughed with joy, and the formerly blind people in the crowd broke their white-tipped canes across their knees and wept with relief or shouted in sheer joy, and those who could-n't speak a word practiced mumbling and forming words, making up for lost time and conversations.

The disciples stood in a field of miracles and forgot that Jesus is con-cerned with the whole person—each one's need for spiritual, emotional, and physical health, as well as his or her daily need for food. The disciples gath-ered together seven loaves and two small fish and stepped into another mir-acle—that of feeding the crowd with little more than what one man could hold in his hands, a few loaves and two fish. Yet they all ate and were satis-fied. The God who heals is the God who provides food abundantly. But still, Jesus admonished His disciples that they were the ones who were to feed the hungry—supernaturally.

Missionaries and aid agencies fly tons of food every week into remote areas in order to feed victims of famines caused by droughts, poor agricultur-al practices, and flooding. Sometimes the food doesn't make it or gets rerout-ed to another location. Some days, missionaries stand crying tears of despair, as they face the masses of starving children, knowing that they have noth-ing—not even a loaf of bread for their own children to eat. And they look to Jesus and say, "Where will we get enough bread to feed such a crowd?"

One woman, Heidi Baker, a missionary in Mozambique, knows the answer to that question. She has been there for a long time, and through the years she has learned not to weep in despair but to rejoice, knowing that her Father always provides. When the sights and sounds, the snotty tears of the masses, overwhelm her; when thousands stand in front of her seeking food; when the overwhelming sickness, open sores, and smells of death assault her, she redirects her attention onto the face of Jesus.

"Just focus on His face. You will only make it to the end if you can focus on His face. Focus on His beautiful face. You can't feed the poor, you can't go to the street, you can't see anything happen unless you see His face. One glance of His eyes, and we have all it takes."[1]

Once, when her Chihango Children's Ministry in Maputo faced severe persecution, the entire staff was given 48 hours to vacate their buildings and move out of town. And so they worked non-stop for 48 hours to clear out everything they could, lest it be confiscated or stolen when they left. They had no idea what to do with the children who came to their center. The children had no idea what to do either. And so more than a hundred children followed Heidi and Roland Baker to the gate of their small apartment; some flooded into the house, while others stood with their faces pressed against the gate, just standing there.

In fact, the Bakers' own two children stood amidst the chaos and exhaustion as overwhelmed as their parents. Heidi looked over the crowd of children inside her house and those spilling onto the street, and she thought she was going to snap. She had neither the food nor the pots to cook the quantities of food that these children required. Just then, a woman from the U.S. Embassy across the street knocked on her door. She thought she would just stop in with a little dinner for the Bakers and give them some chili and rice—just enough for the four of them.

Heidi said, "We hadn't eaten in days. I opened a door and showed her all our children. 'I have a big family!' I pointed out tiredly but in complete and desperate earnest. My friend got serious. 'There isn't enough. I must go home and cook some more!' But I just asked her to pray over the food…. We began serving and right from the start, I gave everyone a full bowl. I was dazed and overwhelmed. I barely understood at the time what a wonderful thing was happening. But all our children ate, the staff ate, my friend ate, and even our family of four ate…. Because He died, there is always enough."[2]

According to additional reports that have been given by staff and volunteers who have worked with the Bakers' ministry, the multiplication of food has occurred more than once. Many people have personally witnessed these miracles.

Raising the Dead

Elijah the prophet holed up in a widow's house, waiting for the moment when the drought would break. Grateful that God had moved miraculously on behalf of a widow, he not only had a place to stay but received the ongoing miracle of multiplication of food when there was little to be had.[3] One day, the widow's son died; and with his death, the widow realized there was no one who would provide for her in her old age, no one to comfort her. Elijah, moved by the Spirit of God, stretched himself over the boy, prayed for him, breathed life back into him, and restored him, completely alive and well, to his mother.

Later, his prophetic successor, Elisha, was called upon to raise his benefactor's son from the dead.[4] His faith had been elevated by his predecessor's success in raising the dead. And, having learned from Elijah's modeling, a certain technique of prayer for raising the dead, Elisha went to work. And the woman's son came back to the join the land of the living.

Centuries later, Jesus came to town. He knew the stories of Elijah and Elisha, but seemed reluctant to employ the techniques they used. He decided to break the mold and teach the people that true authority transcends technique. He had probably heard certain physicians in town debate with the Pharisees regarding the merits of a mere touch or command, which certainly would demonstrate the authority of a greater prophet. The grumbles of the intelligent, speculating that the old prophets' stories read like mere accounts of mouth-to-mouth resuscitation, probably reached Jesus, as well.

Presented with an opportunity to raise a little girl from the dead, Jesus, knowing He is the Prophet of all prophets, the very Son of God himself, simply prayed the child back to life.[5] The people reacted all along the spectrum of belief—some said the child never died, while others shouted the miracle of resurrection from rooftop to rooftop, passing the story throughout the country.

Later, Jesus saw a casket passing by and a heartbroken widow wailing about her child who was lying inside.[6] Certainly, if Jesus raised this man from the dead, the crowd could not say he had never died. After all, he is already in a casket on the way to the burial ceremony. So, prompted by the Holy Spirit, Jesus commanded life back into the body of the man and went on His merry way.

Still the societal debate raged over the authenticity of the miracles. This time, the Pharisees and physicians likely said, "The first one was questionable—after all, there were very few people in the room with Jesus when He allegedly raised the girl from the dead or, more likely, woke her from her slumber. The second one was a bit more realistic but still, the man had been allegedly dead less than 24 hours. It could have been a fluke. Maybe Jesus heard him thumping from inside the casket, wanting to get out; so He stopped the procession when He realized the mother's cries drowned out the thumping and pretended to raise him from the dead by merely opening the casket. What I want to see is that man Jesus, pull a rank and stinking corpse out of a grave and bring him back to life. Then I'll believe Jesus can, in fact, raise the dead."

And so, when Lazarus died, Jesus waited. And waited. And waited until the fourth day, when the corpse was rank with rot and decay. Just before the miracle of the century unfolded, He turned to Mary and proclaimed, "I Am the resurrection and the life…."[7] Then, Jesus called forth Lazarus, an undeniably dead man, from his grave while a group of Pharisees stood by, mouths agape, trembling, as the fear of God coursed through their veins.

Now I don't believe Jesus conducted miracles just for show or felt like He had to prove anything to anyone, especially to the Pharisees of His time. The resurrections He conducted were precursors to His own. The miracles testified to Jesus' true authority and the message of salvation. I use them here to reveal how long it takes your average "intellectual" and skeptic to finally believe that God has sent us models and mentors and His very own Son to show us that we, too, have this all surpassing power resident with us—power to heal the sick, cast out demons, and raise the dead.[8]

A few believers are already getting the message. They are walking in the understanding that they, too, can pray with resurrection power because within them lives the One who is the resurrection and the life, the One who said, *"If you believe, you will receive whatever you ask for in prayer."*[9] Even in our day, women are receiving back their loved ones from the dead and children are being restored and given a future and a hope, as their faith moves Heaven.

Reinhard Bonnke, a well-known international evangelist stood preaching in a Nigerian church, completely oblivious to the miracle that was unfolding in a nearby room of the church—a man who was clearly dead had returned to life through the prayers of many. Later, his ministry, Christ for All Nations, received dramatic video footage of the event.[10] The faces of those who prayed, the tears and cries of shock from those who witnessed the breath of life return to the man, the long, slow process of massaging the rigor mortis from the man's limbs, revealed a miracle in the making. What impacted me as I watched the DVD that was released by Bonnke's ministry was the look on the dead man's face as he came to life, dazed and confused. The man's story went something like this:

A Nigerian pastor, Daniel Ekechukwu, had been fatally injured in a car accident near the town of Onitsha, Nigeria, Africa, on November 30, 2001. During a dramatic journey to a hospital in Owerri, Nigeria, he lost all life signs and was later pronounced dead by two different medical staff members in two different hospitals. The latter wrote a medical report and commissioned the corpse to the mortuary.

The primitive Nigerian mortuary where Daniel's body was taken had no cold storage facilities, and so the mortician injected embalming chemicals into Daniel.

But Daniel's wife remembered a verse from Hebrews 11: "Women received their dead raised to life again." She heard about a meeting where evangelist Reinhard Bonnke was going to preach, and proceeded to bring Daniel's body in his coffin.

By then, Daniel had been dead for more than 28 hours. Rigor mortis had fully set in. An ambulance was hired on Sunday morning, December 2, and the casket that contained Daniel's body was taken to Grace of God Mission in Onitsha, where evangelist Reinhard Bonnke was preaching at an afternoon service.

Security would let neither the ambulance, not the accompanying party into the church. She caused such a disturbance that the senior pastor was notified, and his son instructed that Daniel's wife be permitted to bring his body to the church without the casket, and that it be placed in the basement. Daniel's body was laid on two tables pushed together in a Sunday school room.

Some believers gathered around Daniel's body and prayed while Reinhard Bonnke, who knew nothing of the dead body in the basement, preached and prayed. Eventually, people noticed that Daniel's corpse twitched, and then irregular breathing started. The attendant believers began praying fervently, and because his body was stiff and cold, they began massaging his neck, arms, and legs. When those in the sanctuary got word that a dead man below was coming back to life, the basement room was soon jammed with people. Suddenly Daniel sneezed and arose with a jump. And he slowly came back to consciousness.

Many other missionaries, such as Heidi and Roland Baker and David Hogan, and indigenous pastors around the world, have similar stories of dead people coming back to life in areas where they minister. Some of them experience visions of Heaven and hell and return with not only an amazing testimony of resurrection but a message and life calling as well. Others are simply restored to grieving mothers and fathers. As faith rises, so do the accounts of miracles. But in places where skepticism abounds and Western rational world views prevail; and where people believe in the utter sanctity of the medical profession that provides diagnoses for more diseases than it can cure, we see little in the way of dramatic miracles. Why is that? Matthew 13:58 gives us a clue: *He did not do many miracles there because of their lack of faith.*

Miracles of Healing

There are places in North America where miracles of medical healing abound. In fact, the healing movement has become so integrated into Charismatic and Pentecostal churches that most churches see at least a miracle or two per year. Some churches experience many more. Healing evangelists and prophetic voices across the nation predict that the next couple of decades will cause us all to sit up in awe and wonder at the vast number of healings, miracles, signs, and wonders that will shout to the world that Jesus is alive and well and the Holy Spirit is moving in.

In the meanwhile a few pioneers of healing focus on releasing healing on the home front and gather documentation of authentic healing miracles as they go. They are ones who truly know that the gifts of the Holy Spirit are for everyone. Healing does not depend on the faith of a healer any more than the salvation of another depends on the faith of an evangelist. The gifts of God may be released through anyone.

Mahesh and Bonnie Chavda, pastors of All Nations Church in North Carolina, are pioneers of healing evangelism who document and verify healings that take place regularly in their meetings. The secret to their success lies in knowing that Jesus desires to heal, that His atonement provides for our healing, and that the corporate church has a responsibility to minister to one another in love. They call their church to pray and fast for a greater release of healing to their members and, as a result, they see continuous results.

An article I wrote about them for Charisma magazine reveals the story of one family whose son was healed of a neurological condition called Tourette's, after the church called a corporate fast on the boy's behalf.[11]

Peter and Monica Floyd discovered the power of that corporate anointing when the church placed their son Michael at the head of the prayer list and called the members to a 21-day fast. Michael had been diagnosed with Tourette's syndrome, a neurological condition that causes verbal and motor tics and includes symptoms of Attention Deficit Hyperactive Disorder and obsessive-compulsive tendencies (repetitive thoughts and behaviors a person cannot control).

For six years, Michael's tics worsened until he had one almost every second and had to be taken out of school. He endured rounds of medication to correct symptoms, but they caused either rapid weight gain or emaciation as a side effect. At one point, Michael couldn't swallow or breathe.

"After almost four years of seeing a lot of different specialists and counselors, we were drained," Peter says. "The church had already done a lot of praying for us, but they decided to pray and fast for 21 days."

Not long after the fast ended, the Floyds were sitting down to dinner when Peter looked at his son and said, "Hey, we haven't seen any tics," Peter recalls.

"Here at home we'd gotten used to them and didn't know the exact moment they stopped," he continues. "It was a matter of weeks before we realized they were totally gone."

His pediatrician believes Michael's healing is a miracle. But the specialists said that Michael could simply be in remission and asked the Floyds to wean him slowly off the medications he was taking. It's been a year since Michael has been off all medication, and the tics have not come back.

Mahesh says of healings such as Michael's that are occurring at the church: "The community is being trained to love and welcome the anointing and honor the King of glory. The more we have learned to have corporate grace, the better it is."

Kathryn Kuhlman, the foremost healing evangelist of the 20th century, did more to challenge the unbelief of a nation than any other evangelist in our time. For every doctor who verified and documented that God had healed someone of something the medical community was powerless to cure, another doctor rose up in disbelief. Yet, the sheer numbers of documented miracles of healing that occurred during her meetings created an atmosphere of faith that caused many to believe that God is compassionate and powerful. Still, she believed that she did not do the healing. She had no ability to create a miracle. It was the Holy Spirit—who is available to any who would ask. Her biographer wrote this about the secret of Kathryn's success—that she merely recognized what God was doing; the power wasn't hers.

Kathryn's gift in the miracle service was not the gift of healing; rather, it was the other gifts of the apostle Paul listed in his letter to the Corinthian church—"faith" and the "word of knowledge" (1 Cor. 12:1). Kathryn was not a healer. The "gifts of healing, which Paul talked about, Kathryn believed, came only to the sick. It was the sick who needed the gift of healing. All she had was faith to believe and a word of knowledge concerning where that gift had been bestowed. For this reason, she said over and over, "I am not a healer. I have no healing power. No healing virtue. Don't look at me. Look to God."

Yet during those miracle services when the wave of faith crested, and the presence of God actually invaded the building—inhabiting the praises of His people—Kathryn could suddenly begin to recognize healings that were occurring in the auditorium. It was the trademark of the miracle service. Her critics called her "psychic." Allen Spraggett of the *Toronto Star* said she was "clairvoyant." Kathryn, however, knew it was simply the power of the Holy Spirit, which was available to any person who would pay the price.[12]

All churches everywhere and all individuals who are open to the Holy Spirit are destined to see miracles, and they are capable of releasing miracles or healing to others. Whether God comes in a great whoosh of power that releases thousands upon thousands of miraculous healings throughout a region or not, we all have the Holy Spirit who desires that we extend our hearts and hands to others and pray the prayer of faith that says, "Be healed in the name of Jesus Christ." When more people do that, more miracles will be seen in our communities. The gift of healing, as Kathryn says, does not depend on our power, but on His.

Beyond Our Reality—or Not?

If mere humans can do the same miracles that Jesus did—such as healing the sick, casting out demons, raising the dead—what about the odd things that Jesus did? Can we do those as well? We expect that a ghost or the resurrected body of Jesus would be able to pass through a closed door on Earth. (See John 20:19, 26.) But how odd is it that His natural body apparently dematerialized as He passed through a crowd unseen and untouched, as if no one could see or feel His bodily form? Could we do that, too, in an extreme situation where a mob is out to apprehend and kill us?

Is it not strange that His resurrection body can assume an unrecognizable form (see Mark 16:12) and walk about on Earth? And how bizarre is it that He can enter a human being on Earth and become "Christ in you" (2 Cor. 13:5)?

What about Jesus letting Peter walk on water without a life jacket (see Matt. 14:25-30), can we do that, too? Well then, why not fly from one place to another without a plane or a car when the Lord wills it? If God can part the Red Sea, as it is recorded in the Book of Exodus, why can't a man drive his car underwater, through a raging river, safely to the other side? Or fly his motorcycle off a cliff, as he escapes terrorists in the jungle and suddenly discovers that he was miraculously, safely transported a great distance to a road very close to his home?

Jesus is Lord of all. (See Acts 10:36.) All things are in subjection to Him. (See Ephesians 1:22.) Odd things, even bizarre things, are completely within His realm of authority. After all, He is the Creator of the universe. The universe still bends to His will.

But will your will bend toward His? Will to believe and let your unbelief give way to faith—faith that sees and receives the greater things—things that you cannot even imagine.

Endnotes

1. Baker and Baker, *Always Enough*, 52.

2. 1 Kings 17.

3. 2 Kings 4.

4. Mark 5.

5. Luke 7.

6. John 11:25.

7. Matthew 10:8.

8. Mark 11:24.

9. For more information, the DVD may be obtained from the ministry Christ for All Nations.

10. Julia Loren, "Anointed to Heal," *Charisma* Magazine, January 2006.

11. Jamie Buckingham, *Daughter of Destiny* (Gainesville, FL: Bridge-Logos, 1999), 226-227.

12. R.T. Kendall, *The Anointing* (Nashville, TN: Thomas Nelson Publishers, 1999), 163.

CHAPTER 12

Glimpses of What's to Come

BY JULIA LOREN

One day, the heavens will open to Christians and non-Christians alike—on the street, not just in the church or in a conference. The manifest Presence of God will be so tangible that people will be healed in an instant and demons will flee; and angels will appear and come and go among us, releasing words, visions, and directions while we stand in gaping astonishment that Heaven has come to Earth. People will shake and fall under the power of God when Christians release the Kingdom of God in the workplaces and restaurants of their cities. Stadiums and public places will be filled with people preaching and releasing the power to heal. Government offices around the world will fling open as policymakers shout, "Bring that Christian in here—I need a prophetic word of wisdom."

Is this really a glimpse of what is to come as the supernatural realms of Heaven invade Earth? Or are extreme prophets just running their mouths trying to sensationalize faith and stir up a little more expectation?

The Kingdom of God is so near; it is as close as your own heartbeat. The experiences I have just mentioned have happened and are happening. We need only look inward to realize that Christ is in us and we can release His

Presence, His light, His authority over sickness and disease, and all principalities and powers and rulers of this age will bow to Him. We need only reach out and touch the world with the Presence of God in us.

What is it going to take to raise our level of faith to match His Word?

What if God were to suddenly move in Charismatic and evangelical meetings, creating a fusion of God's Spirit and man's that leads us all into a deeper abandonment of ourselves and causes us to explode with supernatural love and power? What if we all became walking spiritual encounters for unbelievers? What if we released the Presence of God and radiated Christ in a dark world? Would you resist this move? Or would you embrace it?

How close do you want to come to the bonfire of God's love and encounter spiritual experiences that you never dreamed of having? It begins with receiving greater revelation of the power of the Word of God. And it moves into dynamic encounters with the Holy Spirit that build our capacity to desire more of Him and lessens our focus on ourselves.

Supernatural Experiences Released Through the Power of the Word of God

The closest place you can turn to for an impartation of revelation and an instant encounter with God is the Word of God. His Word is alive and active, and it ministers to you as you read. His Word can seem like a hammer that breaks the hardest heart one day; and the next day, His Word flows into you like a sweet balm, soothing your deepest ache.

A friend of mine ventured into a monastery a few months after his wife died in order to seek solace in a silent retreat. His only contact would be a monk who provided spiritual direction every morning. The monk advised him to read a certain passage in the gospels and to go there in his imagination as he read. "Walk with Jesus, listen to Him address the people, imagine the scene, the sights, the smells, the people. Ask God for a deeper revelation of His Word and the word that He is speaking to you through that passage."

My friend took the passage and meditated on it daily. At first he chewed on the theological and symbolic significance he found there. Then he dared to venture a little closer and considered what Jesus looked like, how compassion rose up in Him, moving Him to touch the masses and heal them. And as the week wore on, he discovered that his heart took over and the story became alive to him.

On the last day of his retreat, while meditating on the passage, he felt himself lapse into a little dream-like state and saw the Lord turn, take him into his arms, and release the warmth of His embrace. Suddenly, he knew that somehow his imagination had given way to a vision where Jesus pulled him from the crowd, signaled him out, and let him weep on His shoulder. Afterward, he realized that Jesus would always be there for him, always waiting for him to pull away from the crowd and spend a moment with Jesus. Jesus now seems as near to him as his own heartbeat.

Moving that closely into the Word launched him into an encounter that enabled him to gain a different perspective on the nature of God. And the perspective shift was this—Jesus wasn't the ogre who took the love of his life. Rather, He is a compassionate Friend who weeps when he weeps and laughs with him, and remains to walk and talk with him so that he is never alone. God is ever present and always willing to release a revelation of His Presence.

The Holy Spirit speaks through the Word and gives us revelation of the deep truths that are hidden in the Word. If we want to increase our capacity for authentic encounters with God, spiritual experiences, and revelation, we need to spend time with His Word.

According to R.T. Kendall, in his book, *The Anointing*:

"...God gave us the Bible yesterday. But the Holy Spirit applies it today. And if we are open to the immediate and direct witness of the Spirit the Bible will be doubly real to us.

"...The Holy Spirit continues to speak—clearly, directly, and immediately through prophecy, word of knowledge, vision, and audible voice. But He will never, never, never conflict with or contradict anything in the Bible but only make it clearer!

"The Holy Spirit speaking today is not new revelation or in competition with the Bible. The proof of the Holy Spirit's voice or manifestation will be that it vindicates and magnifies the Bible."[1]

Take time to meditate on a passage of Scripture and invite the Holy Spirit to release revelation of the nature of God, His character, and His thoughts of you. You may just find yourself catapulted into an extraordinary vision of who He is to you today.

Supernatural Experiences Released Through a Revelation of the Glory of God

Moses met face to face with God who descended in a cloud of glory that enveloped the tent of meeting. And his face radiated the Presence and love of God long afterward. Centuries later, Jesus ascended to glory. Today, He is increasingly releasing and imparting that glory, changing us, enlarging our capacities to see and understand more of Him. "…*We, who with unveiled faces all reflect the Lord's glory, are being transformed into His likeness with ever-increasing glory, which comes from the Lord who is the spirit.*"[2]

How much glory can you presently handle?

Not only are we cleansed and purified in glory (see Isa. 6:5), but we are being changed into His likeness. We are meant to transform "from glory to glory." We are meant to change as we look Him straight in the face and worship the King of glory. Slowly, through the years, we come into His Presence and discover our old nature giving way, as we become the persons we were created to become. Yet sometimes, God accelerates the process and descends in a cloud of glory that causes us to radiate the Presence and love of God long afterward.

According to Canadian revivalist Todd Bentley, founder of Fresh Fire Ministries:

The very word for *dwell* and *glory* occurs over 50 times in the book of Exodus alone and every time it's referring to the manifest Shekinah abiding glory that you can touch, taste, see, feel and experience in the natural. Every time Moses went into the tent of meeting, the glory cloud was there

(Num. 20:6). All the people witnessed the glory. They could see it on the tabernacle as a cloud and as a pillar of fire. I believe that when we prepare the sanctuary in the way that pleases God, He will pour out His glory and dwell in our presence so intensely that we won't even have to say anything. We'll just walk into the building and we're in the cloud of His glory. I believe that there is a place where God's glory can become so manifest that when we walk down the street, the sick get healed and when we walk into a factory the unbelievers get saved. When we sit on the train the presence and the glory lingers in such a measure that the whole train gets saved![3]

Like Moses, we must encounter God's glory first, in order to become carriers of His glory. The greatest, most pure revelatory encounters and spiritual experiences occur when you find yourself in an atmosphere infused with God's glory. We need to seek His face, pray for a release of God's glory, and embrace it when it comes. Then, as we bask in His glory, Christ in us, the hope of glory, can overflow through us to the world.

Becoming a Spiritual Experience that Releases the Brilliance of His Presence

In Christ and in His Word, there is no shadow of turning, no shifting shadows of light and darkness. In Him is light. He is the light of the world. And we are the light of the world. We are meant to become a walking spiritual experience and the world encounters God in us, the hope of glory. Having stood in the tent of meeting saturated in glory, our faces radiate with His love and Heaven touches Earth through us.

Many apostolic and prophetic voices in our day state that we can release His Presence and glory right now. The following particularly give us the keys that will enable us to become walking spiritual experiences, releasing His glory wherever we go:

James Goll: One time when I was "resting" in the Lord's presence, the Holy Spirit said, "I want to teach you to release the highest weapon of spiritual warfare." I continued to listen as I knew there must be more...He continued, "I will teach you to release the brilliance of My presence." In a moment, it seemed all theological debate on the issues of spiritual warfare was answered. What is His highest weapon? Why, He is!...He wants us to be gatekeepers so we can release the brilliance of His great presence![4]

Mark Chironna: We aren't trying to get into the Holy of Holies, we're there. We need to release it into the atmosphere. We are living from the inside out. The more you understand God the less you have a separation consciousness. I carry the Glory of God. I can release God rather than wait for God to show up.[5]

Kim Clement: There is coming a fusion between God and man so that no man is seen—only God and His Glory.[6]

Bill Johnson: Jesus recognized that "virtue" left His body when a woman touched the hem of His garment out of her desperate need for healing. At the Gate Beautiful, Peter said...such *as I have give I to you*. Jesus taught His disciples...*freely you have received, freely give*. What were they to give? What was drawn from Jesus' body by the woman? It was the anointing—the manifest presence of the Holy Spirit.[7]

One of the great joys of enjoying the presence of the Holy Spirit in our lives is learning how He moves. As we learn to recognize the flow of life through us, we can better learn to release His presence into a given situation. We can do this intentionally through laying on of hands, declaration, and prophetic acts (actions that are inspired by the Holy Spirit, but are in and of themselves unrelated to the outcome—i.e., Moses striking the rock brought forth water from it for Israel to drink). Learning how to release the Holy Spirit into specific situations makes it easier for us to see what the Father is doing, therefore following the example that Jesus set for us.

In other words God is in us and He wants out! God is in us now and He is coming with ever-increasing measures of glory that will so saturate us that it will seem like the Presence of God and man are fused together. Learning to release the Holy Spirit to others will come easily as the anointing of His Presence flows from us.

It is possible to experience this now. For the past two years I have entered into a greater understanding of what these prophetic voices are trying to explain to us. They are truths that are more caught than taught, and they are accelerated by soaking in an atmosphere of His Presence.

Praying for people in church and seeing the Presence and power of God move on their behalf is normal for me in my Christian milieu. More than a year ago, however, I discovered, much to my chagrin, that I was accidentally releasing the Presence of God in the workplace and it wouldn't shut off. The spiritual dynamics that followed me as I worked on several overseas contracts startled me. My job skills had opened doors to minister in the places where God called—not in the cocoon of the church or the nest of my home, but into the midst of very dark places in Europe and Asia. And yes, the people I talked with were saved, healed, delivered, and touched by God's tangible Presence and His overwhelming love.

Most of the time they didn't know I am a Christian; until they started shaking and crying and asking me what was up with the strange sensations they felt in my "office." I saw some amazing things, as God walked with me and moved through me; and as I released His prophetic words and power to others; or others simply found that they had walked into a "power zone of God's Presence" and reacted to the Presence of God within me.

While working overseas, I became extremely aware that what I carried within me instantly and undeniably shifted the environment around me. While I had experienced this on rare occasions in the past, now, His Presence would not and could not be turned off whenever I ventured off to work. As a result, I often found myself in uncomfortable positions that could have resulted in my immediate dismissal. But God covers what He initiates. His love for others is so great, that He will move Heaven and Earth, brush aside the "giants in the land," and break all the protocols of man, to touch the hearts of those He is reaching out to that day.

Once I caught on to what was happening when others came into my/His Presence, I realized that I could intentionally release His Presence to whomever I desired and learned to harness His power more effectively. However, it wasn't until I attended a Fusion Conference[8] held in Albany, Oregon, that I fully understood what was happening to me and through me.

Lance Wallnau's prophetic insights that were given during that conference helped lessen my fear, clarify my understanding, and taught me how to direct the flow of His Presence more effectively. Here are that key points I picked up from Lance. Let them serve as prophetic words of wisdom, as we glimpse what is to come:

- God is sending us on missions and assignments where we don't want to go. He calls us to release Heaven there. Professionals can do this even on a bad day. We have the authority to bring into the present what we see in the future. The greater weight of glory on Earth today is pulling Heaven to Earth.

- Get to the place where you are not shaken [by what you see and hear around you].

- What you are carrying shifts the environment around you. The lesser authority yields to the greater authority. The person with the dominant process can take over the frequency of the room or the group. The depressed or angry one will impact the group, or you can bring them under the authority of the anointing in your life.

- We have a kingdom "radius of Heaven." It is as close as your hand. Atmospheres are things you shape, not things you respond to.

- We are carrying the capacity to release the supernatural. We have the kingdom within—a force of righteousness, peace, joy, love, power, and authority.[9]

We are carrying the capacity to release the supernatural. When a Spirit-filled believer walks through the door, the atmosphere shifts! We have the Kingdom within—the force of righteousness, peace, joy, love, power, and authority—and it will accidentally flow from us at the oddest times and displace the internal and external forces that trap unbelievers in a cycle of despair.

The Presence of God in me and the radius of Heaven surrounding me were strengthened by the time I spent at home and at church, soaking in God's powerful Presence. All of that year, I came home to recharge, and a few weeks later, I left again to go to Europe or Asia and I released His Presence to a dark and hungry world. God and I fused together, as I soaked in His glory like a sponge and wrung it out on anyone nearby. Christ in me grew stronger and released the hope of glory to others, with or without my conscious consent.

Warnings about Shifting Shadows of Glory

How much glory can you presently handle? Learning how to handle the glory of God also involves being aware of how dangerous it is to manipulate God's glory or attempt to glorify ourselves when we use our authority to release His Presence and power.

Prophetic minister Rick Joyner gives us two warnings that call attention to how easily the enemy can shift the shadows of confusion and darkness over the brilliance of God's glory. In particular, he warns us about "charismatic witchcraft" and "the religious spirit." He claims that the danger does not come from those who are *having* prophetic revelations, or releasing God's Presence, but from those who have been *inflated* by the experiences.

Regarding witchcraft, Rick writes in his book, *Overcoming Evil*:

> One prominent form of white witchcraft, which is common in the Church, can be described as "charismatic witchcraft." This has nothing to do with the Charismatic Movement, but is a pseudo-spirituality. It often uses this guise to gain influence or control over others or situations. It is a source of many false prophecies, dreams, and visions that can ultimately destroy or neutralize a church, or bring the leadership to the point where they overreact so as to despise prophecy altogether. Those using this form of witchcraft will almost always think that they have the mind of the Lord which gives them the greater authority. They will therefore conclude that the leadership, or anyone else who contradicts them, are the ones in rebellion.[10]

Regarding the shifting shadows of religious spirits, he writes:

Colossians 2:18-19 indicates that a person with a religious spirit will tend to delight in self-abasement and will often be given to worship angels or taking improper stands on visions he has seen. A religious spirit wants us to worship anything or anyone but Jesus. The same spirit that is given to worshipping angels will also be prone to excessively exalting people.

We must beware of anyone who unduly exalts angels or men and women of God, or anyone who uses the visions he has received in order to gain improper influence in the Church. God does not give us revelations so that people will respect us more, or to prove our ministries. The fruit of true revelation will be humility, not pride.[11]

Glimpses of What's to Come

Those who cultivate a humble abandonment to the Lord and purpose to give Him all glory will soon discover that they have become this century's emergent Church who overflows with the healing gifts and miracles of the Holy Spirit. Already, we are seeing glimpses of what is to come as more people are stirred to faith and action and more places are becoming churches and communities that are known as places where God's Presence dwells.

Open visions and dreams that God has given me over the years bid me leave these questions for you to answer:

What if a group of young adults standing around chatting idly about nothing in particular happened to be so filled with the Presence of God that the power of God zapped others who just happened to walk by?

What if suddenly one would catch the eye of a person walking ten yards away, point at him, and release the power of God and a prophetic word that reveals the secrets of that passerby's heart; then drift back into the group's conversation like nothing had just happened because it happened all the time?

Would these young adults be hanging around the foyer of your church oozing God's Presence that released heaven's power and prophesied and healed and left individuals strewn about on the carpet as the unsuspecting churchgoers realized they ventured too close to the "power zone"? Or would they be hanging out in your town accidentally zapping people into salvation as they hung around the outside of a movie theatre? Would you, or one of your children, be hanging with them?

What if you were standing on the platform of a train station and suddenly everyone around you gasped as they stared at the sky? The heavens had just rolled back, revealing a shocking vision that everyone saw simultaneously—believers and unbelievers alike. One person, who had experienced many supernatural experiences over the years, was able to keep his wits about him long enough to step inside the station, grab the loud speaker, and lead everyone in prayer for salvation. Then everyone fell to his or her knees weeping and praying because of that great and terrible corporate vision. Would you be the one gaping and staring at the sky or would you be the one who has the nerve to lead the crowd in a prayer of salvation and intercession as a city or a nation comes to Christ in a single day?

Who are those who shine with the glory of God and become walking spiritual experiences for others? Those who covet being in His Presence, soak in His love, quiet their souls and allow the Lord to change them, transforming them from glory to glory.

Arise, dear reader, and shine. For your light, the glory of God will rise upon you!

Endnotes

1. 2 Corinthians 3:18.

2. http://www.freshfire.ca/teaching_details.php?Id=117

3. James Goll, *Revival Breakthrough Workbook*, 73.

4. Mark Chironna, Fusion Conference, Albany, OR, August 2006.

5. Kim Clement, Fusion Conference, Albany, OR, August 2006.

6. Contributed by Bill Johnson specifically for inclusion in this chapter.

7. Fusion Conferences are held through an alliance of speakers that include Kim Clement, Mark Chironna, and Lance Wallnau. For more information see www.fusionexperience.org.

8. Lance Wallnau, Fusion Conference, Albany, OR.

9. Rick Joyner, *Overcoming Evil in the Last Days* (Shippensburg, PA: Destiny Image Publishers, 2003), 82-83.

10. Rick Joyner, *Overcoming Evil*, 153.

11. Rick Joyner, *Overcoming Evil*.

CHAPTER 13

Discerning the Origins of Supernatural Experiences

BY JAMES GOLL

As we begin to round the corner, we note that we have already gone down the lane and walked through the rooms of Miracles and Glimpses of What's to Come. Indeed, it has already been one incredible, investigative trip that we have been on together.

"What's left?" you ask, as we head down the final stretch of the road less traveled. Well, actually we have saved the crux of the matter for the very last. You are just now about to receive your very own compass to help you navigate through life's field of many experiences. What you are about to pick up in this chapter might just save your life from a big crash and enable you to successfully complete your course.

We will now turn our attention to the practical A, B, C's of *Discerning the Origins of Supernatural Experiences*. Ready? Let's move right ahead!

Sources of Revelation

The Scriptures indicate that spiritual revelation or communication comes from any one of three sources: the Holy Spirit, the human soul, and the realm of evil spirits. The need for discernment in this area is obvious.

The Holy Spirit is the only true source of revelation. (See 2 Peter 1:21.) It was the Holy Spirit who "moved" the prophets of the Old Testament and the witnesses of the New Testament. The Greek word for "moved," phero, means "to be borne along" or even "to be driven along as a wind."[1]

The human soul is capable of voicing thoughts, ideas, and inspirations out of the unsanctified portion of our emotions. (See Ezekiel 13:1-6; Jer. 23:16.) These human inspirations are not necessarily born of God. As Ezekiel the prophet said, they are prophecies "...*out of their own hearts....* Woe unto the foolish prophets, that follow their own spirit, and have seen nothing*" (Ezek. 13:2-3 KJV).

Evil spirits operate with two characteristics common to their master. They can appear as "angels of light" (or as "good voices"), and they always speak lies, because they serve the chief liar and the father of lies, satan. Messages delivered through evil spirits are often especially dangerous to people who are ignorant of God's Word or inexperienced in discernment, because satan loves to mix just enough "truth" or factual statements in with his lies to trick gullible people. Just think of it as tasty bait carefully placed in the middle of a deadly trap.

Acts 16:16-18 tells about a slave girl with a spirit of divination who *spoke the truth* about the disciples, but got it from a satanic source. When apostle Paul eventually had heard enough and was irritated within, he commanded the spirit of divination to leave her.

In a world of imperfect people, God-given revelation can be mixed with competing information from sources that are *not* of God. People functioning as prophetic mouthpieces or visionaries are imperfect instruments, though vital to the Church today.

None of us are immune to the effects of outward influences on our lives. Even though God's Spirit is in union with our spirit, we can be strongly affected in our spirits and souls by such things as the circumstances of life; our physical or bodily circumstances; by satan or his agents; and very often by the other people around us. (See 1 Samuel 1:1-15; 30:12; John 13:2; 1 Corinthians 15:33.) The solution is to "test" every source and aspect of the revelation—whether it be a dream, apparition, spoken word, or other type. First, we should test ourselves with a series of self-diagnostic questions.

The Self Test

1. Is there any evidence of influences other than the Spirit of God in my life?

2. What is the essence of the "vision" or revelation? (How does it compare to God's written Word?)

3. Was I under the control of the Holy Spirit when I received the vision?

   a. Have I presented my life to Jesus Christ as a living sacrifice?

   b. Have I been obedient to His Word?

   c. Am I being enlightened with His inspiration?

   d. Am I committed to doing His will, no matter what it is?

   e. Am I yielding my life to the praises of God or to critical speech?

   f. Am I waiting quietly and expectantly before Him?

The Source Test

The next step is to test whether the image, prophetic message, or vision received is from our own soulish arena, from satan's realm, or from God. Dr. Mark and Patti Virkler, founders of the Christian Leadership University in Buffalo, New York, offer some excellent guidelines in this area in their landmark work, *Communion With God.* They teach that "The eyes of your heart can be filled by self or satan or God."[2] The following guidelines are adapted from a table in the Virklers' study guide.[3] First are three general instructions:

1. I am to cut off all pictures put before my mind's eye by satan (see Matt. 5:28 and 2 Cor. 10:5), using the blood of Jesus.

2. I am to present the eyes of my heart to the Lord for Him to fill. In this way, I prepare myself to receive. (See Revelation 4:1.)

3. The Holy Spirit will then project on the inner screen of my heart the flow of vision that He desires. (See Revelation 4:2.)

Testing Whether an Image Is From Self, Satan, or God

A. Find its origin by testing the spirit. (See 1 John 4:1.)

SELF: Was it primarily born in the *mind*? Does it feed my ego or exalt Jesus? What does it resemble?

SATAN: Does the image seem destructive? Does it lure me away?

GOD: Is it a "living flow of pictures" coming from my inner-most being? Was my inner being quietly focused on Jesus?

B. Examine its content by testing the ideas. (See 1 John 4:5.)

SELF: Does it have ego appeal? Is self the centerpiece or is Jesus the One who is lifted up?

SATAN: Is it negative, destructive, pushy, fearful, and accusative? Is it a violation of the nature of God? Does it violate the Word of God? Is the image "afraid to be tested"?

GOD: Is it instructive, uplifting, and comforting? Does it accept testing? Does it encourage me to continue in my walk with God?

C. Check its fruit by testing the fruit. (See Matt. 7:16.)

SELF: The fruits here are variable, but eventually they elevate the place of man in contrast to the centrality of Christ.

SATAN: Am I fearful, compulsive, in bondage, anxious, confused, or possessing an inflated ego as a result of the encounter?

> *GOD*: Do I sense quickened faith, power, peace, good fruit, enlightenment, knowledge, or humility?

Nine Scriptural Tests

Here is a list of nine scriptural tests by which we can test every revelation that we receive for accuracy, authority, and validity. The following truths are for all of us—whether you are an acknowledged seer prophet or an everyday believer in the Lord Jesus Christ. Let's drop the plumb line of God's Word in our lives!

1. *Does the revelation edify, exhort, or console?* *"But one who prophesies speaks to men for **edification** and **exhortation** and **consolation**"* (1 Cor. 14:3 NASB). The end purpose of all true prophetic revelation is to build up, to admonish, and to encourage the people of God. Anything that is not directed to this end is not true prophecy. Jeremiah the prophet had to fulfill a negative commission, but even his difficult message contained a powerful and positive promise of God for those who were obedient. (See Jeremiah 1:5, 10.) First Corinthians 14:26c sums it up best: *"Let all things be done for edification"* (NASB).

2. *Is it in agreement with God's Word?* *"All Scripture is given by inspiration of God"* (2 Tim. 3:16a KJV). True revelation always agrees with the letter and the spirit of Scripture. (See 2 Corinthians 1:17-20.) Where the Holy Spirit says, "Yea and amen" in Scripture, He also says, "Yea and amen" in Revelation. He never, ever, contradicts himself.

3. *Does it exalt Jesus Christ?* *"He will glorify Me; for He will take of Mine, and will disclose it to you"* (John 16:14 NASB)). All true revelation ultimately centers on Jesus Christ and exalts and glorifies Him. (See Revelation 19:10.)

4. *Does it have good fruit?* *"Beware of the false prophets, who come to you in sheep's clothing, but inwardly are ravenous wolves. You will know them by their fruits..."* (Matt. 7:15-16 NASB). True revelatory activity produces fruit in character and conduct that agrees with the fruit of the Holy Spirit. (See Ephesians 5:9 and Galatians 5:22-23.) Some of the aspects of character or conduct

that clearly are not the fruit of the Holy Spirit include pride, arrogance, boastfulness, exaggeration, dishonesty, covetousness, financial irresponsibility, licentiousness, immorality, addictive appetites, broken marriage vows, and broken homes. Normally, any revelation that is responsible for these kinds of results is from a source other than the Holy Spirit.

5. *If it predicts a future event, does it come to pass?* (See Deuteronomy 18:20-22.) Any revelation that contains a prediction concerning the future should come to pass. If it does not, then, with a few exceptions, the revelation is not from God. Exceptions may include the following issues:

   a. The will of the person involved.

   b. National repentance—Nineveh repented, so the word did not occur.

   c. Messianic predictions. (They took hundreds of years to fulfill).

   d. There is a different standard for New Testament prophets than for Old Testament prophets whose predictions played into God's messianic plan of deliverance.

6. *Does the prophetic prediction turn people toward God or away from Him?* (See Deut. 13:1-5.) The fact that a person makes a prediction concerning the future that is *fulfilled* does not necessarily prove that person is moving by Holy Spirit-inspired revelation. If such a person, by his own ministry, turns others away from obedience to the one true God, then that person's ministry is false—even if he makes correct predictions concerning the future.

7. *Does it produce liberty or bondage? "For you have not received a spirit of slavery leading to fear again, but you have received a spirit of adoption as sons by which we cry out, 'Abba! Father!'"* (Rom. 8:15 NASB). True revelation given by the Holy Spirit produces liberty, not bondage. (See 1 Corinthians 14:33 and 2 Timothy 1:7.) The Holy Spirit never causes God's children to act like slaves, nor does He ever motivate us by fear or legalistic compulsion.

8. *Does it produce life or death?* "Who also made us adequate as servants of a new covenant, not of the letter, but of the Spirit; for the letter kills, but the Spirit gives life" (2 Cor. 3:6 NASB). True revelation from the Holy Spirit always produces life, not death.

9. *Does the Holy Spirit bear witness that it is true?* "*As for you, the anointing which you received from Him abides in you, and you have no need for anyone to teach you; but as His anointing teaches you about all things and is true and is not a lie, and just as it has taught you, you abide in Him*" (1 John 2:27 NASB). The Holy Spirit within the believer always confirms true revelation from the Holy Spirit. The Holy Spirit is "the Spirit of Truth." (See John 16:13.) He *bears witness* to that which is true, but He rejects that which is false. This ninth test is the *most subjective* test of all the tests we've presented here. For that reason it must be used in conjunction with the previous eight objective standards.

God's Word tells us that we must prove all things and hold fast to that which is good. (See 1 Thessalonians 5:21.) At all times we must seek the Lord's wisdom while refusing to use "wisdom" as an excuse for fear. We must be careful not to become offended at the genuine things that the Holy Spirit is doing, no matter how strange they may appear to us. Divine revelation and visionary experiences come in many different forms, and it is vital that we understand how to discern the true from the false.

Now I know that some of you are waiting for me to dish out "some of the deeper things" to you by this point. But from my perspective, I would be remiss not to make sure these foundational truths are laid well before taking us further on our "mystical journey." With this in mind, we would do well to study the 15 "wisdom issues" that follow. They will help us learn how to wisely judge the various forms of revelation we will encounter in our adventure with Christ.

Fifteen Wisdom Issues

1. *Search for proper exegesis and scriptural context.* One of the most important issues concerning wisdom is our interpretation of Scriptures—or proper exegesis. Many times, "prophetically

gifted" people seem predominantly to take a type of loose symbolic interpretation of the Scriptures. Although there are different schools and methodologies of interpretation, we should look for the historical context from which the Scripture is speaking. Wisdom suggests that individuals with revelatory gifts should consult teachers, apostles, and pastors for additional clarity on scriptural interpretation. *"Study to show thyself approved unto God..."* (2 Tim. 2:15 KJV). Walk with others!

2. *Focus on Jesus.* Manifestations of the Holy Spirit should not take center stage—*Jesus* is our central focus. While giving ourselves to the purposes of God, the movements of the Holy Spirit, and revelatory experiences from Heaven, let us not jump on just any bandwagon. Sometimes people will jump into anything that's moving because they lack security and a proper biblical foundation. Remember the simple test: "Does this experience lead me closer to Jesus Christ?"

3. *Major on the "main and plain" things.* Manifestations are not our primary message. In the mainstream of evangelical orthodoxy, our emphasis is to be on the "main and plain" things of Scripture: salvation, justification by faith, sanctification, etc., followed by the consequential experiences revealed in people's testimonies of how they are advancing in their relationship with God and the community of believers.

4. *Follow biblical principles—not the rigid letter of the Law.* Some things fall into a "non-biblical" category. This does not mean that they are wrong, "of the devil," or contrary to the Scriptures. It just means that there is no sure "biblical proof text" to validate the phenomena. (There was no "proof text" to justify Jesus' spitting in the dirt and anointing a man's eyes with mud either—but it was obviously "right.") Don't stretch something to try to make it fit. Realize there will not be a Scripture for every activity. What is important is making sure that we follow the clear *principles* of the Word of God.

5. *Build bridges.* In "times of refreshing and supernatural experiences," keep in focus the reality that there are other sincere believers who are not as excited about it as we are. This is normal

and to be expected. Some of the disciples, such as Thomas, were less excited about the Resurrection than others, but they all stood for Christ in the end. We must be careful to keep ourselves clean from spiritual pride and arrogance, and devote ourselves to building bridges to our "more cautious" brethren through love, forgiveness, understanding, and kindness.

6. *Honor and pray for leaders.* Realize that every leadership team of a local congregation or ministry has the privilege and responsibility to set the tone or the expression of the release of the Spirit in their gatherings. God works through delegated authority! Pray for those in authority with a heart and attitude that is clean before God. Ask that they be given God's timing, wisdom, and proper game plan. (Be careful and hesitant to apply the label of "controlling spirit" or similar titles to leaders! Most leaders are sincere believers who simply want to do what's best for the overall good of their particular flock—and remember, they are God's appointed and anointed.)

7. *Be aware of times and seasons.* Is anything and everything supposed to happen all the time? Apart from a sovereign move of God, I think not. Ecclesiastes 3:1 (KJV) tells us, *"To every thing there is a season, and a time to every purpose under the heaven."* The Scriptures vividly depict "Pentecost meetings," but they also include clear admonitions from Paul on how to walk with those in the "room of the ungifted or unbeliever," as well. We should never use our freedom to purposefully offend others. I personally believe that it is in line with God's Word to have specific meetings for predetermined purposes. The leading of the Spirit works both ways. We can predetermine by His guidance that certain gatherings or sessions are oriented as "prophetic or life-in-the-Spirit gatherings." But also be hungry for and welcome those spontaneous occurrences when His manifest Presence is ushered in even when we don't expect or plan it.

8. *Let love rule.* The "unusual and rare" is not to be our consistent diet, nor will it ever replace the daily Christian spiritual disciplines. If all a person does is "bark like a dog" and quits reading the Scriptures and relating properly to other members of the

local church, then most likely some other spirit is at work. Perhaps the individual has simply lost focus and needs a word spoken in love to help him or her maintain spiritual equilibrium in the midst of a mighty outpouring. Whatever the case, let love always be the rule.

9. *Maintain balance.* There is no exact science for figuring out all the manifestations of the Holy Spirit. When something is unclear, we should not over-define what we do not understand. There is a godly tightrope of dynamic tension between the reality of subjective experience and biblical doctrine. Let us strive to maintain our balance! There is a tension—it is supposed to be there!

10. *Understand the relationship of divine initiation and human response.* Is all this demonstrative activity (laughter, crying, shaking, falling, etc.) necessarily from God? I specifically call these "manifestations of and to the Holy Spirit" for a very good reason. Although some of these external, visible, and audible signs are divinely initiated, we must admit that some of them are human responses and reactions to the Holy Spirit's movement upon us or upon others close by. Divine initiative is followed by human response. This is normal. We must also make room for ethnic and different cultural displays of our affection to God. Every gift comes from God but becomes expressed through a variety of clay pots!

11. *Be known by your fruits.* Although we want to bless what we see the Father doing, let us also direct this blessing into fruitful works. If we have been truly activated by the Holy Spirit, then we must channel it into *practical works* that express our faith. Let us channel this energy from a "bless me club" into a "bless others" focus that feeds the hungry and ministers to the poor, the widow, the orphan, and the single parent. Channel God's river of revelatory blessing into a life of evangelism, intercession, worship, and other things that display the passion and compassion of Jesus for people.

12. *Perceive the works of God and the motives of man.* Although the phenomena of manifestations and prophetic encounters have

occurred in revivals throughout Church history, I doubt that we can make a case for any of these individuals *willing* these things into being. These experiences were equated with receiving an anointing for power in ministry and as tools of radical means whereby God brought personal transformation.

13. *Control your flesh and cooperate with God.* Self-control is one of the fruits of the Spirit. (See Galatians 5:23.) Too many of us have forgotten it or thrown it out the window! Nowhere in the Scriptures are we told that we are to "control God"—we are told to control "self." The fruit of self-control is to conquer the deeds of the flesh—lust, immorality, greed, etc. We are to *cooperate* with and yield to the Presence of God and *control* the deeds of the flesh.

14. *Be alert and aware.* Let us search the Scriptures, review Church history, seek the Lord, and receive input from those who are wiser and more experienced than we are. Seasoned believers know that the enemy always tries to "club" Christians over the head after they have had an encounter or experience, in hopes that they will become confused, discouraged, and bewildered. We must continually arm ourselves for battle. This is a real war. These radical, revelatory visitations are not just "fun and games." They come to lead us into greater effectiveness for our Master!

15. *Avoid spiritual ditches.* There are two deep ditches we should avoid. First, we should watch out for *analytical skepticism*, which will cause us to be offended by what we do not understand. The other deadly ditch is *fear* (of man, rejection, fanaticism, etc.). Both of these "ditches" have a common fruit: criticism. Consider this nugget of wisdom that was spoken to me some years ago:

"If you can't jump in the middle of it, bless it. If you can't bless it, then patiently observe it. If you can't patiently observe it, then just don't criticize it! Do not stretch out the rod of your tongue against those things you do not understand!"

I remember so well when the Holy Spirit spoke that phrase to me. It saved my neck then, and it might just save yours from a judgmental and critical attitude as well in the future. *"Do not stretch out the rod of your tongue against those things you do not understand!"* Another way of saying it could be, "It's the worst time to be a know-it-all!"

Thank God for the gift of the Spirit that is called a word of wisdom! Some common sense along the way is a big help as well! Oh my, and O God! Whew, glad we got that out of the way!

Rounding the Bend

Let's recap what we just accomplished and then round the bend toward home! In this chapter, we have investigated the Sources of Revelation, Nine Scriptural Tests, and 15 Wisdom Issues. Don't just read this material as just another good "To Do List." Rather, chew on these concepts and engraft them into your soul. These principles are worth meditating on and reviewing to make sure the plumb line of God's Word is dropped true and sure in your life and ministry.

Let's build a house for the Lord that is built to last—one that will withstand the winds and storms of time and pressure. With that in mind, turn with me now to the close of this fun-filled and wisdom-filled book, as we contemplate *Seeing Jesus Only!*

Endnotes

1. Goll, James, *Understanding Supernatural Encounters Study Guide*.

2. Dr. Mark and Patti Virkler, *Communion With God*.

3. Dr. Mark and Patti Virkler, Study Guide.

CHAPTER 14

Seeing Jesus Only!

BY JAMES GOLL

Let's begin our last chapter by reading the words of the disciple Mark, who saw and recorded very many amazing spiritual experiences. The following is from Mark 9:1-8, and it concerns what took place on the Mount of Transfiguration. It changed his life forever!

> And Jesus was saying to them, "Truly I say to you, there are some of those who are standing here who will not taste death until they see the kingdom of God after it has come with power" (Mark 9:1 NASB).

> Six days later, Jesus took with Him Peter and James and John, and brought them up on a high mountain by themselves. And He was transfigured before them; and His garments became radiant and exceedingly white, as no launderer on Earth can whiten them. Elijah appeared to them along with Moses; and they were talking with Jesus. Peter said to Jesus, 'Rabbi, it is good for us to be here; let us make three tabernacles, one for You, and one for Moses, and one for Elijah.' For he did not know what to answer; for they became terrified. Then a cloud formed, overshadowing them, and a voice came out of the cloud, 'This is My

beloved Son, listen to Him!' All at once they looked around and saw no one with them anymore, except Jesus alone (Mark 9:2-8 NASB).

Out of the Rubble of Zion

Some years ago, I went on a journey to visit the famous Zion, Illinois, where Alexander Dowie lived and ministered in the late 1800s through the turn of the century. Dowie was mightily used of the Lord in profound working of miracles and gifts of healings. He built a model city outside of Chicago, Illinois, that was quite a center for the faith in its heyday. Many know that this ministry eventually went into error, as some began to call Dowie the Elijah who was sent from Heaven. Worship of the vessel, pride and doctrinal error set in. The downfall was as great as the height of its short-lived success.

On the heels of that failure, the Lord raised up out of the rubble of Zion a quiet witness of those who sought the manifested Presence of Jesus. The primary leaders were Martha Wing Robinson and a dear man called Elder Brooks. They and others with them, established what became known as the Zion Faith Homes.

I remember visiting the Zion Faith Homes, where you could still sense the Presence of our dear Lord Jesus Christ. I reaffirmed that day that I wanted my life to be centered, not in gifts primarily, but on the man Christ Jesus the Lord—the Head of the Body of Christ! To this day, that is the goal of my life, and I trust it is yours, as well—to be so close to Jesus so as to only cast one shadow.

While visiting the Zion Faith Homes, I picked up a copy of the Letters of John G. Lake to Elder Brooks and Elder Brooks wisdom-filled reply that was penned in 1916. The lessons included in these letters were stunning then, and they are perhaps even more stunning today.

As I contemplated the closure for this catalytic book, I thought there could be no better way to do so than to scorch your life with these writings, hoping they would ruin you like they did me! So take a deep breath, because here we go!

John G. Lake's Letter to Elder Brooks and His Reply

The following are two letters that were written many years ago. One is by the fabled miracle worker **John G. Lake** and the other is by **Elder Eugene** Brooks of the Zion Faith Homes, in Zion, Illinois. I am posting them here because they present, in their substance, a recurring problem of the Christian ministry—as well as of the life of any follower of Jesus Christ. That problem is the enormous need that is latent in the life and experience of those whom God blesses and uses. So many need to understand how to go on with God, how to retain their life with Jesus, and how to grow in it.

This is especially true in these days of what seems to be an overemphasis—in some quarters—on great works and great gifts. I say it's an overemphasis because of the under-emphasis in even some of the greatest of the leaders of our time, upon the growth in God of the daily life of the child of God. *It is a startling fact that in many cases, Christians and Christian workers do not know what to do and how to proceed on and into the fullness of God.* This is an almost unbelievable common failure! *So many talk and teach about "prayer," who do not actually practice in their private lives a vital preoccupation with God!* Or, they gradually lose out in their walk with God by becoming too much involved in goings and doings and/or in efforts to become "great" or "greater."

Anyone who does not realize his need to be alone with God daily will surely find himself in a wilderness, facing a spiritual loss and vainness, as the spirit of this world opposes advance and seeks to render void the fruitfulness of his or her life, which was begun in the wonder of the power of the Holy Spirit. These letters are offered as studies in spiritual contrasts. They will be greatly rewarding to any who are willing to read, study, ponder, and digest what is expressed in them.

John Lake and Elder Brooks were both mighty men of God—each in his own way and calling—as their letters clearly show. And those of us who knew them both quite intimately can add their testimony that such an estimate is true.

Letter Written to Rev. and Mrs. Brooks by Rev. John Lake (June 16, 1916):

For some days, I have been moved by the Spirit to write to you. At the time of our marriage, I felt that God had really laid upon your souls the burden of my need in God. As I moved out in faith at that time, endeavoring to trust God for physical strength and guidance and grace from heaven to accomplish His will, He richly blessed my soul and our work was accompanied by the power of His Spirit.

While at Philadelphia, the Spirit of the Lord came mightily upon me for healing and wonderful healings took place. Later we came to Spokane, Washington. The first door God opened there, strangely, was a door in what is known here as the Church of the Truth, a new thought body.

Their pastor was formerly a Universal preacher. He had seen Christ through Christian Science teaching. He was a hungry soul. He invited me to preach at his church! I said to him, "My message is not yours. I preach Christ and Him crucified." He replied, "Brother, preach your own message and as much of it as you want to. You are in the hands of the Spirit of God."

After the first sermon, he invited me to take one of the healing rooms in their church and pray for the sick throughout the week. God gave wonderful healings! The church was mightily moved. It was a new manifestation of the power of God to them. I was invited to teach their week day classes on the subject of the baptism of the Spirit. God showed me four persons in the church at that time who would receive the baptism. We ministered there about six months, then started our own work about Feb. 1, 1915.

The first lady from the Church of the Truth to be baptized in the Spirit was Mrs. P. She received her baptism at the first service we conducted in our own hall. At the close of the Sunday morning service, the Spirit fell on her and she was baptized in the presence of the congregation.

Mrs. P. told me that five years before, while in great agony of soul, she fell on her knees and cried out for deliverance and light and help saying, "Oh God, is there no one anywhere who can bring me the light my soul needs and show me God as my spirit craves?" And the Spirit spoke to her and said, "Yes, in Johannesburg, South Africa." On the day of her baptism, as she was under the power of the Spirit, the Lord reminded her that He had fulfilled His promise to her, and that I had come from Johannesburg, South Africa, in response to her soul's call and the soul call of those who needed God.

Another lady from the Church of the Truth, Mrs. F., was likewise baptized in the Spirit. The Spirit revealed Christ and the blood and His cleansing power. They have been beautiful souls, as also the other two.

In connection with our work…we maintain healing rooms, which are open from ten a.m. to four p.m. every day, where the sick and otherwise needy souls come for prayer. We also have a hall that is connected with the healing rooms where we have our week day and week night meetings. Our Sunday services are held at the Masonic Temple with Sunday School in the morning, preaching at eleven a.m., and the large public service at three p.m. Our work here has been characterized with wonderful healings and many of them. When I wrote the stories of the wonders God was performing in Africa to America, the people largely said, "We do not believe it." Satan tried in many ways to make the world believe that it was not a fact. But our work here has been under the eye of such competent witnesses of such high character—and so many of them— that satan can no longer deny the stories that God has done. The news has reached all of the Pacific Coast states. People are coming, not only the sick but teachers (who are particularly from among the Truth people of the coast country), to inquire about what it is, what is the difference, what do we mean when we talk about the baptism of the Holy Ghost, and how do you get it?

During the year of 1915, some 8,030 people were healed. Mr. Westwood ministers with me in the work and has the adjoining healing room. Mr. S. P. Fogwill, formerly a deacon of Zion City, is also with me. He makes the calls from home to home throughout the city all day with the Ford car. Usually we minister to one hundred persons per day, sometimes more…sometimes less.

Among the remarkable cases of healing are three of recent occurrence that I want to give to you. They are out of the usual order of healings and in my judgment, belong to the class of miracles of creative order.

One is Mrs. Pn., a trained nurse and graduate of Trinity Hospital in Milwaukee. She was operated on and the generative organs (womb and ovaries) were removed last July. In November, she was operated on again for gall stones. After the operation, the bile broke loose and flowed from her body in quarts—to such an extent that death was imminent. Indeed, during the time she was prayed for, she passed into the state of a coma, apparent death, and for about a half an hour there was no evidence of life and no breath passed her lips. Mr. Westwood was with her. He had been with her all night. It was about 4 AM. The Spirit of God took gradual possession of her being in such power that she was healed entirely of the gall stone difficulty. Her generative organs regrew and last month she became a perfectly normal woman! Mrs. Pn. Is now the matron of our Divine Healing Home.

The second case is that of Miss K., a victim of glandular tuberculosis. She was operated on 26 times and was treated by 56 different physicians—and finally left to die. One after another abandoned the case. In one of her operations, an incision was made in the lower abdomen. This was done in an endeavor to remove a great quantity of pus that had formed in the body. On account of the tubercular state of her flesh, the wounds would not heal nor hold stitches. Three times she was opened and sewed up, but without avail. The consequence was that a normal movement of the bowels could not take place. This condition lasted for six and a half years!

While down in the city, she fainted on the street. They were about to take her to St. Luke's Hospital for an operation when she became conscious and refused to go. She came to our home and spent the night with us. We prayed for her. On the next Sunday, as she sat in the tabernacle in the afternoon service and public prayer was being offered, she said it seemed to her as if a hand was placed inside of her abdomen and another hand on her head. The voice of the Spirit spoke within her soul and said, "You are healed." She arose from her chair and became perfectly normal!

Number three. Mrs. L., the wife of a Main Street merchant here, fell down some stairs ten or twelve years ago, which caused a prolapse of the stomach, bowels, and female organs. She became an invalid. After several years of operations and suffering, she was attacked with rheumatics and became a helpless cripple.

When the doctors had failed, she was recommended to take bath treatments at Soap Lake, one of the hot lakes in Washington, where the water is very hot and very much mineralized. The treatments had this strange effect—that the disease left her body and centered entirely in the right leg! A formation of bone (as big as a large orange) came on the inside of the right leg and the bone of the leg began to grow until the leg was three inches *longer* than the other one, and the foot became almost an inch *longer* than the other one!

Her lungs had fallen in through tuberculosis. She was prayed for one day in the healing rooms. As she went out to get in the car, she was amazed to discover that her lungs were raising up and her chest filling out. She was perfectly and instantly healed of that!

Later, while I prayed for her concerning the lump in her leg, the Spirit came upon her powerfully and she burst into great perspiration, which ran down her person into her shoes! The leg which was three inches longer than the other one at the time, *shortened* at the rate of an inch a week and in three weeks was perfectly natural and the same length as the other! The foot also *shortened* in length and now she wears the same size of shoe on both feet and her legs are of equal length!

God wants to do something new in connection with my work! It is not clear to my soul yet just what it is. Finances have been tight lately. There has not been the usual flow of financial help. Healings have not been so powerful for some three weeks. My spirit is disturbed. *I recognize it as one of the stirrings that come to the soul previous to a change in the character of the work and ministry.* I feel the need of your prayers. I know that God put me on your hearts. I know I am on your hearts still and will always be, for I believe God has laid the burden of intercession upon you dear ones for my life. I may not always see the guidance of God as you see it, but I desire to assure you of my deep personal love for you all, and the bond in the Holy Ghost with you that is intense and powerful. I want your prayers!

Our work has extended into the country round about. We now have a congregation at Bovill, Idaho; another at Moscow, Idaho, the seat of the state university; another at Pullman, Washington, where the Washington Agricultural Schools are located; and another congregation in the north part of Spokane, Washington, aside from the central work.

Beloved, you know that we can trust God to apply to the soul that discipline that is necessary for its subjection to God. As I look back over the way, though it seems hard, I can see that every step of the way has been necessary for my soul's discipline—not only that God's humility might reign in me, but that God's power might be made manifest through me and my faith strengthened in God.

I feel I have never yet attained that place in God where I can accomplish the real life work that He desires through me. There is a broader ministry that God wants accomplished. I feel He has called me to it, but the way has never been opened so far, nor have I felt that my soul was really ready for it.

I have given you a good deal of detail concerning myself, for John Lake has always been a good deal of burden to himself, and I feel that I want your loving prayer and holy faith in my behalf, that the real will of God may be done in me and through me to the glory of God. God bless you! Give our love to all the dear ones.

Your Brother in Christ,

John G. Lake

Reply to John Lake's Letter by Elder Eugene Brooks (July 1, 1916):

My Dear Bro. Lake,

Your long and interesting letter was received and read with much pleasure. We were exceedingly glad to hear from you and to know that God has been so abundantly blessing you. I do praise Him for all He is doing in and through His people.

We have been in severe strain of work for some weeks—spending as much as 14 hours a day at times. It did seem as if your request would have to go unheeded, for we knew that a short prayer would not meet the demands in your case, but the Lord said we were to have a three hour prayer for you. In order to get it, we dismissed our usual meeting last night and called the people in the three homes together and prayed for three hours, strong and powerful. I'm sure our God has heard that cry and we believe that God will manifest the answer in the way and at the time of His choosing.

We do not need to tell you that we love you and greatly desire that you should measure up to the divine requirements, therefore no apology is needed for a little word of admonition. My soul seems to sense a possible error you are making in reference to your self and your work. I do not say that I am correct at this point, but I have the soul sense that you have your eyes in the wrong direction. You say, "God wants to do something *new* in connection with my work." I do not doubt that. But what is it? Is it enlargement? Development? Aggression? Gifts and dominion? It may be all of these or none of them, but one thing is true— that if your eyes get on these, somehow you will fail.

While I do not claim wisdom for these words, yet I am quite sure of the correctness of the statement that no man can be used as largely as you have indicated and not be treading on most danger-ous ground.

And while it is true that greater conquest, enlargement, dominion, etc. may be intended by the Lord, *one thing is absolutely necessary if these victories are to be continued—that* **humility** *genuine, deep, and lasting shall be yours.*

You know that a man may be called and greatly anointed for a cer-tain work and yet not be as powerful in God as some other not so greatly called. But you have learned that the man thus largely called must find that grace and depth in God or lose his steward-ship and disgrace his name and profession? *God needs certain works to be done and calls whom He will to do it, but He will sacrifice the work to save the worker. With God the worker is important; with man the work is important. God has His eye on the man; the man has his eye on the work.* Your letter shows that you have the vision somewhat mixed though. You see God and you see your need, but you also see other things and these other things *needing* you.

The real vision is to see "Jesus only" and to see nothing else! Not Jesus and— just Jesus. The "single eye" sees none but Jesus; the double eye sees Jesus <u>and</u>.

If I could put into words the soul sight of this, you would get the idea and seek to impart it, but it is an experience, not a doctrine. It is the absolute sufficiency of Jesus for *every need* and the utter uselessness of every human effort. Just as long as there are <u>things</u> and <u>doings</u> in our vision, Jesus cannot be so mighty. When He alone is seen, He *takes care* of the things and doings. We *try* and fail until we are willing to give up and admit that we cannot—then we may turn to Him.

My brother, we are absolutely useless without Him! What if we have been so used a bit when we were not recognizing Him? That does not prove our sufficiency, but His grace. He knew we were blind and was therefore patient, but our blindness and folly must be exposed and we fail—then awaken to find *our springs had all been in Him all the time!* It is the folly of the natural man to suppose that <u>he</u> is doing it until his conceit is exposed and then he finds that God made a vessel to honor because He had need. When the vessel took glory to itself, He broke the vessel that He might make it again.

Now you know as well as I the things I am saying. Then why do I say them? Just to stir up your "pure mind."

But there is one thing which you perhaps do not know as well as I—the unfailing and only way to attain that desired end. You are the one called and equipped (because of the need) without much effort on your part. I not being thus called must needs find at the foot of the cross what was imparted to you at the start, because of the need. Is God unrighteous? Not at all. Then sometime, somewhere, you too will have to go down at the foot of the cross to retain that which has been imparted for the time of need, or you will find yourself someday to be that "broken vessel." No, I by no means indicate you should do as I do, nor by any means go the way I go, but I do say that go what way you may, you have got to go on your knees. Nor do I think you would have to spend the time in prayer that we do, for your call being different makes the requirement different. *But certain it is that if the prayer closet is neglected because of the stress of work, God will neglect the work sometimes.*

We can't argue ourselves out of the victory with the thought that God will excuse our declension in prayer because we are so engaged in the vineyard. When we turn to the life of our Lord and find Him leaving the multitude (who had come to be ministered to) and going off to pray—we have to admit that there is no excuse left.

But surely I have exceeded the limitations of propriety. I simply intended to say a few loving words by way of remembrance, and lo, I have been preaching to you at a wild rate. Still, I have not said the thing yet I desire to say, for I did wish to just hold up Jesus and make you look at Him from every angle and see how transportingly beautiful He is—how all sufficient He is—how He fills all— meets every requirement—satisfies every longing—is Himself the equipment for every service! Oh, John Lake, there is no other need of ours in this world or that to come but Jesus. I know I am not making it clear, and I can't, but it is true all the same.

It is so true that it is supreme folly to look for, desire, or be tempted with ought else! If He is "The Way," we can't get lost. If He is "The Life," the devil can't kill us. If He is "The Truth," we can't be deceived by lies. What do we need besides Jesus then? If everything proceeds from Him—if all things culminate in Him and if He is the embodiment, the fulfillment, and the consummation of all things—then why should we seek after or even *think* of anything else?

No, I haven't told you yet and now I despair of doing so, for Jesus is so infinitely wonderful that all words fade when referring to

Him. Oh, my Brother John, I once looked for <u>power</u>—wanted equipment; sought <u>usefulness</u>—saw gifts in the distance—knew that dominion was somewhere in the future, but glory to God! One by one these faded, and as they faded, there was a form—a figure emerged from the shadows which became clearer and more distinct as these things faded. When they had passed, I saw "Jesus only."

The Lord bless thee, my brother, and fulfill all His purposes in thee. Our very earnest love to you and your dear wife.

All the saints greet thee in love. My wife and I are among them.

In the Bonds of Christ

Eugene Brooks

Reflecting on the Letters

Is not Jesus the most beautiful and amazing person you have ever met? I imagine you agree with me or you would not even be reading this book. But perhaps you have gotten caught up in the maze of many good things to do that you have lost your gaze upon the wonder of the man Christ Jesus.

I have lost my way from time to time, and have needed an occasional chiropractic adjustment to help me get back into proper alignment. It is so easy to get our clothing caught in the machinery of ministry, work, the cares of this life, and keeping up your approval ratings that you miss the very reason you got into this to start with. It's all about love. It's all about having a passionate, life-giving relationship with our Father through the man Christ Jesus the Lord! I want more of Jesus!

Like the three disciples we read about earlier, though Elijah and Moses might even appear before me in some extreme spiritual experience, I want to see Jesus only!

In fact, right now, I want to give you an opportunity to reset the calibration of your heart to see Jesus the Lord. If this echoes the cry of your heart, then pray this simple pray right along with me.

Heavenly Father, by the power of the Holy Spirit, change my heart! Bring my vision back into focus. I want to see Jesus! I want to be a passionate worshiper of God. I choose to turn the gaze of my heart from primarily focusing on gifts and ministry into a consecrated devotion of your Son. Forgive me for not giving Jesus first place. Help me see Jesus more clearly for your glory and honor. Amen and Amen! Praise the Lord!

It's a Both And!

First Corinthians 14:1 states that we are to pursue love and yet earnestly desire the spiritual gifts, especially that we may prophesy! It is not that on one hand we have the gifts of the Spirit and on the other hand we have the fruit of the Spirit. They are not two separate camps—or at least it is not supposed to be that way.

In God's economy, it is a "both and!" So let's make sure this point is clear. We are to be people who hotly pursue with a passionate yearning the spiritual gifts, while keeping love as our aim! We can do that, can't we? We can have character to carry the gifts and wisdom for life's journey. God wants nothing less. So why settle for powerless Christianity?

We can have both fruit and power. Let's go for the double in this generation. Let's see the shifting shadows removed and walk in the light of authentic, power-filled, apostolic Christianity. Let's see this Christianity cover the Earth as the waters cover the sea, for the glory of our marvelous God and Savior—Christ Jesus the Lord!

The world is waiting for a generation of authentic believers in Christ who are filled with power, wisdom, and character. They are worth it! Jesus is worth it! Let the light of God shine and the only shadow that is seen be His!

BIBLIOGRAPHY

Baker, H.A. *Visions Beyond the Veil*. Kent, England: Sovereign World, 2000.

Baker, Roland and Heidi. *Always Enough: God's Miraculous Provision Among the Poorest Children on Earth*. Grand Rapids, MI: Chosen Books, 2002.

Buckingham, Jamie. *Daughter of Destiny*. Gainesville, FL: Bridge-Logos, 1999.

Clement, Kim. *Secrets of the Prophetic*. Shippensburg, PA: Destiny Image Publishers, 2005.

Crowder, John. *The New Mystics*. Shippensburg, PA: Destiny Image Publishers, 2006.

Davis, Paul Keith. *Books of Destiny*. North Sutton, NH: Streams Publishing House, 2004.

Goll, James. *Revival Breakthrough Study Guide*. Franklin, TN: Ministry to the Nations, 2000.

Johnson, Bill. *When Heaven Invades Earth*. Shippensburg, PA: Destiny Image Publishers, 2003.

Joyner, Rick. *Overcoming Evil in the Last Days*. Shippensburg, PA: Destiny Image Publishers, 2003.

Kendall, R.T. *The Anointing*. Nashville, TN: Thomas Nelson Publishers, 1999.

King, Patricia. *Spiritual Revolution*. Shippensburg, PA: Destiny Image Publishers, 2006.

Loren, Julia. *Shifting Shadows of Supernatural Power*. Shippensburg, PA: Destiny Image Publishers, 2006.

Michaelson, Johanna. *The Beautiful Side of Evil*. Eugene, OR: Harvest House Publishers, 1982.

Morse, M.D., Melvin with Paul Perry. *Closer to the Light: Learning from the Near Death Experiences of Children*. New York: Villard Books, 1990.

Morse, M.D., Melvin with Paul Perry. *Transformed by the Light: The Powerful Effect of Near Death Experiences on People's Lives*. New York: Villard Books, 1992.

Nee, Watchman. *The Latent Power of the Soul*. New York: Christian Fellowship Publications, 1972.

Otis, George. *The Twilight Labyrinth*. Grand Rapids, MI: Chosen Books, 1997.

Randolph, Larry. *Spirit Talk: Hearing the Voice of God*. Wilksboro, NC: Morning Star Publications, 2005.

Robinson, Mickey. *Falling to Heaven*. Cedar Rapids, IA: Arrow Publications, 2003.

Roundtree, Anna. *The Heavens Opened*. Lake Mary, FL: Charisma House Publishers, 1999.

Tari, Mel. *Like a Mighty Wind*. Green Forest, AK: New Leaf Press, 1978; permissions: newleafpress.net.

Walters, David. *Children Aflame*. Macon, GA: Good News Fellowship Ministries, 1995.

NOTES

_____

_____

_____

_____

_____

_____

_____

_____

_____

_____

_____

For More Information

Dr. James (Jim) W. and Michal Ann Goll are the cofounders of
Encounters Network. They are members of the **Harvest International
Ministries** Apostolic Team and contributing writers for **Kairos Magazine**.
James is also the Director of **PrayerStorm**, an instructor in the **Wagner
Leadership Institute**, member of the **Apostolic Council of Prophetic Elders**
and a member of **The Call Board**. James and Michal Ann have four wonder-
ful children and live in the rolling hills of Franklin, TN.

James has produced numerous Study Guides on subjects such as
Equipping in the Prophetic, Blueprints for Prayer and Empowered for
Ministry all available through the Encounters Resource Center.

BOOKS BY JAMES W. AND MICHAL ANN GOLL

FOR MORE INFORMATION CONTACT:

Encounters Network
P. O. Box 1653
Franklin, TN 37075
Office Phone: 615-599-5552
Office Fax: 615-599-5554
For orders call: 1-877-200-1604

For more information to sign up for their
Monthly E-mail Communiques,
visit their web site at www.encountersnetwork.com
or E-Mail: info@encountersnetwork.com

Additional copies of this book and other
book titles from DESTINY IMAGE are
available at your local bookstore.

Call toll-free: 1-800-722-6774.

Send a request for a catalog to:

Destiny Image₀ Publishers, Inc.
P.O. Box 310
Shippensburg, PA 17257-0310

*"Speaking to the Purposes of God for This
Generation and for the Generations to Come."*

**For a complete list of our titles,
visit us at www.destinyimage.com**